MEDICARE MAMA'S®
— GUIDE TO —

MEDICARE
AND SOCIAL SECURITY
RETIREMENT

MEDICARE MAMA'S® GUIDE TO MEDICARE AND SOCIAL SECURITY RETIREMENT

SYLVIA A. GORDON, JD

Paperback ISBN 979-8-9922140-0-0
Ebook ISBN 979-8-9922140-1-7
Audiobook ISBN 979-8-9922140-2-4

Library of Congress Control Number: 2025904488

Printed in the United States of America

AUTHOR'S NOTE

DEDICATION

To my large, loud, and wonderful family
that makes my life so colorful and fun.
Working in our family businesses has
been one of my greatest blessings.

TABLE OF CONTENTS

INTRODUCTION

Welcome to the wild world of Medicare and Social Security, where getting older is like winning a golden ticket to a complicated and confusing maze.

Whether you're here to decode drug plans or avoid late penalties, this book is your trusty guide. It won't always be smooth sailing, so expect some twists and turns. But don't worry, I'll walk you through all the tricky stuff. Who knows, you might even laugh (or cry) along the way.

I've added some bonus resources you can access with the fancy QR code below.

A little about me.

I've spent my career as the president of one of the nation's largest insurance distribution companies, Gordon Marketing, which is known as an FMO or NMO. Prior to that, I was an Estate Planning attorney, and prior to that, I was a stay-at-home mother to four amazingly ornery children. I've been a member of the Forbes Financial Council, a Certified Senior Advisor and a national speaker on Medicare. I've hosted a weekly segment on Fox TV KTBC, and published many articles, blogs, and White Papers on all things Medicare.

I've trained thousands of independent insurance agents that have helped retirees all across the nation. I've also personally helped many retirees in my hometown.

Now I help millions over social media where I go by the name Medicare Mama®.

You can learn a little bit every day by following my daily one-minute retirement videos @MedicareMama on TikTok, Instagram, Facebook, and YouTube @themedicarefamily.com.

My parents started helping people with Medicare insurance in the 1980s, now my son is running this company, **THEMEDICAREFAMILY.COM**. Truly an old-fashioned family company headquartered in central Indiana and licensed in all 50 states.

Now a little about the book!

Just so we are clear, this is not a scholarly masterpiece.

I created this guide filled with stories[1], plain language, and no heavy jargon. You have a super computer in your pocket to easily fact-check my work.

---

1   The real stories from our clients are the heart of this book. Their experiences will help you steer clear of common mistakes. (Don't worry I've changed the names of the innocent — and not-so-innocent).

Please note that I can't possibly cover it all in one book.

This is a **guide, not an encyclopedia!** For the nitty-gritty, you'll need to visit **MEDICARE.GOV** and **SSA.GOV**.

💡 *The government websites can be hard to understand and navigate!*

When you finish this book, I invite you to join our private Facebook group @TheMedicareFamily and catch my weekly Medicare Monday live streams. It's a great way to keep learning after the book ends.

Happy retirement!

Sylvia

Sylvia A. Gordon, JD / Medicare Mama®

CHAPTER 1
FEELING OVERWHELMED?

If you are a nervous wreck about Medicare and retirement, you are not alone! Most people feel exactly the same when they start learning about retirement. With all the decisions you have to make about Medicare, Social Security, and other retirement options, it's normal to feel lost.

But don't worry, you are in the right place. I'll break a lot of this down and try to make the process fun. I am here to help you navigate your retirement and hopefully take away some of the stress you are feeling.

A few notes before we jump in.

While you can read this book cover to cover, I designed each chapter to be read on its own. You will find some material repeated so you can jump around and just read the parts you need right now.

In this book, I'm going to use some generalizations and simplifying language, because trying to write out every alternative is impossible. For educational scenarios, I will use terms for a married couple in a typical male and female relationship. I will assume the wife is younger and has a lower income than her husband.

- Yes, I know that women can marry younger men.
- Yes, I know that women can be the primary earners.
- I'm also aware there are many types of couples.

- I also know that some people never get married.

I'm not trying to offend anyone. I'm simply here to help. These shortcuts save me from repeatedly writing he/she/they in every scenario.

Another note, all the costs I list in this book are for 2025. They will all go up. Every year. Some years are worse than others. Refer to our website **THEMEDICAREFAMILY.COM** where all information is updated in real time.

With that out of the way, take a deep breath. Even if you know nothing about this stuff, it's going to be OK. Yes, you have many critical decisions to make, not just about your healthcare, but also about Social Security and retirement in general. For most people over 60, this is an intense and daunting period of learning. **But you aren't on your own**.

And even if you had learned this at 18, you would still have to re-learn it today.

This stuff is dry.

It's very confusing.

There are changes each and every year!

Everyone, regardless of their intelligence or education, starts at square one. You are not behind. You are the same.

Be aware that I can't make it all make sense, because we are dealing with the government and often $1 + 1 = 4$ just because they say it does. I can explain it, *but I can't make it make sense.*

Now, let's get started!

DO YOUR OWN HOMEWORK

A lot of people will have advice for you, but don't take any short-cuts offered by friends or family. This is your life. You need to do the homework!

The majority of my clients usually feel very comfortable with my expertise and quickly want to stop the educational part of this process. They say, "I trust you. Can we cut this short, and you just tell me exactly what to do?"

I could, but I won't.

There is no one right answer for every person. There is no best insurance company or plan. There is no right way or perfect age to retire.

I have an opinion, and thousands of others will have *other* opinions.

The next thing I typically hear is, "Just tell me what you'd do yourself."

That will not help you. We are not the same. We don't have the same health or budget. We don't have the same genes or live in the same zip code. (Yes, location really does matter when it comes to Medicare.)

For what it's worth, here is my personal plan:

- I'll draw Social Security as soon as I'm not working over the annual income limit, probably around 62–64. I'll invest the money aggressively, as I won't need it to live on.
- I'll buy a Medicare Supplement Plan G, a Part D drug Plan. If my daughter wasn't a dentist, I'd buy a dental plan too.
- I have a whole life insurance policy with Living Benefits to cover a nursing home stay.
- I have an irrevocable trust to shield my assets from probate and the threat of lawsuit or Medicaid Estate Recovery.
- I retired to Florida (no income taxes) and live there for at least 183 days each year and spend the summers in Indiana.
- I have a 401k, IRA, and Roth IRA that I probably won't touch till I have to take money out at age 75.
- I'm healthy, but heart attacks, diabetes, and bad joints run in my family.

See, that didn't help you. Your plans will be vastly different.

The next question I'm often asked is, "OK, since it is not a one-size-fits-all situation, what would YOU do if you were ME?"

Before I can think like you, I need to know if you like to gamble. I have gone to Las Vegas for Medicare meetings at least twice a year for the last 20 years. I gambled *once*. $1 slot in the airport (and I won $5). I don't like to gamble, but you might take on more risk. That matters because making these decisions are all about gambling.

If you gamble that you will live into your 90s, you shouldn't draw Social Security at age 62. You need to wait to max it out at 70 because you'll need it longer.

If you gamble that you will stay healthy and need minimal healthcare, buy a Medicare Advantage plan. You will save around $200 a month if you never use it, plus you can earn money back on some plans.

If you think you'll never take prescription drugs, you can gamble and go without a drug plan. Think how much money you'll save if you never get sick!

Once your house is paid off, you can gamble and go without property insurance. You could, but most won't. Why not? **That's a gamble most don't want to take.** But people take way more risks with their health insurance for some reason.

Our health is our most important asset! We all know that we are likely to get sick at some point. Our houses, on the other hand, may never require a homeowner's claim. Insure as much as you can comfortably afford to. My motto is: Buy insurance and hope you'll never have to use it.

My mom liked to say, "No one should complain when they spend hundreds of dollars a month, for years, and never used their health insurance. They should be rejoicing that they stayed healthy!"

This doesn't mean you should take on too much insurance either. Only you know how much you can afford and what risks run in your family. I've told many people that they are insurance poor and should consider dropping some coverages that an over-exuberant agent pushed them into. Too much is not as bad as too little, but it is still bad!

Our goal is to educate you and help you enroll into plans you feel comfortable with and can afford. This requires a long conversation about your life. The more we know about your situation, the more we can tailor our recommendations to you. We'll still be here for the rest of your life as your healthcare needs change (and all the insurance plans change).

Living on a fixed income in a world where insurance prices always go up each and every year is challenging. It's up to you to tell us when you are struggling to pay for your insurance. Our nightmare is you just stopping your coverage instead of allowing us to help you find something more affordable.

DON'T WAIT FOR THE GOVERNMENT

The government doesn't do much to help you learn about Medicare. It's all in your hands!

They provide a website and a great informational booklet called Medicare and You each year. I'm not being sarcastic, the booklet really is well written and easy to understand. I'm a fan. But I also know the majority of our clients instantly throw it in the trash. I also know the government would love to stop producing and sending these expensive booklets out annually to save money. Just like they stopped sending annual Social Security statements to most people years ago.

There are a few things the government will do to prepare you for Medicare.

- You can sign up for an account at **MEDICARE.GOV** and they will send you helpful emails.

- The government staffs Medicare offices in all states to provide volunteers to answer questions in an unbiased manner (these volunteers are not insurance agents and can't sell you anything). These offices are called different names depending on your state, but you can search State Medicare Help Programs to find one near you.

- The Medicare app is helpful! It's free and easy to download. Get it to see what is covered.

- You can call 1-800-Medicare with questions about coverage, etc. *but I'm warning you, it is as likely you'll get the wrong information as the correct information.* Congress did a study that bore this out. We have a problem with both the employees at Medicare and Social Security giving incorrect or incomplete information. Be your own advocate and call them at least three times. See if you get the same answer twice. This is sad, but you've been warned.

OUR HAPPIEST CLIENTS FOLLOW THESE STEPS

1. Start by watching our free 30-minute Medicare Workshop. No need to register, you can watch it any time. You can quickly get to it by scanning the QR code at the start of the book.

2. Self-enroll into Medicare A and B on **SSA.GOV**.

3. Once you have your Medicare ID number, book an appointment with our team to choose your other insurance coverages.

4. Prepare a list of your drugs, dosages, doctors, and questions. We research plans in your area and present you with many options.

5. Choose the plans you feel most comfortable with.

6. Enroll into your other coverages.

7. When questions pop up down the line, email or call our Client Care Team at 1-800-970-1964.

8. Book an annual review with our Client Care Team each fall to see if your plan still meets your needs.

9. Sleep well at night knowing that our team will be here. My family has done this for 45 years!

IS MEDICARE GOING AWAY?

No. It's not going away.

The media loves to stir up fear with headlines that Medicare is going to run out of money very soon. *Don't plan on ever getting Medicare or Social Security!* is a common clickbait headline.

But don't fret! For those readers who are years away from age 65, rest assured that Medicare will be here for you.

It *will* continue to change as the population continues to age and costs continue to spiral. Medicare is one of the largest and most established government programs in the U.S., serving tens of millions of retirees and individuals with disabilities. Yes, Medicare faces funding challenges, but there are many ways to modify the program and still keep it viable.

Medicare is unlikely to disappear any time soon!

It has strong bipartisan support, as it's highly popular among the public. Any political attempt to eliminate or drastically reduce Medicare would likely face significant opposition from voters, especially since it serves a crucial role for older Americans who depend on it for healthcare. Retirees vote!

Every day 11,000 people turn 65. Thanks to the Baby Boomers, the number of people relying on Medicare is increasing rapidly. Eliminating the program would leave millions of seniors without affordable healthcare options, *a politically and socially untenable situation.* It will likely require bipartisan support to get any modifications into law. It's hard, which is why major changes are rare.

💡 *Medicare and Social Security make up the biggest part of the federal budget. We spend more on Medicare than we do on national defense.*

Would one (or both) political parties love to pare down the cost of Medicare? Yes (and yes). It can be political suicide to push the topic of Medicare cuts, just ask former House Speaker Paul Ryan, who was known for advocating for major changes to Medicare.

The last big changes to Medicare came in 2003. Over 20 years ago we got the Medicare Part D drug program under President George W. Bush. It's taken us 22 years to see the next major change to Medicare with the cap on drug costs that begins in 2025. A big change every 20 years!

Yes, funding is a problem for both Medicare and Social Security for two simple reasons:

- We live longer.
- Families have fewer kids which means fewer adults to work and pay into the system.

Will benefits be cut for both programs in the future? Yep.

Will you be grandfathered in? Maybe.

Does anyone know what the future of these programs looks like? It's all speculation.

But it is unlikely to go anywhere!

MEDICARE FUNDING

> Let's briefly touch on the funding of Medicare.
> It's boring but important, so I'll keep it short.

Funding for Medicare comes from a variety of sources. The different components are financed in different ways and revenue sources intended for one part of the program cannot be used to pay for another part.

Funding includes:

- Payroll taxes.
- General tax revenues.
- What you pay for your Part B (and sometimes Part A) premiums.

If you are a typical W-2 employee, 1.45% of every income check you get goes to Medicare FICA (Federal Insurance Contributions Act), and your employer pays the other 1.45%. If you are self-employed, you pay the entire 2.9%. Higher income employees pay a higher tax on their earnings. Your FICA payroll taxes account for the majority of your Part A funding.

Part B is financed primarily through general tax revenues and monthly beneficiary premiums. A few years ago, they decided to increase the cost of Medicare for those considered to be high earners. The income-related monthly adjustment amount (IRMAA) is a fee some beneficiaries may have to pay for Part B and Part D plans. This surcharge is now bringing in money for Medicare that we didn't have 20 years ago.

🔆 *A lot has to change in the future for both Medicare and Social Security programs to continue to meet their obligations. It is not politically popular to gut these programs, so our lawmakers keep avoiding the topic so as not to tank their reelection. But the needed changes will come!*

POINTS TO REMEMBER

- Listen to your friend's advice but make decisions that are personal to your unique location, medications, doctors, and budget.

- Everyone's retirement choices will be different.

- Which insurance you should buy is a gamble, so buy the best insurance that you can comfortably afford.

- Only you know how comfortable your budget is. Don't get talked into something you can't afford.

- Budget for prices to go up each year!

- Medicare has a funding issue which means that benefits are likely to go down and prices are likely to go up in the future, but for now, it's just speculation when change will come.

- Every politician has a plan to shore up Medicare.

- It's going to take bipartisan support to make any major change to a program this big and important!

CHAPTER 2

THE PARTS OF MEDICARE

Medicare is the nation's health insurance program for seniors and the disabled. It serves those aged 65 and older, those who are disabled at any age, and those who suffer from End Stage Renal Disease (ESRD) or Lou Gehrig's Disease (ALS).

Medicare currently consists of four parts:

- Part A (Hospital)
- Part B (Medical)
- Part C (Medicare Advantage)
- Part D (Prescription Drugs)

You don't need to understand everything in this book, but you should know how these four parts work:

Part A is called Hospital Insurance. It covers you while you are under inpatient care in a hospital or hospice. Most people can enroll in Part A at age 65 at no cost, though you will still have a deductible and other costs. If you don't have 40 work credits to get Part A at no cost, you can pay for it. How much you'll have to pay is based on how many work credits you do have.

Part B is called Medical Insurance by the government, but that makes no sense. We call it Doctor Insurance even though it covers more than just doctor visits. Part B covers things outside of a hospital, like doctors, labs, CAT scans, and outpatient surgeries. Part B has an annual deductible, and you'll pay 20% of the total bill.

Part C is Private Medicare known as Medicare Advantage. It usually rolls A, B, and D into one plan called Part C. Prices and designs vary, but a $0 monthly premium plan with no deductible is very common.

Part D is the *only* thing that Medicare ever did that is easy to remember. D stands for Drugs. Part D is a private insurance plan you buy to cover your prescription medications. It has a monthly cost, annual deductible, and copays for each prescription.

- For Parts A and B, you'll enroll directly with the government on **SSA.GOV.**
- For Parts C and D, you'll enroll directly with a broker — like my family — or with the insurance company. Not the government.

You must enroll into government Medicare A and B *before* you can purchase a Medicare Supplement or enroll into a private Medicare Advantage plan. You only need Part A or B to be able to purchase a Part D plan.

Medicare Supplement Plans, like Plan F or G are different from Medicare Parts A, B, C, and D. Private supplemental insurance fills the gaps in government Medicare A and B. You can't have a Supplement *and* Medicare Advantage. More on this later.

If you are feeling drowsy, hang in there, I'm almost done with the basics. Parts A, B, C, and D are really all you need to memorize, the rest you can read and forget as long as you understand the basics and know where to go for help when you have questions.

I'll cover these topics soon, but here is a quick summary of some of the terms I'll be using frequently:

Enrollment Periods are different timelines when you can enroll or change plans. There are many enrollment periods! When you move or have unusual circumstances, you'll need to use a **Special Enrollment Period** to change your plans.

Medicare Supplement plans, also called Medigap plans, are *private insurance plans* issued by insurance companies that are designed to cover the gaps in Medicare Part A and Part B coverage. Plans are alphabetical A – N. Some plans you may have heard of are no longer available.

Medicare Advantage plans are private insurance plans you can get to administer your government Medicare A and B. These types of plans have many names and often include Part D drug coverage and extra benefits you won't find in government Medicare.

The **Medicare Savings Program** may help you pay for some or all of Part B if your income and assets are low enough. Every state offers this type of program.

IRMAA (income-related monthly adjustment amount) is a surcharge you may pay if your income is high. This requires you to pay more for Parts B and D for one year at a time.

Dual Eligibles are people who qualify for financial assistance through their state's **Medicaid** program. Millions of people have both Medicare and Medicaid and are eligible for different plans and have different enrollment rules.

There are an immeasurable number of other terms that pertain to Medicare (you'll find more in the glossary), but these are the ones you should become familiar with. Even if you know you want to go with a Medicare Supplement at age 65, please learn about Medicare Advantage plans, too. It's likely that at some point in the future, you'll move into that type of plan.

QUALITY COVERAGE

There's a common misconception that Medicare is bad insurance. **Generally speaking, Medicare is very good insurance for what you**

pay for it. It is often far superior in coverage and cost to the insurance you had prior to age 65. If you come to Medicare from the Affordable Care Act / Obamacare, you will be shocked at how low the deductibles and out-of-pocket costs are!

🔆 *The Affordable Care Act (ACA) is also commonly referred to as Obamacare. No, the term "Obamacare" is not a slur. It originated as a colloquial way to refer to the ACA, the healthcare law enacted during President Barack Obama's administration in 2010. Initially, it was often used by critics of the law as a critical label. Over time, however, even President Obama embraced the term, stating, "I like it. I do care." The government has used this term on its own website!*

How could Medicare be better than your work insurance? Many work plans have a very high deductible, from $2,000 to $5,000 per year. A Medicare Supplement Plan G will have an annual Part B deductible of only $257 this year! Most work insurance plans have a limited network while government Medicare has no network.

HOW TO QUALIFY FOR MEDICARE

To qualify for premium-free Medicare Part A at age 65, you or your spouse must have worked and paid into Social Security FICA payroll taxes for at least 10 years (they don't need to be consecutive years) to earn the 40 credits. This is the same requirement to qualify for Social Security retirement benefits. To qualify for Medicare, you must be age 65, or on Social Security Disability if you are younger than 65.

STAY-AT-HOME MOMS

"I don't have 40 credits to qualify for Medicare, what do I do?"

This is the most popular question I get from people who are worried about their spouse's retirement. Stay-at-home moms (or people who never worked) can qualify for premium-free Part A benefits on their spouse's work record. To qualify, you must have been married for at least one year, you must be at least 65, and your spouse must be at least 62. (Remember, I'm using generalized terms.)

- If you were a stay-at-home mom and are married to a younger man, you may not be able to enroll into Medicare when you turn 65 if he is not yet 62. You are not penalized for not taking Medicare at age 65 because *you were not eligible*.

- Qualification can also be based on the work record of a deceased or divorced spouse if the marriage lasted long enough (10 years if divorced, 9 months if deceased during the marriage).

If you lived with your partner for 30 years and your state doesn't recognize common law marriage, you can still qualify for Medicare. Just get married! After only 1 year of legal marriage, you become eligible for Medicare as a spouse (assuming you are 65 or older).

💡 *If you were not in the work force and your spouse or ex-spouse always worked under the table (and fraudulently avoided FICA taxes), you may not be eligible for Medicare. If you are close to having 10 years and 40 credits to qualify for benefits on your own work record, you may have to work a few more years to qualify.*

FOREIGNERS MAY QUALIFY TOO

Non-U.S. citizens can qualify for Medicare under certain conditions. Medicare eligibility is primarily based on legal residency and work history in the United States. Here's a breakdown of how foreigners can qualify for Medicare:

Legal Permanent Resident Status (Green Card Holders)

- They must be at least 65 years old.

- They must have lived in the U.S. for at least 5 continuous years immediately before applying for Medicare.

- There is still a work requirement. To qualify for premium-free Medicare Part A, they or their spouse must have worked and paid Medicare taxes in the U.S. for at least 40 quarters (10 years). If they do not meet the 40 quarters of work requirement, they may still be able to buy into Medicare A by paying premiums (but it is expensive).

Spousal Qualification

Foreigners may also qualify for Medicare based on their spouse's work history. If the spouse is eligible for Medicare, the foreign spouse may qualify for Medicare at age 65 *based on their spouse's work record.*

No Medicare Coverage for Visitors

Foreign visitors to the U.S. (those on temporary visas such as tourists or short-term workers) generally do not qualify for Medicare, regardless of age or health condition. Medicare is for U.S. citizens or lawful permanent residents who meet the specific eligibility criteria mentioned above.

FICA PAYROLL TAXES

If you are employed, you pay 6.2% for Social Security and 1.45% for Medicare FICA each pay period. Your employer matches this. But if you are self-employed, you pay the full amount of both portions: 12.4% + 2.9% = 15.3%.

I find it strange that Medicare FICA is paid on every last dollar of wages you earn, but Social Security tops off at a certain income each year. For 2025 it is $176,100, which means the rich are only paying Social Security FICA on a fraction of their income. Raising this income cap is often mentioned as a solution to the funding problem.

> Congress is toying with raising payroll taxes
> to raise money for both programs.
> It's not popular, but it is being discussed.

If you worked, you paid into Medicare (or you should have). Medicare FICA ate up a lot of your paycheck. Because of this, most people assume that Medicare will be *FREE* at age 65. It comes as a shock to many that only one Part of Medicare (Part A) is premium-free. I don't call it free because you did pay into it your whole working career. Medicare Parts B and D have a monthly cost unless your income and assets are low enough to qualify for financial assistance.

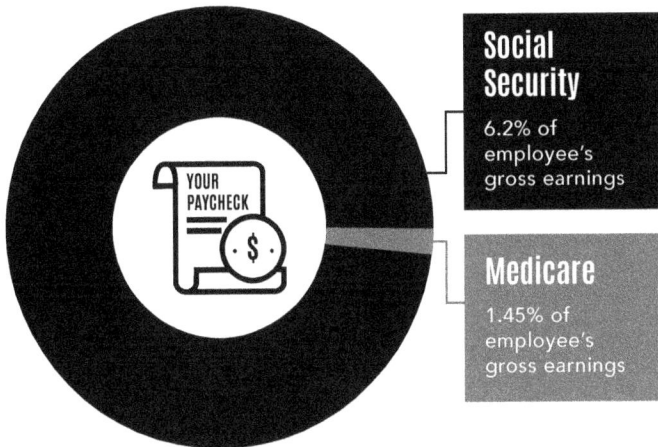

YOUR PAYCHECK

Social Security
6.2% of employee's gross earnings

Medicare
1.45% of employee's gross earnings

Total taxes deducted from paycheck: 7.65%
Your employer matches your contribution.
If you are self-employed, you pay all of it.

💡 *Unlike Social Security, you don't get more Medicare benefits if you worked longer and paid in more via your FICA payroll taxes. Everyone who qualifies for Medicare gets the same benefits.*

THESE SERVICES ARE "FREE"

I'll give credit where credit is due. Government Medicare offers a lot of free care and screenings to find illness early and help keep you healthy.

> Sadly, Medicare does NOT provide a free, comprehensive annual physical.

Many people have had access to a free annual physical through their work insurance and are shocked to find out the government doesn't provide this too. Yes, treating cancer is more expensive than an annual physical, but Medicare doesn't want to pay for 60 million physicals each year.

Note that most private Medicare Advantage plans do offer a free physical. The for-profit companies want to keep you healthy more than the government does!

Even though you won't get an annual check-up, you will receive a Welcome to Medicare visit!

"Welcome to Medicare" Visit Explained

This free visit consistently underwhelms people. It is not a physical, it is more like an introduction to some of the care that Medicare offers. During this visit, you mostly just talk to your doctor about your needs and possibly get some counseling on how to prevent disease.

There is a small bit of care happening. Your doctor will check your weight, height, vision, and blood pressure. You'll be asked if you have depression or any trouble navigating your daily life.

Your doctor will ask if you have healthcare legal documents such as a Power of Attorney and Living Will. This is important, as many people are unaware of the value of these types of documents.

So, while your welcome visit may be underwhelming, Medicare still offers a lot of free preventative care, like:

Bone Mass Measurements – Near and dear to me since I have Osteoporosis and get this scan myself. Even if you are not yet suffering from Osteopenia or Osteoporosis, bone mass measurements are critical preventative care. Especially if you are at risk due to a slim build.

Cardiovascular Screening – These screenings check your heart and vessel health through a variety of tests. Heart attacks run in my family, so we are hypervigilant about our heart health.

Most Vaccinations – As long as your doctor accepts Medicare assignment, most vaccinations are free, including:

- COVID-19 vaccines
- Hepatitis B vaccines for persons at increased risk of hepatitis
- Influenza (flu) vaccines
- Pneumococcal vaccines
- Vaccines directly related to the treatment of an injury or direct exposure to a disease, such as rabies.

Vaccines for shingles, tetanus, pertussis, and RSV are not covered by government Medicare A and B. However, they are covered under Medicare Part D — with no copay or deductibles!

Glaucoma Screening – Medicare does not provide an annual wellness exam to check your eyes. You'll have to pay for that on your own. However, it will cover a glaucoma screening every year, if you fall into one of these groups:

- You have diabetes
- You have a family history of glaucoma
- You're African American and 50 or older
- You're Hispanic and 65 or older

You will still pay your portion of the Part B cost.

Colonoscopy – Medicare pays for a screening every 10 years, or every 2 years if you are at high risk.

Pap Smears – This screening is covered every 2 years. I pay for my own annually since I've known too many younger people who have been diagnosed with cervical cancer.

> The average doctor spends very little time with each patient!

You need to go to every doctor appointment prepared with a list of questions and concerns. The more research you do in advance — and the more honest you are with your doctor — the more productive your visit will be. Understand what Medicare will and won't pay for so you can decide which tests you can afford to pay for.

Use the **MEDICARE.GOV** app and keep your annual *Medicare and You* guide handy. You'll need these references for the rest of your life.

POINTS TO REMEMBER

- Government Medicare, also known as Original Medicare, is composed of Parts A and B.

- Parts C and D are private insurance plans.

- You must work and pay into Medicare FICA payroll taxes for 10 years to qualify for premium-free Part A.

- If you didn't quite earn all the credits for premium-free Part A, you can pay for it.

- You may qualify based on your spouse's work record if you've been married for at least 1 year.

- If you qualify due to a former spouse's work record, your marriage had to have lasted at least 10 years.

- There are coverage holes in Medicare A and B, so most people buy private insurance too.

- You may qualify for both Medicaid and Medicare.

- Foreigners may qualify for Medicare.

- Medicare offers a lot of great preventative care for free.

CHAPTER 3

WHEN, WHERE, AND HOW TO ENROLL

Medicare and Social Security are sister programs. They are similar, but different. People make a lot of assumptions because the age to get Medicare is 65 and the age to get your full social security *used to be age 65.* You sign up for Medicare at the Social Security office and they take the cost of your Medicare Part B premiums automatically out of your Social Security check. It is confusing. Remember, I can't make it make sense.

You can easily apply for government Medicare A and B online at **SSA.GOV**. The Social Security Administration handles the back end; **MEDICARE.GOV** handles claims and health related questions.

Setting up an online account at **MEDICARE.GOV** and **SSA.GOV** allows you to avoid long waits to talk to government employees that are likely to give you incorrect information. You can also use the website to update your address, change payment methods, check to see claims information, and more. Plus, you will be able to see your claims information on your Medicare site.

Now that I've explained the basics, let's dive into when and how you can sign up.

💡 *I use the term Government Medicare to draw attention to the fact that Medicare Advantage is Private Medicare. The government uses the term Original Medicare.*

WHEN TO ENROLL

Many people think Medicare *automatically* starts at age 65. They just wait for their Medicare card to arrive in the mail. Unless you are already collecting any type of Social Security benefits, you will *not be automatically enrolled* into Medicare Parts A and B. You have to enroll.

For the people who are drawing a Social Security benefit at least 4 months prior to turning age 65, Medicare enrollment is automatic. Only about 30% of people are drawing Social Security prior to age 65.

The rest of retirees need to do these 4 things:

1. Figure out if you need to enroll at age 65 (some don't).

2. Determine when to enroll (if it's not age 65).

3. Enroll yourself into government Medicare A and B.

4. Figure out your next steps (other coverages that you'll need and enroll).

💡 *At age 65, if you received your Medicare ID card in the mail but you do NOT want Medicare yet, because you are still covered on your own or your spouse's health plan, you can choose to turn down Part B (and save the monthly cost). Flip your welcome letter over for details on how to return your card.*

You can begin your application up to 3 months prior to the month you turn 65. Go to the SSA's Medicare Benefits page and select **"Apply for Medicare Only."** It shouldn't take you more than 30 minutes to apply.

Here are some common reasons people encounter problems while enrolling:

1. **Incorrect Personal Information.** If there are discrepancies between the information provided during enrollment (like name, date of birth, or Social Security number) and what's on file with the Social Security Administration, it may cause issues.

2. **Not Eligible for Medicare.** People who haven't worked enough quarters (or haven't paid Medicare taxes long enough) may not qualify for premium-free Medicare Part A, which could cause confusion or complications during the enrollment process. You should be able to set up payment for Part A when you enroll.

3. **Abbreviations.** Sometimes the SSA website may glitch if you use abbreviations in your street address. Spell it all out (Street, Lane, Avenue, etc.).

4. **Previous Enrollment Mistakes.** If there was an earlier attempt to enroll that didn't go through correctly, it could result in conflicting applications or errors in the system. You'll need to apply in person to sort this out.

If you are still working and have medical coverage, you don't need to sign up for Medicare right away.

DOCUMENTS YOU MAY NEED

IMPORTANT: The SSA won't accept photocopies.

To apply for government Medicare Parts A and B, you probably won't need to supply any documents. If they do need documents, you can mail them to the Social Security Administration or take them into a local facility. I caution you against mailing or faxing anything to the SSA as they have a habit of losing things, which can put you into a time crunch.

When you need anything done in a hurry, take it in person. If you are not in a hurry, use certified mail, never regular mail.

Some of the documents the SSA may require:

- Proof of age (such as a birth certificate).
- Proof of U.S. citizenship or legal residency (like a passport or green card).
- A record of your employment history (such as a W-2 form).
- Marriage certificate.
- Military service history.

Your birth certificate verifies your eligibility based on age. Your W-2 form helps determine if you've worked long enough under Medicare-covered employment to qualify for premium-free Part A (10 full, but not consecutive years). Your marriage certificate is needed if you qualify for Medicare off your spouse's work record.

WHERE IS MY ID CARD?

After you've enrolled, you'll wait for your Medicare ID card to arrive by mail. Sadly, with so many applying each day, an outdated computer system, and overworked federal employees, mistakes are made. Many of our clients have waited patiently for Medicare cards that never arrived.

Wait for 8 weeks, but no longer than that! If you haven't received your card by then, a call to the SSA will find your application and set it back on its way to get processed.

For example, the processing time for Medicare Part B applications typically ranges from *1 to 3 months*, starting from when the Social Security Administration receives your application.

Note that things are a little slower if you apply to begin Medicare at the very end or very beginning of a calendar year. During the rest of the year, I frequently hear from people who applied online and got their Part B ID number in their online account within a week.

💡 *It's best to apply as early as possible, especially if you're nearing your 65th birthday or the end of your Initial Enrollment Period. You can apply 3 months in advance of the month you reach age 65.*

You'll receive a welcome package with your red, white, and blue Medicare card in the mail. The envelope is addressed *from Medicare*. It's not a durable credit card type of plastic. It's a cheap, paper card that easily gets damaged in your wallet. The government doesn't want you to laminate it (although I've done that for countless clients). Just buy some type of plastic cover to protect it, because you'll need this card for the rest of your life.

Once you have your Medicare card (or can see the info online) you are ready for your next steps.

💡 *If you set up an account at Medicare.gov you can often find your Medicare ID number there much faster than waiting for them to mail you your card. It's often available online within a week!*

MEDICARE EASY PAY

If you enroll into Part B *and are not drawing* Social Security, you will be billed for **3 months at a time**.

This quarterly payment is almost $600. This is unpleasant and comes as a surprise for most people. You do have an option to have the monthly cost of Part B deducted from your checking or savings account through Medicare Easy Pay.

You can find the Medicare Easy Pay **Form SF-5510** online.

You can file two ways:

1. **Online** – You'll need to create an account if you don't already have one. Log in to your **MEDICARE.GOV** account, select My Premiums, then change to My Medicare Easy Pay.

2. **By mail** – Mailing or faxing anything to Medicare is NOT my recommendation. Yes, you can mail it, but they may claim they never received it. If you still want to go this route, then print and fill out the form. You'll need to include information from your Medicare card and bank details, which you can find on a blank check. If you're using a checking account, you'll need a voided check. Mail the completed form to the Centers for Medicare & Medicaid Services below:

Centers for Medicare & Medicaid Services
Medicare Premium Collection Center
P.O. Box 979098
St. Louis, MO 63197-9000

Once you return this form, it can take 6 to 8 weeks to process. Until it's processed, you must continue to pay your quarterly bill.

Once your form is successfully processed, your Medicare Premium Bills will state "THIS IS NOT A BILL" in the upper right corner, so you know that your automatic deductions have begun.

From there forward, your premiums will be deducted from your bank account, *usually on the 20th of each month*. It will appear on your bank statement as a CMS Medicare Premium Automated Clearing House (ACH) transaction. If you file this form when you first apply for Medicare Part B — 3 months prior to turning 65 — Medicare may not process it on time. You may end up owing 2 to 3 months' premiums because they didn't get the ACH into effect.

After the initial deduction, 1 month's premium is the maximum deduction you'll see each month on your statement.

When you begin receiving payments from Social Security, your **Medicare premiums will automatically be deducted** from that amount instead of the bank account you set up through Medicare Easy Pay. *But this could take 1 or 2 months to switch over.*

On a similar note, you can have your Medicare Part D drug premium automatically withdrawn from your Social Security check too. I'll explain Parts C and D more, but since this section is about payments, let's be clear that the government is *slow*. If you sign up to have your Part D premiums deducted from your Social Security account, it can take a few months to take effect.

If you switch plans — which you eventually will — it can take a few months for them to begin taking the deductions for the new company and stop the payments to the old company.

WHEN WILL YOUR MEDICARE COVERAGE START?

Most people apply for Medicare when they turn 65. This is called your **Initial Enrollment Period (IEP)**. It lasts for 7 months, starting 3 months before you turn 65, and ending 3 months after the month you turn 65.

For example, if you turn 65 in June, your IEP begins the first day of March and ends the last day of September.

The date your coverage starts depends on the month you sign up. You could sign up any time during your 7-month IEP. When you sign up, you will choose a start date, which is often the first day of the month that you turn 65.

1. If you applied in the 3 months prior to age 65, Medicare starts the first day of the month you turn 65.

2. If your birthday is on the 1st, your coverage starts on the 1st of the *prior month.*

3. If you waited to apply until your 65th birthday, your benefits start on the *1st of the next month.*

4. If you applied 2 months after your birthday, *Medicare starts the 1ˢᵗ of the following month.*

5. If you waited to apply until 4 months after your birthday, *you waited too long*! You'll have to wait to enroll until January.

Initial Enrollment Period

The Initial Enrollment Period (IEP) is the first time you can sign up for Medicare.

3 months before your 65th birthday   The month of your birthday   3 months after your 65th birthday

If you wait to apply on the last day of the month (but still within your IEP) your coverage can still start on the next day, the first day of the next month. You won't have any ID cards, but if you get sick, you'll have coverage.

But don't procrastinate! Start the enrollment process 3 months before you want Medicare to start to make your enrollment smooth and stress-free.

Since most people will pay out-of-pocket for Medicare Part B, if you enrolled and found out later that you didn't need to, you can cancel it. But first, be sure that you don't need Medicare.

WHAT IF I DON'T WANT MEDICARE?

While many people take Medicare at age 65, many more do not. More and more people are continuing to work indefinitely. This delay won't harm you as long as you have Creditable Coverage **at work (more than 20 employees).**

If you are working past age 65, how you proceed with Medicare depends on *where* you work:

1. If you are self-employed or working for a small company with **fewer than 20 full-time employees**, you should enroll into Medicare Parts A and B. If you don't, you'll face a late penalty.

2. If you work for an **employer with 20 or more** employees you do NOT have to enroll into Medicare.

3. If you are **self-employed** and on Obamacare (ACA), you might be getting a tax subsidy based on your income. That subsidy goes away once you are eligible for Medicare. You'll need to enroll into Medicare once you become eligible or face a late penalty.

Go to Chapter 9 to learn more about Creditable Coverage and working past 65.

If you don't want Medicare when you turn 65, you don't need to provide notice to anyone that you'd like to delay enrolling into Medicare. Just go about your life and enroll when you are ready.

However, if you are receiving any type of Social Security or Railroad Retirement Board benefits, you'll need to notify the SSA prior to turning 65 and say that you do NOT want to be automatically enrolled into Medicare.

💡 *By law if you receive Social Security benefits and are eligible for Medicare, you must also have Medicare Part A.*

You may get a great job offer with health insurance and no longer need Medicare. Typically, you don't benefit by keeping Medicare Part B as long as your employer has 20 or more employees. So why continue to pay about $200 per month when you don't need it?

When Is My Special Enrollment Period?

| While you have coverage from an employer | OR | The 8 months after your coverage ends for Parts A and B | The 63 days after your coverage ends for Parts C and D |

You can easily disenroll from Medicare Part B by filing **Form CMS-1763** to terminate Medicare.

You will typically keep Medicare Part A if you go back to work. But if your new job allows you to contribute to an HSA, you can't keep Medicare Part A. More on HSAs in Chapter 22.

I have a client, we'll call him Larry, who has enrolled and disenrolled a few times. Larry gets a job, then loses it. He doesn't need Medicare while he has coverage through his employer, but his industry isn't stable. The fact that he's been in and out of Medicare doesn't hurt him.

Everything is triggered by enrollment into Part B, but you only get one lifetime Golden Ticket. Meaning, the first time you enroll, you can get any Medicare Supplement regardless of health. But the following enrollments, you must be healthy enough to qualify to get a Medicare Supplement (unless you live in one of the states that always allows it).

AVOIDING MEDICARE SCAMS

Scammers are getting sophisticated. So, here's what you need to know.

Scammers need your 11-digit Medicare number to charge Medicare for fake claims. They will try to trick you into giving it out over the phone.

One of these scams goes like this: Someone will call you and tell you that you need to replace your cheaper paper card — the one the government sent you — with a new plastic chip card, similar to a credit card. This is a good scam because I'd like to have a more durable Medicare card. The cheap paper one wears out fast! Then they ask you for your Medicare number. Once they have that, they bill your plan with fake charges and walk away with the money.

Medicare will never call you to ask for your number. Please, read that again. Medicare will never call you to ask for your number.

Also, the government doesn't charge a fee to issue you a new card and it does not offer a plastic version of the Medicare card.

You need to protect your Medicare number. Don't give it out to anyone except people who need it and are trusted, such as doctors. Don't give it out over the phone if someone claims to be from Medicare, because (say it with me) Medicare will never call you to ask for your number.

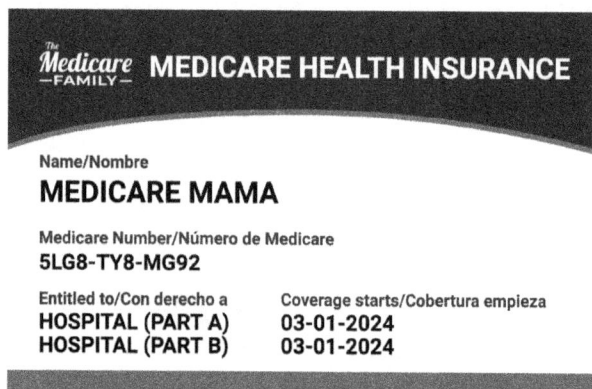

The **Medicare** **MEDICARE HEALTH INSURANCE**
—FAMILY—

Name/Nombre
MEDICARE MAMA

Medicare Number/Número de Medicare
5LG8-TY8-MG92

Entitled to/Con derecho a | Coverage starts/Cobertura empieza
HOSPITAL (PART A) | **03-01-2024**
HOSPITAL (PART B) | **03-01-2024**

LOST OR STOLEN MEDICARE CARD

Since your Medicare card *no longer contains your Social Security number*, it's fine to keep it in your wallet. (Please don't keep your Social Security card in your wallet.)

If you lose your Medicare card, simply log into your Medicare account to print a new official Medicare card at **MEDICARE.GOV**. The Client Care Team can help walk you through this process.

If your card number is stolen, or you lose your card, call Medicare immediately at 1-800-MEDICARE (1-800-633-4227).

POINTS TO REMEMBER

- Medicare starts the first day of the month that you turn 65.

- If your birthday is on the 1st day of the month, it begins the month prior.

- If you are drawing any type of Social Security benefit 4 months prior to turning 65, you will be automatically enrolled.

- If you don't want Medicare and were automatically enrolled, contact the SSA to disenroll.

- If you are not auto-enrolled, the month Medicare starts is based on the month you apply.

- Medicare charges you for 3 months of Part B premiums at a time unless you sign up for Medicare Easy Pay.

- Medicare Easy Pay will allow the SSA to draft 1 month of Part B premiums from your checking or savings account each month until you start drawing Social Security.

- If you are drawing Social Security, your Part B premiums must come out of your Social Security check.

- If you don't want Medicare, you don't have to notify the government. Just don't enroll.

- If you enrolled and later realized you don't need Medicare, you can disenroll and re-enroll later.

- If your card number is stolen, report it immediately!

CHAPTER 4

HOW MUCH WILL IT COST?

In this chapter, I'll break down the costs of Medicare's different parts and give you a better idea how to budget for retirement. From premiums and deductibles to potential out-of-pocket costs, I'll try to simplify your options so you can make the decision that feels best for *your health and wallet.*

There are a lot of choices. The combination of coverages you choose will depend on your health, budget, location, family history and comfort level.

Here are some popular options that people use to get the right balance of coverage and cost:

- Government Medicare only.
- Government Medicare + Part D drug plan.
- Government Medicare, Part D + Plan G.
- Plan G, Part D + Stand-alone Dental, Vision, & Hearing Plan.
- Private Medicare PPO or HMO.
- Private Medicare PPO or HMO + Hospital Indemnity plan.
- PPO, Hospital Indemnity + Cancer Plan.

PREMIUM ESTIMATES

Medicare Part A

For most people, **Medicare Part A** is paid up by age 65. If you didn't work and pay into FICA for 10 years, you will have to pay some or all the cost of Part A. The actual price is based on how many FICA Medicare credits you have. If you have fewer than 39 credits but more than 30 credits, you'll pay $258 per month for Part A. (Remember, all estimates in this book are for 2025.)

💡 *Many government employees do not pay into Social Security FICA, but still pay into Medicare FICA and qualify for Medicare Part A.*

Medicare Part B

The majority of people will pay the standard premium for **Medicare Part B**, with those considered to be low income paying $0 per month, and those considered to be high income paying more. The standard Part B monthly price in 2025 is $185. This amount goes up every year about $10 to $15 per month.

If you are a high earner, you may pay considerably more for Part B. Read about IRMAA in Chapter 8.

Medicare Part C

Almost every county in the nation has some type of Medicare Advantage plan available (most of Alaska does not!). This is called **Medicare Part C** or **Private Medicare** or **Medicare Advantage.** Medicare Advantage plans became famous for offering $0 monthly plans, but in some areas, especially rural ones, you might find that these plans do charge a monthly premium. Larger cities often have the most affordable Part C plans or even plans with no monthly cost, while more remote locations will have fewer options.

But $0 does not mean free. You still pay, just in a different way.

You still must pay for Medicare Part B, but there may be no additional cost to enroll in one of the Part C plans. While some plans do have a monthly cost of $20 to $120 per month, many plans do not. *Price will always be based on your location and plan choice.*

The costs add up when you *use* your insurance. You'll pay a separate fee for every service (remember, many preventative services are free), up to an annual maximum. The maximum out-of-pocket (MOOP) is the most important and overlooked part of Medicare Advantage. Remember MOOP because it will help you determine which plans to choose.

Medicare Advantage plans may include a drug benefit. The plans that do not include a drug benefit are designed for veterans and spouses who are eligible for a richer drug benefit through the VA or TRICARE For Life. The vast majority of people will purchase a Part C plan that includes a Part D drug benefit.

🔅 *Warning: You cannot purchase a Medicare Advantage plan without a drug benefit and then purchase your own stand-alone drug plan! Doing this will terminate your health plan and you'll be left with only drug coverage.*

Medicare Part D

Depending on where you live, you may have access to a drug plan that costs from $0 to $150 per month. The monthly price pales in comparison to the copays, but we will use an average of $37 a month as a ballpark estimate for budgeting reasons. If you want to budget more accurately, you'll need to know the copays for each medication you take. If you take a lot of prescriptions, you won't pay more than $2,000 for the year (your MOOP). You can sign up for the Medicare Prescription Payment Plan (M3P) to spread out the cost over the year.

Medicare Supplement Plan G

Supplemental plans base their rates on age, gender, and location making it hard to estimate a price. If you are a woman turning 65 in most of the Midwest, in 2025, you could get a Medicare Supplement Plan G from $100 to $300 per month. A man in the same area turning 65 will pay at least $30 more per month.

New York is the most expensive state for Medicare Supplement plans. You can expect to pay double what a person in the Midwest would pay.

We are licensed in all states and can help explain what is available to you.

Medicare Supplement Plan N

This plan is typically $30 to $40 less per month than Plan G.

Stand-Alone Dental Plan

Medicare A and B do not cover dental care. There are many dental insurance plans available, and the premiums vary by the state you live in, your age, and what type of benefit you purchase. Unlike a Plan G, which will have the same benefit regardless of which insurance company you work with, dental benefits are drastically different from company to company. One company may only offer $1,000 of annual coverage while another company may offer up to $5,000 of coverage. You will need to shop around.

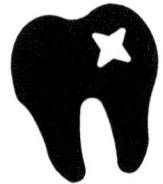

A woman turning 65 who is from the Midwest can expect to pay about $35 to $45 per month for a plan with $2,000 of annual coverage.

Cancer Plan

If cancer runs in your family, I recommend a separate cancer policy, even if you have great insurance. Many of the costs associated with cancer are non-medical, such as travel out of state, time your spouse must take off work, and modifications to your house or car. A cancer plan is a lump sum of money *paid directly to you to use as you wish* for all these extra costs. Or you can use it to pay your out-of-pocket costs on a Medicare Advantage plan.

The cost of a cancer insurance plan for a 65-year-old female in the Midwest can vary based on several factors, including the insurance company, the level of coverage, and the specific state. Price ranges:

- **Low Coverage** (around $10,000 to $20,000 in benefits): Premiums typically range from **$20 to $40 per month**.
- **Moderate Coverage** (around $30,000 to $50,000 in benefits): Premiums typically range from **$40 to $75 per month**.
- **High Coverage** (above $50,000 in benefits): Premiums typically start around **$75 per month** and go up from there.

PREMIUM SCENARIO

Sandy is turning 65 in 2025. She completed her work credits for Part A. She lives in Indiana, Ohio, Tennessee, Kentucky, or Iowa. Here is what she can expect to pay in monthly premiums for 2025.

Part A	$0	**Plan G**	$120
Part B	$185	**Dental**	$40
Part D	$37		

Sandy's monthly estimate for 2025 is $382. If her prescription copays cost more than $2000 each year, she will pay no more than $167 per month in addition to her monthly premiums.

- MOOP for Plan G is $257 in 2025.
- MOOP for Part D is $2,000 in 2025.

Or Sandy could go to private Medicare Advantage, which includes her drug and dental coverage.

Part A	$0
Part B	$185
Part C (includes Rx)	$0

Sandy's monthly estimate is $185 per month in premiums. If she uses her insurance, she will pay additional copays for every service. In both scenarios, she'll pay additional copays for her prescriptions.

How you react to this price summary tells me a lot about the health insurance you have now, prior to Medicare.

- If you are **excited** beyond belief, you have either no insurance or ACA / Obamacare. You may be self-employed and expect the worst because you are paying twice that for your current coverage.
- If you are **irritated** by this price, you typically work for a huge corporation that still offers rich health benefits.
- If you just look **confused**, you are likely on your spouse's insurance and are not really sure how much of that coverage is attributed to you.

These are rough price estimates. For a personal quote for plans in your area, book a free appointment with our team online at **THEMEDICAREFAMILY.COM** and let us help you.

FILLING IN THE GAPS

Most people don't stop at government Medicare Parts A and B. Many fill the gaps with supplemental insurance, also called Medicare Supplement coverage.

💡 *A Medicare Supplement and a Medigap Plan are the same thing with a different name because this isn't confusing enough.*

Many people add up the costs of Parts A, B, and D and call it a day. They estimate that $300 per month is enough coverage at a price similar to what they were paying for their work health plan. They resist Medicare Supplements and Medicare Advantage. They often change their minds later, especially after a major illness, and the system is designed to let them back in, under certain circumstances.

> Healthy people are quick to think government Medicare alone is enough, because they haven't seen the prices of healthcare.

Healthcare in the U.S. is ridiculously expensive. You do not want to go it alone with government Medicare A and B only. I repeat this a lot because I feel strongly that I'll be able to help someone out there from making this mistake. Because government Medicare A and B have some big holes!

They don't cover:

- Long-term care in a nursing home $$$$$
- Prescription drugs that you self-administer $$$$$
- Dental care $$$
- Annual healthy eye exams or prescription glasses $
- Cosmetic surgery $$$
- Massage therapy $
- Routine physical exams $
- Hearing aids and exams for fitting them $$
- Travel expenses when your care is out of the country $

There is no maximum out-of-pocket on government Medicare. I firmly believe that all the people hurling complaints against Medicare Advantage would benefit from learning this one point!

Medicare Part B pays 80% of all your care outside of a hospital. This sounds great. But having to pay the remaining 20% for several rounds of chemotherapy and radiation is very, very expensive. What if you need dialysis 2 to 3 times a week? Or you could need even more expensive care such as a transplant!

Yes, I am trying to scare you.

Everyone on only government Medicare A and B should be scared of their potential out-of-pocket costs.

There are many different types of treatment with varying costs from wildly expensive to outrageous. If you need an air ambulance to save your life in an auto accident, that helicopter ride to the hospital can easily cost $75,000. You'd only pay 20% of $75,000.

Wait! *Only* 20% is still $15,000. Then you'd also pay a couple thousand dollars for the hospital deductible. Then you'll pay 20% for weeks of therapy and doctor's visits. *It adds up fast and there is no MOOP!* That is why people choose to supplement government Medicare with private insurance.

Unless you have other health insurance that will pay in addition to Medicare (like VA, TRICARE, FEHB, etc.), I never recommend that you enroll in Medicare A and B as your only coverage.

POINTS TO REMEMBER

- Most people qualify for Medicare Part A premium-free because they worked long enough or their spouse qualified.

- If you don't have 40 credits to get Part A without a premium, you can buy Part A, but it is expensive.

- Most people will pay for Medicare Part B.

- Some pay more or less than the standard monthly Medicare Part B premium based on their income.

- Medicare Part D has a monthly premium. You must enroll with a private insurance broker, not with the government.

- Medicare Part C may have a monthly premium depending on what plans are available in your area.

- You must enroll into a Medicare Part C plan with a private insurance agent, not through the government.

- Enrolling in government Medicare alone has unlimited financial risk.

CHAPTER 5

MEDICARE AND DISABILITY

Medicare isn't just for people over 65. If you are under 65 and disabled, you may still qualify, but the rules are different.

If life has handed you some unexpected physical challenges, you don't have to wait until you're 65 to access Medicare. If you qualify for **Social Security Disability Insurance (SSDI)**, you're also on a path to Medicare, giving you essential coverage long before retirement age. In this chapter, I'll explain how the process works, how long you'll need to wait, and what steps to take to make the most of it.

:🔆: *Just because you consider yourself disabled or your doctor told you that you are disabled, doesn't mean you can qualify for SSDI. You must go through the process to get formally declared disabled before you are eligible for benefits.*

GETTING SSDI IS HARD

You've likely heard terrible stories of how long it takes and how hard a process it is to get approved for SSDI. Those stories are true. I don't explain that process in this book as it is a book unto itself. If you think you might need to apply for SSDI, my best advice is to consult with an attorney that specializes in this area (not a dabbler).

Not every disabled American can qualify for SSDI. For instance, if you're a stay-at-home parent who has spent years raising the kids but never earned a paycheck, you won't be eligible for SSDI. To get SSDI, you have to have paid into Social Security through your work for a minimum number of years. Unlike with regular Social Security retirement benefits or Medicare coverage where you can qualify through your spouse's work record, SSDI usually requires you *to have worked and contributed on your own.* So, unfortunately, even if your spouse paid into the system, that doesn't help when it comes to SSDI eligibility.

You need to understand the term **substantial gainful activity (SGA)**. You know you were hankering for another acronym! As much as I try to eliminate acronyms — and I never use this term in my videos — some are necessary. So, let's dive into this one.

SGA is when someone makes enough money from working that the government thinks they no longer need disability benefits. If you make too much money, the SSA might stop your benefits because they think you can support yourself.

Imagine you have a lemonade stand, and you make just a little bit of money — Social Security says that's okay, and you can still get your benefits. But if your lemonade stand becomes super popular and you start making a lot of money, the SSA might say, "Wow, you're doing so well! You don't need our help anymore."

In 2025, the SGA limit for most people is **$1,620 a month**, which means if you earned more than that, your disability benefits could have been stopped. But if you're blind, the limit is a bit higher at **$2,700 a month**.

If you are on disability benefits, confirm the annual limit EVERY YEAR with the government before you work and risk losing your disability benefits!

THE 24-MONTH WAIT

If you are approved for both SSDI and Medicare, it typically takes **24 months** on SSDI before your Medicare coverage finally kicks in. Folks often get frustrated, thinking they should get Medicare right away, but that 2-year wait was the political trade-off that made it possible.

While you wait for Medicare to kick in, and if you don't have spousal insurance, you can still try to get coverage with Medicaid. (Read more about Medicaid in Chapter 22.)

Once the 24-month wait is over, you may discover that you can't afford Medicare. If that's the case, Medicaid may be the solution. There are many different levels of Medicaid that can help cover Medicare premiums, copays, and other costs. If you qualify for both Medicare and Medicaid — called "Dual Eligible" — Medicaid can help fill in the gaps where Medicare leaves off, making healthcare more affordable and accessible. Read more about insurance for Dual Eligibles in Chapter 15.

SOME EXCEPTIONS TO THE RULES

Under certain circumstances, you don't need your own work history to qualify for Medicare. If you have a severe condition like **Lou Gehrig's Disease (ALS) or End-Stage Renal Disease (ESRD)**, you can qualify for Medicare before age 65, even if you don't have enough work credits yourself. In these cases, you may be able to qualify based on your spouse's or parent's work history, provided they've worked enough to meet the Social Security requirements.

In the case of ALS, Medicare kicks in immediately once you're approved for Social Security disability. There's no waiting period at all. On the other hand, if you have ESRD, there is a 3-month waiting period before Medicare coverage begins, even if you're already on dialysis or need a kidney transplant. It's a bit of an odd disparity in the system, but the critical takeaway is that both ALS and ESRD can grant you early access to Medicare, with different timelines depending on the condition.

These are the only 2 conditions that get to skip the waiting period for Medicare. I'm often asked why terminal cancer isn't included, but

I have no idea. A lot of this is a patchwork of rules made at different times and that's why it doesn't flow and make more sense. At least that is my take on it.

💡 *You must be under age 65 to qualify for Social Security Disability.*

AFTER THE 24-MONTH WAIT

Once you've crossed that 24-month finish line, the real relief begins and Medicare will finally start working for you. You'll be automatically enrolled into government Medicare Parts A and B. Your Medicare ID card will arrive in the mail. Here are your choices how to proceed:

1. Stick with government Medicare alone and pick up a drug plan.

2. Enroll in a Medicare Supplement if you live in a state where it's available and affordable to those on SSDI and enroll into a drug plan.

3. Enroll into a Medicare Advantage plan with drug coverage, with the goal to move up to a Medicare Supplement at age 65.

For some on their spouse's work plan, those who qualify for VA benefits, or have federal retiree health benefits, *Medicare may not be wanted.* Since most people have to pay for Medicare Part B, be sure that you want it before you allow it to automatically start and the monthly costs to be drawn from your SSDI check. If you know you won't want Medicare, be sure to call the SSA and tell them *before the 24-month period* is over so you don't have to pay for it if you don't want it. Once the government starts withdrawing Medicare Part B premiums from your SSDI check, you won't be able to get that money back.

"But what if I later change my mind? Am I penalized for not taking Medicare after 24 months?" You could be if you didn't have employer group health insurance with at least 20 employees. If you did incur late penalties say, at age 45, your late penalties are wiped away at age 65.

Medicare Supplement State Rules Vary

When your Medicare coverage starts you may be upset to learn that you are not able to purchase a Medicare Supplement Plan G *in your state*. While some states require insurance companies to offer some or all plans to those on Medicare due to SSDI, it is not a federal mandate.

These states **don't** require insurance companies to offer a Medicare Supplement plan to those on SSDI under age 65:

- Alabama
- Arizona
- Arkansas
- Idaho
- Indiana
- Iowa
- Kansas
- Kentucky

- Louisiana
- Michigan
- Mississippi
- Montana
- Nebraska
- Nevada
- North Dakota
- Oklahoma

- South Carolina
- South Dakota
- Tennessee
- Texas
- Utah
- Virginia
- West Virginia
- Wyoming

If your state is not on this list, don't do a victory dance yet. Your state may allow the insurance companies to *charge significantly higher premiums* for those under 65 than they charge for beneficiaries who are 65 or older.

> For many, Medicare Supplement Plan G
> will be out of reach until age 65.

Most disabled people will purchase a Medicare Advantage plan *until they turn 65*. After 65, they often move to a Medicare Supplement plan for as long as they can comfortably afford the price. Later, they typically move back to Medicare Advantage. Told you it wasn't easy!

SOME GOOD NEWS

Late penalties are temporary. If you stay on your spouse's work coverage but it isn't creditable coverage, you will be penalized with late

Medicare B and D penalties. Some good news is that all penalties are erased when you turn 65. You will get a new IEP as if you were enrolling into Medicare for the first time.

There's a second open-enrollment period. Regardless of your state's rules for those under 65, once you turn 65, you enter a new 6-month open enrollment period where you are guaranteed access to all Medicare Supplement plans, regardless of your health conditions or disability status! Sadly, too many people are unaware of this and miss this window. Mark it on your calendar!

DISABLED ADULT CHILD BENEFITS

If you're trying to get Medicare based on your parent's work history, the key is qualifying for SSDI through something called **Disabled Adult Child (DAC)** benefits.

Here's the gist:

If you became disabled before turning 22 and haven't worked enough to qualify for SSDI on your own, you might still be able to get it through your parent's work record. To make this happen, your parents need to be retired, receiving Social Security benefits, or deceased. Plus, you'll need to meet Social Security's definition of disability and have been disabled before age 22.

Once you're approved for SSDI through your parent's work record, you're on the path to Medicare, but like everyone else on SSDI, *there's a 24-month waiting period before your Medicare coverage kicks in.* This allows disabled adult children to access Medicare, even without their own work history, offering some much-needed coverage and peace of mind.

Example: Sarah is 30 years old and has been disabled since she was 20 due to a serious medical condition. She never worked enough to earn her own Social Security work credits, so she can't qualify for SSDI based on her own work history. However, her father, John, has been working for many years and paid into Social Security. John is now retired and receiving Social Security retirement benefits.

Since Sarah became disabled before the age of 22, she can apply for SSDI based on her father's work record. Once she's approved for SSDI under her father's record, she will be eligible for Medicare, just

To be eligible for Disabled Adult Child Benefits, you must meet the following requirements:

☑ **AGE** At least 18 years old but younger than 22

☑ **DISABILITY ONSET** Your disability must have begun before turning 22

☑ **PARENT'S BENEFITS** One parent should receive Social Security retirement or disability benefits.

like any other SSDI recipient. After receiving DAC benefits for 24 months, Sarah will automatically be enrolled in Medicare, giving her access to the same coverage as someone who qualified for SSDI based on their own work history.

In this example, Sarah is able to get SSDI and Medicare because of her father's work history, even though she never worked enough to qualify on her own.

LOSING DAC MEDICARE BENEFITS

Here's how a DAC recipient could lose their Medicare:

1. **Getting Better.** If Social Security decides your disability has improved and you're no longer considered disabled, your SSDI checks will stop. Since Medicare is tied to SSDI, losing those checks will eventually make your Medicare go away too. You might still get Medicare for a while after the SSDI stops, but eventually, it will end.

2. **Working Too Much.** If you start working and making more money than Social Security allows, it could cause you to lose your SSDI. Since your Medicare depends on SSDI, if you keep earning more than allowed for too long, *you could lose Medicare too.* The amount

you're allowed to earn changes every year, so it's good to check what the limit is.

3. **Getting Married.** Sometimes getting married can mess with your benefits. If you marry someone who isn't getting Social Security, you might lose your DAC benefits, which would mean losing Medicare as well. The reason is you are no longer financially dependent on your parents and the government thinks your spouse can now take care of you (unless your spouse is also drawing Social Security). *That sounds harsh, but they do allow you to keep Medicare for almost 8 years before you are cut off.*

In short, you could lose Medicare if your disability gets better, you make too much money, or you get married to someone who doesn't have Social Security benefits. But even if your SSDI stops, they usually give you some time before they cut off your Medicare.

DAC BENEFITS AND DEATH

If the parent of a recipient dies, the DAC benefits don't just stop. In fact, the monthly Social Security benefit might even increase. When a parent who was providing the work record for DAC benefits passes away, the disabled adult child continues to receive SSDI benefits based on the deceased parent's work record.

Your monthly Social Security benefit amount may increase because survivor's benefits for dependents of a deceased parent are *often higher* than those paid out while the parent was alive. You'll still qualify for the benefits and Medicare as long as you meet the original requirements (disabled before 22, still considered disabled by Social Security, and not earning above the limit). So, the death of the parent doesn't end the benefits but can sometimes result in a higher benefit check for you. Read more about Social Security Survivor benefits in Chapter 28.

THE DISABLED SPOUSE - BENEFITS LOOPHOLE

Many families don't realize they might qualify for additional Social Security benefits when caring for a disabled child or spouse. The following example illustrates how spousal and disability benefits can overlap in helpful ways.

Ed started drawing his Social Security retirement at age 62. Ed Jr. was born with Down's Syndrome and will never be able to earn work credits on his own. Based on Ed's work record, his son is now eligible to begin receiving SSDI benefits. Even though Clara, Ed's wife, *is only 55 and not yet eligible to draw her own Social Security benefits*, she can receive benefits as a full-time caregiver for Ed Jr. Their family's benefits are subject to a family maximum limit, but these benefits make a huge difference for families like theirs.

Clara's benefits as a caregiver for Ed Jr. will last as long as she continues to meet the criteria set by Social Security. Specifically, she will keep receiving these benefits as long as:

1. **Ed Jr. continues to qualify for SSDI benefits** based on Ed's work record (which he will likely continue to do, as Ed Jr. has a permanent disability like Down's Syndrome).

2. **Clara remains a full-time caregiver for Ed Jr.** and doesn't engage in substantial gainful activity (i.e., work that would disqualify her from receiving benefits).

Clara's caregiver benefits will likely continue until she either reaches age 62 and becomes eligible for her own Social Security retirement benefits, or Ed Jr.'s situation changes (for example, if he no longer qualifies as disabled, which is unlikely given his condition). Once Clara reaches 62, she could transition to drawing either her own Social Security retirement benefits or spousal benefits, whichever is higher.

Additionally, **if Ed Jr. were to lose his SSDI benefits for any reason,**

Clara's benefits as a caregiver would also stop, since her benefits are tied to Ed Jr.'s disability status. However, this would only happen if Ed Jr. no longer qualifies as disabled or starts earning too much income, both of which are rare in cases like his.

TICKET TO WORK PROGRAM

Many people find that they can't live on their SSDI payment and need to try to go back to work. They are not sure they can hold down a job, but they want to try. The Ticket to Work program offers job training and support, career counseling, and help finding a job (the government wants you off SSDI). The best part of this program is that you can give work a try without losing your SSDI benefits!

Here's how it works:

1. **Stay on SSDI and Medicare**. While you are participating in the Ticket to Work program, you can continue to receive your SSDI benefits and keep your Medicare coverage, even while you're trying to work.

2. **Trial Work Period.** You can try working for **9 months** without losing your SSDI benefits, no matter how much money you make! This is called the **Trial Work Period.** You only get one Trial Work Period in your lifetime while you are on SSDI. During this time, you get to keep your full Social Security checks and your Medicare, just like before.

3. **Extended Period of Eligibility**. After the Trial Work Period ends, you have another **36 months** where you can still keep your Medicare and your SSDI benefits if your monthly earnings stay below the Substantial Gainful Activity (SGA) limit. If you go over the SGA limit during this time, your SSDI benefits might stop, *but you can get them back if your earnings drop below the limit.*

4. **Keeping Medicare.** This is critical. Even if your SSDI benefits stop because you're earning too much money, you can still keep your

Medicare coverage for at least 93 months (over 7 years) after your Trial Work Period ends!

This program is designed to help people with disabilities get back into the workforce without the fear of immediately losing their benefits if things don't work out. If you are thinking about this program, look up the Red Book. This is a guide the SSA publishes with all the details for those on SSDI. You'll be prepared for the Ticket to Work program after reading the Red Book!

POINTS TO REMEMBER

- If you are approved for Social Security Disability, you will be automatically enrolled into Medicare after 24 months (some health conditions receive benefits sooner).

- Medicare isn't free just because you are disabled. You need to pay for Part B unless you qualify for assistance.

- Most states won't allow you to enroll into a Medicare Supplement plan if you are under age 65.

- A few states do allow those on SSDI to buy a Medicare Supplement, but the prices are often prohibitive.

- At age 65, those on SSDI can get any Medicare Supplement plan regardless of their health as if they have never been on Medicare previously.

- Dual Eligible. If you have both Medicare and Medicaid, Medicaid can help you cover your Medicare premiums, copays, and more.

- The Ticket to Work program allows you to try to get off SSDI and work without losing your benefits or Medicare.

- You can get one 9-month Trial Work Period in your lifetime where you can work and get your SSDI payments.

- Disabled Adult Children can get SSDI and Medicare based on a parent's work record if the child became disabled before age 22.

CHAPTER 6

LATE ENROLLMENT PENALTIES

Late enrollment penalties are worse than you think. It's very important to do things in the right order at the right time.

Medicare Parts A, B, and D can each have late enrollment penalties. If you are late to enroll and don't qualify for a Special Enrollment Period, you could pay any or all these premiums depending on what kind of coverage you choose and when you sign up.

MEDICARE PART A PREMIUM PENALTY

- Most people don't have to pay for Part A at age 65. But if you have to pay a premium, the penalty is 10% per year if you fail to enroll on time.

- The Part A penalty charges you for twice the number of years you delay enrollment. If you are 1 year late, you pay the penalty for 2 years. If you are 2 years late, you pay the penalty for 4 years.

MEDICARE PART B LATE PENALTY

- The penalty for Part B is 10% for each 12-month period you delay enrollment.

- You have to pay the penalty every month for as long as you have Part B.

- Good news! If you're under 65 and disabled, the penalty *ends once you turn 65* as you'll have another **Initial Enrollment Period** based on your age.

- If you qualify for Medicaid, or certain state help programs, you might avoid the penalty, even if you do sign up late.

- If you have proof you were given wrong information by your employer or Social Security about when to enroll, you can appeal the penalty.

Medicare Part B Late Penalty

The Medicare Part B late penalty is 10 percent of your premiums for every 12 months you delay enrollment.

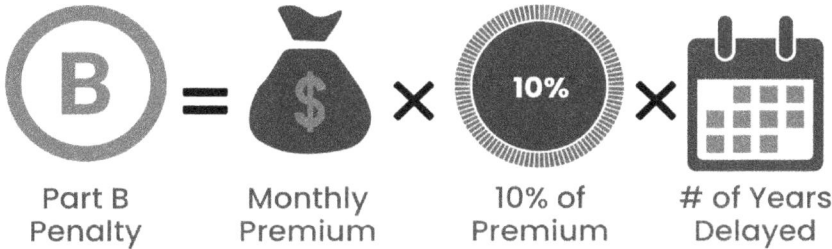

B	=	💰	×	10%	×	📅
Part B Penalty		Monthly Premium		10% of Premium		# of Years Delayed

MEDICARE PART C HAS NO LATE PENALTIES!

If you've been hit with a late enrollment penalty for Medicare, switching to a Medicare Advantage plan won't make the penalty disappear. Even though Medicare Advantage plans are private insurance, the government still tracks any late enrollment penalties you owe. When you join a Medicare Advantage plan, the company running the plan will collect your penalty payments *and forward them to Medicare.*

MEDICARE PART D LATE PENALTY

- The penalty is 1% of the average national Part D premium for each month you delay enrollment, up to a maximum of 12% a year.

- The penalty is always based on the average national Part D premium. *If you enroll into a cheaper plan your penalty doesn't go down.*

You may not have to pay a late part D penalty if you:

- Have creditable drug coverage at work.

- Qualify for the Extra Help program if you are low income.

- Prove that you received *inaccurate or inadequate information* about whether your drug coverage was creditable from your employer.

Let's calculate a sample Part D penalty.

Let's say you delayed enrollment in Part D for 7 months (and you do not meet any of the exceptions listed above). Your monthly premium would be 7% higher for as long as you have Part D (7 months x 1%).

If the average national Part D premium in 2025 is **$36.78** a month, your monthly premium penalty would be **$2.58** per month (**$36.78 x 0.07 = $2.574,** rounded up to **$2.58**).

You pay penalties *in addition to your plan's premium,* even if you enroll into a $0 premium Medicare Advantage plan with drug benefits.

You can't escape the penalty unless you drop Part D. You also won't get a penalty until you enroll into a Part D plan, or a Medicare Advantage plan with drug coverage. If you are 5 years past your enrollment date but still without a Part D plan, you will not be paying a penalty. It starts when your coverage starts.

To avoid these penalties, always make sure you sign up during your enrollment period, even if you are healthy and don't think you need coverage right away.

The Part D penalty summary:

1. **It adds up over time.** For every month you delay signing up for Medicare Part D when you were supposed to, you'll pay an extra fee. This fee is 1% of the average national drug plan cost for each month you were late.

2. **The penalty lasts forever.** Once you get the penalty, you'll keep paying it as long as you have a Medicare drug plan. It doesn't go away!

3. **It's based on average costs.** The penalty is based on a national average drug plan price, not the cost of the plan you choose. So even if your plan is cheaper, the penalty might still be higher.

4. **You can avoid it with other coverage.** If you have a different drug plan from work or another good plan while delaying Part D, you might not have to pay the penalty. As long as it is considered creditable coverage.

5. **You pay the penalty along with your premium.** The penalty gets added to your monthly Medicare drug plan payment, so it's something you'll see on your bill every month.

Avoiding the penalty is simple: sign up for Medicare Part D when you're first eligible, or make sure your other drug coverage counts!

Two Exceptions to Part D Lifetime Penalties:

1. If you mess up and incur any late penalties while under age 65, while eligible for **Medicare due to Disability**, I have good news. *All late penalties will be wiped clean when you turn 65.* You'll get a new Initial Enrollment Period at age 65 as if you'd never been on Medicare.

2. If you qualify for **Extra Help**, also known as the Part D **Low-Income Subsidy (LIS)**, you will not be charged a late enrollment penalty for Medicare Part D.

Medicare late penalties can feel like an extra sting, especially when you're already trying to navigate the complexities of retirement. But the key takeaway is simple: enroll on time!

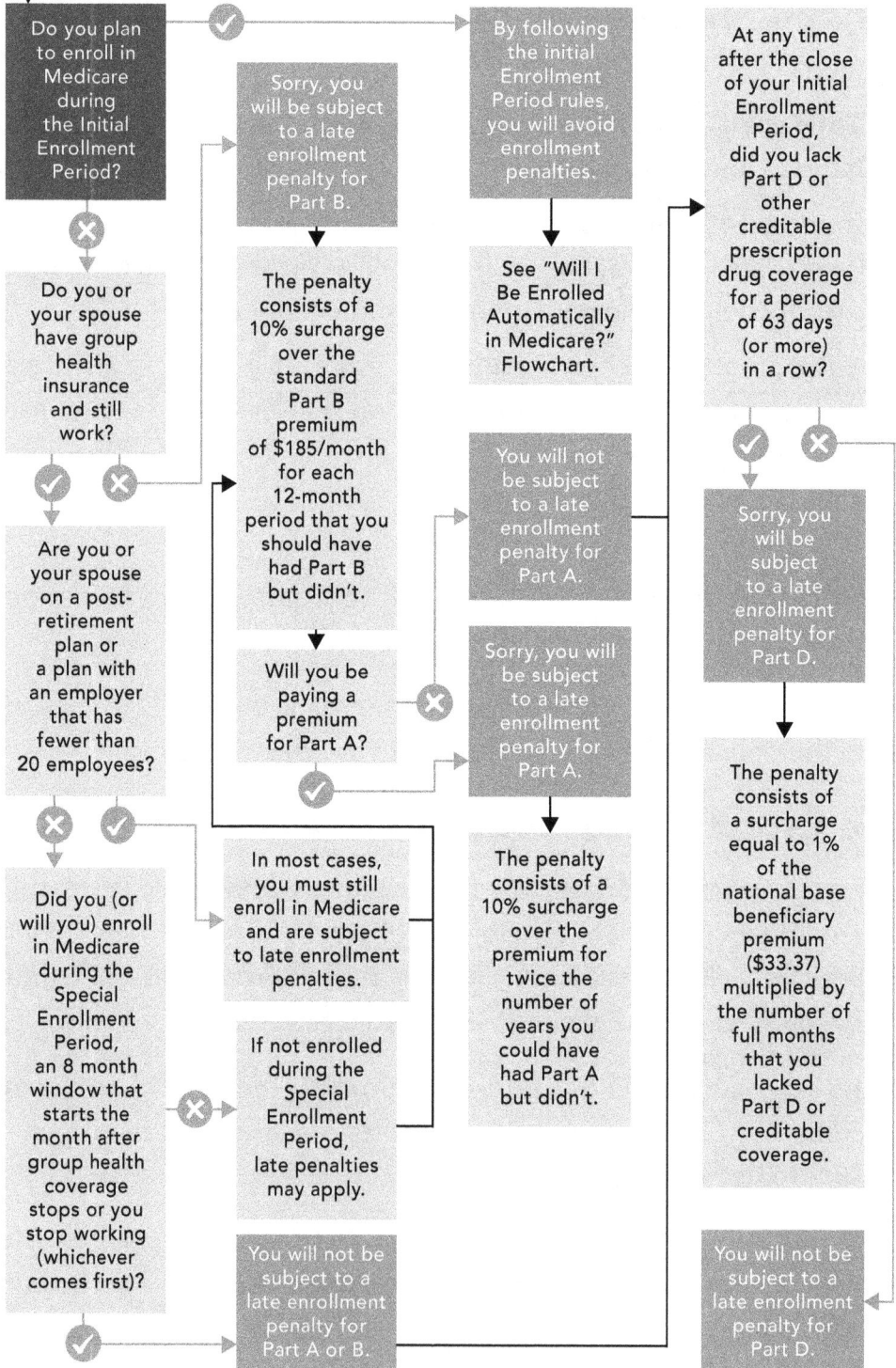

Will I Avoid Medicare Enrollment Penalties?

START HERE

Do you plan to enroll in Medicare during the Initial Enrollment Period?

→ (✓) → By following the initial Enrollment Period rules, you will avoid enrollment penalties.

↓ See "Will I Be Enrolled Automatically in Medicare?" Flowchart.

(✗) ↓

Do you or your spouse have group health insurance and still work?

(✓) / (✗)

Are you or your spouse on a post-retirement plan or a plan with an employer that has fewer than 20 employees?

(✗) / (✓)

Did you (or will you) enroll in Medicare during the Special Enrollment Period, an 8 month window that starts the month after group health coverage stops or you stop working (whichever comes first)?

(✗) → In most cases, you must still enroll in Medicare and are subject to late enrollment penalties.

(✗) → If not enrolled during the Special Enrollment Period, late penalties may apply.

(✓) → You will not be subject to a late enrollment penalty for Part A or B.

Sorry, you will be subject to a late enrollment penalty for Part B.

↓

The penalty consists of a 10% surcharge over the standard Part B premium of $185/month for each 12-month period that you should have had Part B but didn't.

↓

Will you be paying a premium for Part A?

(✗) → Sorry, you will be subject to a late enrollment penalty for Part A.

↓

The penalty consists of a 10% surcharge over the premium for twice the number of years you could have had Part A but didn't.

(✓) → You will not be subject to a late enrollment penalty for Part A.

At any time after the close of your Initial Enrollment Period, did you lack Part D or other creditable prescription drug coverage for a period of 63 days (or more) in a row?

(✓) / (✗)

Sorry, you will be subject to a late enrollment penalty for Part D.

↓

The penalty consists of a surcharge equal to 1% of the national base beneficiary premium ($33.37) multiplied by the number of full months that you lacked Part D or creditable coverage.

You will not be subject to a late enrollment penalty for Part D.

Missing that window can cost you literally thousands of dollars, so it's worth putting it on your radar early. The penalties stick around as long as you have Medicare, so save yourself the hassle by staying informed and getting ahead of those deadlines.

After all, there's no reason to pay more for something that's already yours.

LATE PENALTY AVERAGES

In 2021, 779,400 people — only about 1.3% of Part B enrollees — paid **a Medicare Part B penalty**.[1] On average, their monthly payment for Part B (standard premium plus penalty) in 2021 was 27% higher than it would have been without the penalty.

But it gets worse.

More than three times as many people paid a **Part D penalty** — about 2.5 million people in 2022 (or about 5% of Part D enrollees).

Far fewer people paid a **Part A penalty** because most people qualify for premium-free Part A and do not incur a penalty no matter when they sign up.

---

1   Source: Medicare Annual Report

POINTS TO REMEMBER

- You can and should avoid all Medicare late penalties!

- You may be able to appeal if you have proof you were given bad information from your employer or the SSA.

- Each Part of Medicare has a different penalty calculation.

- The penalties generally last for the rest of your life.

- One exception to the lifetime duration of your penalty is when you incurred penalties while under age 65 due to disability. Your penalties go away at age 65!

- Another exception is if you qualify for Extra Help paying for Medicare Part D your late penalties are waived.

- You can't escape the penalties by enrolling into Medicare Advantage plans.

- If you are drawing Social Security benefits, the government takes the penalties out of your check.

CHAPTER 7

IRMAA

Medicare started charging high earners more for Medicare's Part B and D a few years ago. The program is called **Income Related Monthly Adjustment Amount (IRMAA).** Don't worry, there are ways to plan ahead and possibly avoid paying this surcharge.

For years I've called this the Rich Tax in my videos. The problem is that people get caught up in paying these extra amounts *and they are not rich.* They just did something (sold a property, took a withdrawal, etc.) that caused them to go over the income limit and trigger this surcharge.

MEDICARE'S SURCHARGE FOR HIGH EARNERS

Here are the 5 key things to know about IRMAA:

1. **Extra cost** – IRMAA makes some people pay more for Medicare Part B and D.

2. **Income check** – It's based on how much you earned 2 years ago.

3. **Higher income = higher cost** – There are 5 levels, and more income means more extra charges.

4. **Changes every year** – The amount you pay gets checked and updated each year.

5. **Can appeal** – You can ask for a lower charge if your income drops or your life changes, like retiring.

If you receive an IRMAA determination letter, you will pay extra premiums *for 1 year*. If your spouse is also on Medicare, you'll both pay this surcharge *for 1 year*.

There are 5 levels, and those earning over $500,000 will pay more than $500 extra per month. You can double these amounts for married couples. Check out the 2025 brackets below:

2025 Medicare Premiums*			
2023 MAGI Single	2023 MAGI Joint	Part B	Part D
$106,000 or less	$212,000 or less	$185.00	Plan Premium
$106,000 - $133,000	$212,001 - $266,000	$259.00	$13.70 + plan premium
$133,001 - $167,000	$266,001 - $334,000	$370.00	$35.30 + plan premium
$167,001 - $200,000	$334,001 - $400,000	$480.90	$57.00 + plan premium
$200,001 - $500,000	$400,001 - $750,000	$591.90	$78.60 + plan premium
$500,000 or more	$750,000 or more	$628.90	$85.80 + plan premium

*RATES INCREASE ANNUALLY, SEE UPDATED IRMAA RATES AT THEMEDICAREFAMILY.COM

Medicare looks at your income tax returns from 2 years ago. If you withdrew all your money from your IRA to remodel your house, that was a taxable event. Your income surged — maybe only for 1 year — so you are not considered rich to anyone but Medicare. And that 1 year will trigger this surcharge.

> ### Understanding IRMAA can save you thousands of dollars!

Unfortunately, many accountants are not familiar with Medicare IRMAA. It can be hard to find someone to help you structure a plan to minimize this Medicare surcharge. Typically, if you wait until you're 65 to call us, the damage has been done. What you do at age 63 and 64 may cost you when you enroll. That is why you need to work with a professional to craft a plan.

> Get a plan before you take a large, taxable withdrawal
> from your tax-deferred retirement accounts.

Note: Converting to Roth IRAs is also a common trigger for IRMAA. If the adviser helping with this conversion isn't familiar with IRMAA, find another person to advise you.

If you're still working, you can contribute to your 401(k) (or SEP IRA if you're self-employed). Your contributions will reduce your modified adjusted gross income. Since you only need to be $1 below the threshold, you may be able to avoid IRMAA.

APPEALING IRMAA

Many people are shocked to get an IRMAA determination letter based on their *prior income* because they no longer have that job or income. You can appeal and win an IRMAA determination by filing **Form SS-44** within 60 days of receiving the letter. Show proof you retired with your appeal.

You'll need a "Life-Changing Event" to be eligible to appeal to IRMAA. Here are the standard reasons:

- Marriage, divorce, or death of a spouse
- Work reduction or stoppage
- Loss of income-producing property
- Loss of pension income
- Employer settlement payment

You can also appeal if:

- The IRS data contained an error on your tax return.
- The IRS sent old data, and you'd like them to use newer information on your tax return.

- A beneficiary filed an amended tax return for the year the Social Security Administration used to make the IRMAA decision.

> Do not waste your time filing an
> IRMAA appeal if you don't include proof.

To file an appeal:

1. **Form SSA-44.** This is the official form you'll need to file an appeal. You can easily get this online.[2]

2. **Proof of the Life-Changing Event:**

   ⇨ **Retirement or Reduced Work.** A letter from your employer or recent tax returns showing the change in income.

   ⇨ **Divorce or Death of a Spouse.** Divorce decree or death certificate.

   ⇨ **Loss of Income-Producing Property.** Documentation of the property loss, such as insurance statements or tax forms.

   ⇨ **Loss of Pension Income.** Statements from the pension provider showing the reduced income.

   ⇨ **Employer Settlement Payment.** Documentation of the settlement and its impact on your income.

3. **Tax Returns.** Send in your tax returns from 2 years prior or amended tax returns if corrections were made.

4. **W-2 or 1099 Forms.** If your income went down because you stopped working, send in your W-2 or 1099 forms.

Having proof that your income changed will make it easier to win your appeal, but don't delay. You should submit your appeal within 60 days of receiving your IRMAA determination letter.

---

2   https://www.ssa.gov/forms/ssa-44.pdf.

💡 *Could you appeal for another type of life changing event that is not listed on the Form SS-44? Technically, yes, but you are unlikely to win. Since there are so many possibilities, you can appeal (with documentation). It won't hurt and you could win. But it's unlikely.*

What happens while your appeal is pending?

When you submit an appeal for IRMAA, it typically takes **60 to 90 days** to get a response from the SSA. During this waiting period, you will continue to be charged the IRMAA surcharge based on the original determination they sent to you.

If your appeal is successful, **you will be refunded** for any excess payments made while the appeal was being processed. The refund will typically be applied retroactively to the date the IRMAA surcharge began, and you will receive that money through a direct deposit to your bank account.

TWO MAIN TRIGGERS FOR IRMAA

1. Selling your home, land, or vacation property.

2. Taking large 401(k) or IRA withdrawals.

We will start with home sales.

Maybe you've remarried and are selling to move in with your new spouse, or you might be downsizing from your home to move in with your kids. If the sale of your home makes you a profit that is more than your tax exemption, *it could trigger IRMAA.*

First, let's go over your tax exemption:

When you are **married** and sell your primary residence you've lived in for at least 2 out of the past 5 years, your tax exemption allows you to exclude up to **$500,000** in profits from your taxes.

If you are single, your exemption is only $250,000. It's cut in half. Since house prices have soared in some parts of the country, people are netting profits that exceed their tax exemption. That creates a taxable gain and can trigger IRMAA.

Things you must consider:

- What is the difference between what you bought your house for and what you sold it for?
- What is your tax exemption?
- What profit are you left with?
- Add those gains to your income for the year and see if it triggers IRMAA.
- If so, you'll pay more for Medicare in 2 years. Not now.

> **IRMAA is a cliff. If you are only $1 over, you pay the surcharge for 1 year.**

Let's look at Sharon's situation to see how selling her home might push her into IRMAA territory.

Sharon bought her home in San Diego many years ago and recently sold it. Here is what happened:

Sharon sold her house for $450,000 more than she originally bought it for. As a single person, her tax exemption for the sale is $250,000. This means her taxable gain from the sale is $200,000. Now, let's add that to Sharon's yearly salary of $103,000. This increase in income will push her into a higher bracket, triggering an IRMAA surcharge.

Sharon will need to pay around $400 extra per month for Medicare Part B and about $100 extra per month for Part D. That's an additional $500 per month for the year, totaling $6,000 in extra Medicare costs due to her home sale.

Since IRMAA is recalculated annually, Sharon is not likely to trigger it again. But she could if she isn't mindful of IRMAA when she draws money out of her IRA and 401(k).

💡 *If Sharon moved in with Ted and rented her house out for a few years till they decided to get married, she could lose her tax exemption.*

You do not get the $250,000 tax exemption (or $500,000 for married couples) *when you sell a rental property that is not your primary residence.* The tax exemption applies only to your primary residence, where you must have lived for at least 2 out of the last 5 years before the sale.

When you sell a rental property, you may have to pay capital gains tax on the profit. If you've rented it out for more than a year, it will be taxed at the long-term capital gains rate, which is typically lower than your regular income tax rate.

This all can trigger IRMAA, which may make you decide to keep renting out the property instead of selling it.

Now let's discuss taking large withdrawals from your 401(k) or IRA.

Taking large withdrawals from your 401(k) or IRA can cause you to pay more for Medicare. This is because when you take out a lot of money in 1 year, it increases your taxable income, which might push you over the threshold for IRMAA.

Take Yvonne as an example:

Yvonne is single and makes about $100,000 a year, which keeps her just below the limit for IRMAA. When she retires, she decides to withdraw all her 401(k) at once and put the money in her savings account to "deal with it later." By doing this, her income jumps for the year, landing her above the IRMAA limit. As a result, she now has to pay extra each month for Medicare Parts B and D 2 years from now.

If Yvonne had known this, she could have spread out her withdrawals over a few years to avoid boosting her income too much at once.

It's a reminder that when you're thinking about tapping into your retirement funds, planning ahead can make a big difference in how much you pay for Medicare!

Let's say she took out all her money at age 62. Medicare won't start till 65, so it won't cause IRMAA since it only looks back 2 years. Sure, taking money out of a 401(k) or IRA will always be taxable income, but it won't always trigger the Medicare IRMAA!

💡 Roth 401(k) and Roth IRA withdrawals are tax-free and won't cause any problems with IRMAA.

Are loans from 401(k) accounts taxable?

No. When you borrow from your 401(k), it's treated as a loan, and you don't pay taxes on the amount you borrow. However, you must repay the loan within 5 years or it becomes taxable. You also have to pay interest on your loan.

💡 The sale of a business could also trigger the IRMAA surcharge. You could structure the sale over several years to lower the tax burden and avoid IRMAA. Work with a financial planner before you sell or withdraw anything.

Will filing taxes separately from my spouse help me avoid IRMAA?

Yes, you can file your taxes separately from your spouse if he is the high earner, but it might not always help you avoid the IRMAA surcharge. Medicare uses a different income limit for people who file separately, and this limit is much lower than for couples filing together.

So, even though filing separately might seem like a good idea, it could actually trigger IRMAA for you at a lower income, meaning you'd both end up paying more.

For example, while couples filing together might not pay IRMAA until their income is quite high, someone filing separately could have to pay the surcharge even if their income is not nearly as high.

Let's look at Carl and Maud's taxes.

Carl and Maud thought they'd save money by filing their taxes separately. Carl is the high earner, making over $250,000 a year, while Maud's income is much lower. They figured that by filing separately, Maud could avoid paying the IRMAA surcharge, but it backfired.

Since Medicare uses a much lower income limit for people who file separately, Maud ended up having to pay the IRMAA surcharge anyway, even though her income wasn't that high. *In the end, both Carl and Maud ended up paying more than if they had filed jointly!*

:💡: If Maud's income was far under $100,000, filing separately could save her from IRMAA.

It's a good idea to talk to a tax expert to make sure of the best option for you and your spouse!

FORECASTING IRMAA

Medicare IRMAA increases are tied to a consumer price index (the CPI-U). The government looks at inflation from last August and if it is greater than this August, IRMAA brackets increase. Technically, IRMAA could go down if we had negative inflation.

FINANCIAL PLANNING TO AVOID IRMAA

Planning ahead can help you avoid IRMAA charges in retirement. While most people expect their income to drop, sometimes it goes up due to property sales, withdrawals from pensions, Social Security, or retirement accounts like IRAs and 401(k)s. These withdrawals can increase your taxable income and push you into higher Medicare brackets.

If a lot of your savings are in pre-tax accounts, those withdrawals could surprise you with more income than you anticipated, which could trigger IRMAA. But with some simple planning — like spreading out withdrawals or consulting with a financial advisor — you can manage your income and avoid those extra Medicare costs.

Some financial planning strategies you might consider:

- Make **charitable contributions** to lower your MAGI.

- **Utilize Roth IRA** funds instead of an IRA for some cash withdrawals.

- **Spread out withdrawals** for cash needs across a few years. For example, if you need $80k for a new car, you could take half of the amount from an IRA in December and the other half in January once the new year begins.

- If you have earned income, **continue to make tax-deductible retirement contributions.**

- In lower tax years, convert funds from a Traditional IRA to a Roth IRA via a Roth conversion with the help of a financial advisor.

POINTS TO REMEMBER

- Most people pay the standard Part B and D price each year, but you may have to pay more due to IRMAA.

- You don't have to be rich to get hit with this surcharge if you reap some high capital gains that bump up your total income.

- IRMAA is based on your Modified Adjusted Gross income from 2 years prior.

- IRMAA is recalculated annually.

- IRMAA has 5 income brackets.

- If you recently retired, got divorced, or had another life-changing event, you can appeal within 60 days of your IRMAA notice.

- If you and your spouse file taxes jointly, and you are both on Medicare, you'll both pay IRMAA.

- It may be possible to avoid IRMAA if your own income is low and you file your taxes separately from your spouse.

CHAPTER 8

DELAYING MEDICARE

So, you've hit age 65 but you're still working and wondering if you really need to dive into Medicare just yet. Good news — you might not have to!

If you've got health insurance through your job (or through your spouse's employer), and that company has at least 20 full-time employees, you may be able to hold off on enrolling into Medicare without worrying about those pesky late penalties.

CREDITABLE COVERAGE

This is a term that's often used **incorrectly** in the insurance industry, as well as by HR departments — but fortunately, it doesn't cause any issues if we all agree to *keep using it incorrectly.*

Technically, employer group health insurance isn't and doesn't have to qualify as Creditable Coverage for you to avoid late Part B penalties. Your work insurance can be bad and nowhere near as good as Medicare, but as long as your employer has 20 or more full-time employees, you have no late Medicare Part B penalty. If your company size fluctuates, it's the average size of full-time employees employed at your job over the past year.

Twenty doesn't mean the number of employees on the health plan, but total employees working at the company.

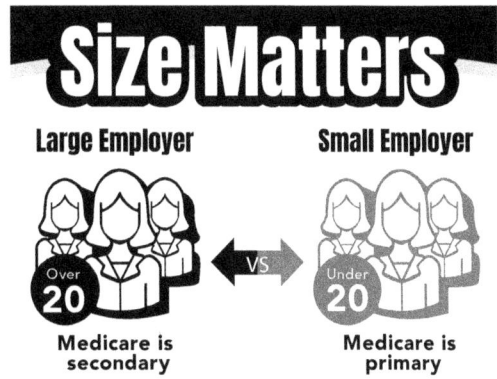

Size Matters

Large Employer vs Small Employer

Over 20 — Medicare is secondary

Under 20 — Medicare is primary

Medicare Part D has a different rule. Your employer group health insurance has to be as good or better than Medicare (which is the true definition of Creditable Coverage), or you'll be penalized for not enrolling into Medicare Part D at 65. Just because your employer has 1000+ employees, the drug benefits must still be as good or better than Medicare Part D.

The true definition of Creditable Coverage – for drug coverage only.

If you're happy with your work insurance at 65 and your employer group health plan has 20 or more employees, don't let the fear of Medicare late penalties pressure you — there's no rule that says you have to retire or enroll in Medicare at 65. You can keep working as long as you like and sign up for Medicare whenever you decide to hang up your hat. *Your enrollment period will open when you leave your job, no matter your age nor the time of year.*

🔆 COBRA can be tricky. It's not the same as staying on your work plan and doesn't count as Creditable Coverage for Medicare Part B (but it does count for Part D). So, if you're eligible for Medicare, it's usually better to skip COBRA and sign up for Medicare instead. If you do take COBRA and are over age 65, you MUST also enroll into Medicare!

🔆 What if your employer drops down to 19 employees? When employee numbers fluctuate, Medicare typically looks at the size of the workforce during the majority of the year or uses a "snapshot" approach to determine whether the employer is large or small.

If you're not ready to give up work just yet, no worries, Medicare will be there waiting for you when you are.

But here's where it can get tricky. Lots of folks aren't sure if their work plan meets the requirements to avoid late penalties, so they enroll in Medicare Part B "just to be safe." This can turn out to be an expensive mistake, especially if you're still paying for your work insurance. Why fork over an extra $200 a month for Medicare Part B if you don't need to? Part B often doesn't add much value when you're still covered by a good work plan.

How do you know for sure if you have creditable drug coverage?

Your employer must **notify you in writing by October 15ᵗʰ** of each year if your drug coverage is creditable. You probably never looked at this notice before, but now it's important. *Start keeping those letters in a file.* You may need them when you retire to prove you don't have late penalties.

This rule determines who pays first (primary payer) if you have more than 1 health plan. It is the number of employees in the company that determines whether a plan is primary or secondary.

If you are working at a small company, with under 20 employees in the company, the government gives your employer a break. **Medicare becomes primary**, meaning it pays first, to save your employer money. That is why you must enroll into Medicare when you turn 65 and want to keep working for a small company. Don't fight me on this.

Let's look at stubborn Bob. We were discussing his options when he said, "I pay nothing for my work plan and it is excellent coverage. Why would I want to pay almost $200 per month for Medicare Part B. No thank you."

Bob ignored my advice, remained on his small group health plan. Three years later, he retired. Then he called our company to get enrolled into Medicare.

Unfortunately, he retired April 1st. Since he is a late Part B enrollee, he can't enroll into Medicare at any time of year, he has to enroll during the first quarter of the year during the **General Election Period**, which begins in January. Because of this, he must go 11 months before his Medicare can begin. And all the while, the clock is ticking on his late penalties.

Bob thinks he saved money by staying on his small employer's health plan. But in the end, he could be punished with late penalties for Part B every month, for as long as he stays on Medicare (likely the rest of his life).

Don't be like Bob.

LOSING WORK HEALTH COVERAGE

(I'll explain the rule and then *what really happens*).

It is illegal for a large employer to kick you off the company health plan when you become eligible for Medicare. Why would your employer want to get you off the plan? Group health plan rates are based on age. **Having older employees causes the entire company's health plan rates to go up**. Every employer would love for you to enroll into Medicare to spare the company the cost of insuring you, but it's illegal for your employer to force or bribe you to leave.

A large employer can legally pay you a monthly bonus for many things, *but not to compensate you for the cost of Medicare Part B*. Do employers do this? Yes. It's a win, win. The employer saves hundreds of dollars a month with you off the large group health plan and you get better coverage at a lower price than you had at work. You are still working but on Medicare not the group health plan.

> It is illegal to incentivize an employee to terminate group health insurance to enroll into Medicare.

💡 *Interestingly, if you want to stay on your small employer's health plan, he can kick you off without facing anti-discrimination laws that protect employees on large group health plans. You can't demand to stay on the plan once you hit age 65 if you are on a small plan.*

RETIREE HEALTH PLANS

A quick word on retiree health plans. If you're not working full-time at 65, your former employer might offer you a retiree health plan. Most of the time, though, they'll require you to sign up for Medicare Parts A and B, since Medicare usually pays first. And trust me, if you don't enroll in Medicare when you're supposed to, that retiree plan probably won't cover your medical bills.

A lot of big employers, and even state governments, are switching their retiree health plans over to **Medicare Advantage plans.** It's all about saving money, and that means shifting some of the costs onto retirees. These plans might not be as cushy as what they're replacing, but that doesn't mean they're bad, you'll just have to compare your options carefully. At the end of the day, we're seeing fewer employers offering those rich Medicare Supplement plans and more leaning into Medicare Advantage. So, if your company still offers a supplement, count yourself lucky and buckle up, *because changes are probably coming.*

All employers are trying to save costs on healthcare, including the U.S. Postal Service. These federal employees are now required to enroll into government Medicare Part B (while other federal employees still are not required to do so).

GROUP PLAN VS. MEDICARE

Just because you *can* stay on your employer's health plan, doesn't mean that you *should*. You must compare prices and benefits with Medicare.

Gather your data to do your own comparison:

Most employers do not pay for all your health coverage.

Find out how much you have to pay for your own portion of your insurance (not including your spouse's coverage).

$_____

Verify what your plan's annual deductible is.

$_____

Compare that to what Medicare Part B would cost you in the year you enroll.

$_____

Add in the price of Medicare Supplement Plan G, N, or a Medicare Advantage plan.

$_____

Add in a Medicare Part D drug plan if you choose a Medicare Supplement plan.

$_____

If the prices are about the same, let the deductible come into play. Many work plans have a $1,000 to $5,000 deductible. What is yours?

Medicare Part B annual deductible in 2025 is only $257.

If your comparison is still a toss-up, look down the list of extra benefits your work plan offers. If your plan has some dental coverage, that may make the decision for you. Remember, Medicare doesn't offer dental coverage, though you can purchase your own coverage for about $45 per month in most states.

> At this point, if you are leaning toward Medicare or if Medicare is hands down cheaper than your current work plan, don't stop there.

Look at your prescription drug coverage. Medicare Part D will not cover your expensive weight loss drug while your employer plan might. Bang! We have a decision. Remain on your employer's group health plan for another year. Plan benefits and prices change annually so you'll get to do this comparison each year until you retire.

If you are planning to continue working and enroll into Medicare because you know the price and benefits will be better than your work insurance, there is one more consideration.

> Due to your income, you may incur IRMAA. This can cause your calculation to lean back towards staying on your work insurance plan and delay taking Medicare!

Lewis is a good example here. He is still working at age 70. I asked him why he isn't on Medicare since his group health plan has a $5,000 deductible. He said he would be paying $500 extra per month due to IRMAA (I was unaware how high his income was). Apples to apples, he is better off staying on his group health plan until he retires. Once his income drops, his IRMAA will go away and he will pay the standard Part B premium.

REASONS TO DELAY MEDICARE

A Younger Spouse

What if you have a younger spouse and kids on your work health insurance plan? Throw everything out the window that you decided above. Your spouse and kids can't follow you to Medicare because there is no family Medicare coverage.

If you retire, your family must go on private health insurance. How much it costs to enroll your spouse and kids into Obamacare often *will determine if you can afford to retire!*

Obamacare is based on expected annual income. Since you are still working, your family likely will pay a lot for private health coverage.

How much is a lot?

The average Obamacare plan costs $483 per month for a 30-year-old, $544 for a 40-year-old, and $760 for a 50-year-old in 2025.

You can go to **HEALTHCARE.GOV** to check out prices in your state. Like all insurance, price varies by plan type and your location. If your younger spouse will need Obamacare when you enroll into Medicare, book your free appointment online at **THEMEDICAREFAMILY.COM.**

If your spouse is not eligible for any type of government tax subsidy, Obamacare may swing the decision back in favor of you delaying Medicare and working a few more years. If you feel your job is too demanding and you must retire, you can use your retirement savings to pay for healthcare till your spouse reaches age 65.

People are reluctant to use IRA or 401(k) money to pay for Obamacare, *but that is what you saved it for: retirement.*

An Older Spouse

In this scenario, you want to keep working. You like your job. The benefits are better than Medicare and your older spouse is able to remain on your work health plan. But should she?

While there are thousands of different group health plans, I'll generalize and say the odds favor Medicare being more affordable than staying on your work plan. If you work for a very large company, you may still have amazing insurance benefits, but every year I see fewer great plans being offered.

This means you can't generalize; you'll have to do the math. Keep in mind your employer usually only pays for some or all your coverage and usually little or none of your spouse's coverage.

If Medicare is cheaper, *and it likely is,* **don't stop there.**

Look at her prescription drugs. I'll use the super popular Ozempic weight loss drug as an example. The Medicare Part D program is prohibited from covering weight loss drugs (it's the same for erectile dysfunction drugs unless they are medically necessary). Ozempic, and similar weight loss drugs, can cost over $1,000 per month. Many employer group health plans cover these drugs! If your plan does, her decision is made. She remains on your work plan until you retire, and she is forced onto Medicare.

💡 *If you decide to leave your employer's group health plan, and later change your mind and want to re-enroll, there is no rule that requires your employer to take you back. They can, but they usually will not.*

PART A AND EMPLOYER INSURANCE

If your company has 20 or more employees, your work insurance will be primary, and it's unlikely Part A will pick up any costs, but it usually doesn't hurt to enroll into Part A along with your employer health coverage.

But some people should delay enrolling into Medicare Part A until they retire. Those are people with a Health Savings Account (HSA) or those who have to pay a premium for Part A (because they didn't work long enough and pay enough into Medicare FICA payroll taxes to get it premium-free). More on Health Savings Accounts in Chapter 22.

So generally, it is a good idea to enroll in Part A when you are eligible, even if you have another health plan.

COBRA AND MEDICARE

COBRA is secondary to Medicare. If you are eligible for Medicare, you must have Medicare and it will pay out first, before COBRA pays.

Mistakes can be a nightmare! The nightmare occurs because people assume COBRA coverage can stand on its own. It is logical to assume that COBRA is creditable since it is the exact same coverage you had while employed. Your employer group health plan was creditable while working, but that same coverage in the form of COBRA after you are terminated is not creditable. **This means being enrolled into COBRA if you are age 65 or older doesn't prevent you from incurring a late Part B penalty.**

COBRA is also very expensive because you are paying the full cost of your health insurance, plus a small administrative fee. While you were employed, your employer paid most or all the cost of your coverage. In most cases, if you are age 65 or older, you are better off NOT taking COBRA and moving fully into Medicare.

Every year, many people like Duane take only COBRA. He thought he could ride COBRA out for a year before starting Medicare. Duane didn't do any research, his HR department sent him COBRA paperwork and he enrolled. He saw how many months he was eligible for COBRA (which can vary by state and your situation) and thought it made sense to stay on COBRA till it ended before enrolling in Medicare.

Then Duane got sick. He found out that COBRA only pays as secondary to Medicare. Since he didn't have Medicare, he had to pay most of his doctor bills! Medicare Part B would have paid 80% of Duane's out-of-hospital care. Since COBRA pays secondary, COBRA only paid the 20% Medicare didn't pay.

Duane had to pay 80% of his total bills and he was fuming mad. "Why did I even take COBRA? Why didn't anyone warn me?" The government says it's YOUR responsibility to learn these rules. Most HR departments do not understand these rules and are unable to warn their employees.

But it gets worse. If you didn't enroll into Medicare in your time period, you will also be triggering a late Medicare Part B penalty.

Look how Duane's errors stacked up:

- Duane was 65 and still worked. He didn't need to enroll into Medicare since he had creditable coverage.

- Duane retired at 66 and took COBRA for a year.

- He had an illness that required him to pay 80% of his medical bills and COBRA paid 20%.

- At 67 Duane enrolled into Medicare. He is 1 year late since he should have signed up when he retired at 66.

- He will pay a 10% penalty for Part B each month for the rest of his life.

- If Part B is $200, he pays an extra $20 each month. But Part B goes up each year and his penalty will go up too!

If you think this makes no sense, you are correct. You have the exact same health coverage you had while actively working. You retired at age 65 and took COBRA because your company offered it to you. Since you saved your notices, you are sure your work insurance was creditable coverage. You were not required to take Medicare while working at age 65. *So how is COBRA not considered creditable coverage?*

It was just an oversight by Congress. It was not intentional. Everyone agrees it should be changed. Yet here we are with retirees every year mistakenly taking COBRA instead of Medicare and later learning they made a mistake that will cost them in the form of a lifetime late penalty.

Just to blow your mind a bit more, **COBRA is Creditable Coverage for Part D** and Duane won't have to pay a late Part D penalty. That is just how the law was written, and it makes no sense.

-ϙ- *I have been on the national insurance FMO Medicare Council through our national insurance organization, NABIP. We have worked for 10 years to get this COBRA problem solved. It's an easy fix that never makes it into law. That could change any year, but for now it is still a problem for retirees.*

POINTS TO REMEMBER

- You can't be forced off your large employer's group health plan when you turn 65.

- You can be forced off a small employer's health plan when you turn 65.

- The magic number of employees is 20. If your employer is under 20, you should enroll into Medicare at 65 or face late penalties.

- Just because you can stay on your 20+ large employer health plan, doesn't mean you should. You might find that Medicare is better and less expensive. Do a comparison.

- If your comparison shows that Medicare offers you better benefits at a lower price than your work plan, you still might want to stay on your work plan if you have a younger spouse.

- There is no family Medicare coverage. Each person must be eligible on their own.

- If you continue to work for a 20+ large employer past age 65, you can take Medicare Part A — unless you have a Health Savings Account.

- *COBRA is secondary to Medicare.* If you are eligible for Medicare, you must enroll into Medicare.

- COBRA is not Creditable Coverage and won't prevent a late Medicare Part B penalty.

- COBRA is Creditable Coverage for Part D.

- Having both COBRA and Medicare is usually not affordable!

CHAPTER 9

MEDICARE SUPPLEMENTS EXPLAINED

In addition to regular Medicare Parts A and B, there are several supplemental insurance policies to consider. In this chapter, I will do my best to break this down and make it easier to understand.

Before we dive in, let's go over some terms.

1. **Open Enrollment** – A 6-month window when you can enroll into any plan without answering health questions.

2. **Guaranteed Issue Rights** – Situations where you are guaranteed to be able to enroll into a plan for special reasons, such as losing your group health insurance.

3. **Medical Underwriting** – When you apply for a Medicare Supplement plan and are not guaranteed regardless of your health, you have to answer health questions to qualify for a plan.

4. **Standardization of Plans** – By law, all insurance companies are required to offer the exact same plan benefits for each Plan A through N. (For example, Plan G is the same regardless of which company you purchase from even though in a few states they don't call it Plan G, benefits are the same in all states.)

GOVERNING LAW MATTERS

Medicare is regulated by both the federal government and the state insurance departments. The **federal government** sets the basic framework, standardizes plan benefits, and provides consumer protections. Meanwhile, **state governments** regulate the sale and pricing of Medicare Supplement policies, enforce state-specific consumer protections, and approve premium increases.

You only need to worry about which rules apply in **your state**. But that's the fun part. The rules can vary dramatically from state to state. Keep this in mind if you plan to move when you retire!

Insurance agents are faced with different rules from state to state. For example, I can't call myself a Medicare Specialist in California even though I have 30+ years of experience and have sat on both the national NABIP FMO Board and the Agent Advisory Board of most of the national Medicare insurance companies. I consider myself a Specialist, just not in California. There, I'm a licensed insurance agent. Period.

The federal laws prohibit me from saying "X has the best benefits this year," but your state law may allow it. There are a lot of gray areas between the two systems.

💡 *The two systems don't talk much. I saw an agent terminated from selling in the federal system due to forging a Medicare Advantage application. That same agent never faced any loss of his state insurance license. The bad agents continue to sell for other Medicare Advantage companies. Keep this in mind when an agent refuses to offer you a plan from a well-known company. The reason he won't sell that product may be because he can't.*

FILLING THE GAPS

As previously discussed, Medicare doesn't cover all your healthcare expenses. A Medicare Supplement plan can help fill in the gaps.

It's kind of like how a school lunch covers only one meal — you have to bring snacks because you know you will get hungry later!

Let's back up with a quick recap:

Medicare Part A is like a big safety net that helps pay when you have to stay overnight in a hospital or nursing home. It begins paying out when your annual deductible is met.

Medicare Part A will help pay for up to 60 days in the hospital. If you need to stay longer, you'll start paying a little bit each day (this is called coinsurance). If you still need to stay after 90 days, you can use special **lifetime reserve days** that are like extra bonus days. You get 60 of these lifetime reserve days, but you can only use them once in your lifetime.

Medicare calls nursing homes **Skilled Nursing Facilities**. If you are in a skilled nursing facility, Medicare Part A covers the first 20 days completely. After that, from day 21 to day 100, you'll have to pay a little bit each day (coinsurance). If you need more than 100 days, Medicare Part A won't cover anything, so you'd have to pay for the rest yourself.

The good news is that some Medicare Supplement insurance plans will cover that deductible for you.

Medicare Part B is like your partner for all the stuff that doesn't require you to stay in the hospital overnight, like doctor visits, tests, labs, x-rays, and things you need to stay healthy, like medical supplies. It covers most of the bill — about 80% — which is a lot, but not everything. That means you're left with 20% to pay out of your own pocket.

Your annual Part B deductible in 2025 is $257 and it typically goes up about $10 per month, each year.

This is where private Medicare Supplement insurance comes in handy. It can cover that 20%, so you're not stuck paying it all on your own. It's like having a backup plan to take care of the rest!

💡 *Remember, there is no maximum amount you can be charged on Parts A and B only! Your out-of-pocket risk is unlimited which is why most people do not stop at Parts A and B.*

MEDICARE SUPPLEMENTS

About 6% of retirees think Parts A and B are enough and go about their lives. A few years later, they get sick and find out they should not have stopped at Parts A and B.

If you are healthy, it's easy to "save" money by not purchasing a Medicare Supplement or drug plan. Afterall, you take no prescriptions and haven't seen a doctor in years! (In my training seminars, I say "A typical man gets his *annual* physical every *10 years*." (The women roar with laughter, because it rings true.)

When you get sick you realize there are many holes in government Medicare. Most people buy private insurance to close some or most of those holes. Private insurance is optional, you get it from a broker like **THEMEDICARE FAMILY.COM** or directly from the insurance companies.

MEDICARE SUPPLEMENT PLANS A - N

MEDICARE SUPPLEMENT INSURANCE PLANS	A	B	C	D	F	G	K	L	M	N
Basic Benefits	■	■	■	■	■	■	50%	75%	■	■
Part B Coinsurance	■	■	■	■	■	■	50%	75%	■	Copay
Skilled Nursing			■	■	■	■	50%	75%	■	■
Part A Deductible		■	■	■	■	■	50%	75%	50%	■
Part B Deductible			■		■					
Part B Excess					100%	100%				
Foreign Travel Emergency			■	■	■	■			■	■
Preventive Care Part B Coinsurance	■	■	■	■	■	■	■	■	■	■

You have a lot of plans to choose from and a good broker will help you understand and navigate these options as a complementary service. Our services are free because we are paid as independent contractors by the insurance companies. Free is good!

Except for a few states, **plans are standardized** and named by letters. Yes, it is awfully confusing that the PARTS of Medicare are A, B, C, and D, and the private insurance PLANS are also alphabetical A through N. It's unfairly confusing. I apologize on behalf of the government. (I don't work for the government, but someone should apologize.)

If you get cancer, need dialysis or a transplant, your bill could easily run in the tens of thousands of dollars and more. But a Medicare Supplement Plan G — the most popular plan in the nation — has an annual maximum you would pay out-of-pocket, which is only $257 in 2025.

There are many Medicare Supplement options. You can choose Plan A, B, C, D, F, G, K, L, M, or N. The vast majority of you will purchase Plan G or N. Because of this, I'm going to focus on Plans G and N in this book.

You may know someone with an old Plan C, F, H, I, or J. Those plans are no longer for sale to people currently aging into Medicare. For now, and this will surely change, Plan G is the go-to plan.

Plan G is standardized by law, so almost every (there is always a weird exception in California that will offer a few extras) Plan G offers the exact same benefits. *But at different prices.*

💡 *Note for Residents of Massachusetts, Minnesota, and Wisconsin: Your states didn't go with the flow and standardize their plans like the rest of the nation. Yes, you can still get a Plan G, but it won't be called Plan G in your state! Same benefits, different names. We work in all states, and we will get you through the name confusions in your state.*

"If a G is a G, and only price separates the plans, it seems pretty simple to just choose the lowest priced Plan G in my zip code."

If it were that simple, we wouldn't be in business. Like an iceberg, a lot is below the surface not visible to the eye.

Medicare Supplements offer you the freedom to enroll in or change your Medicare Supplement policy at any time of the year, *if you are able to answer the health questions.*

Once you have Part B, you don't have to wait until specific enrollment periods to change your Medicare Supplement (like you do with Medicare Advantage and Part D plans).

Medicare Supplement policies are guaranteed renewable.

The company can't cancel you for any reason other than not paying your monthly bill. That is why it is crucial that you set up your bill on auto pay. Too many people neglect to pay just one bill and lose their Medicare Supplement insurance. If they are unhealthy, they will not be able to get their plan (or another Medicare Supplement plan) back without passing the health underwriting process.

When you enroll into Medicare Part B at age 65 (there are different rules while on Medicare due to disability under age 65), you have a **Golden Ticket**. This ticket gives you a 6-month window when you can enroll in any plan regardless of your health!

All your conditions are covered on day 1, with no waiting periods or exclusions of your pre-existing conditions. Every company has to take you, and they can't charge you more than anyone else at your age and gender living in your zip code.

Let me stress this good news: if you are very ill and have not had any health insurance prior to turning 65, you are **not** penalized. You can't be charged

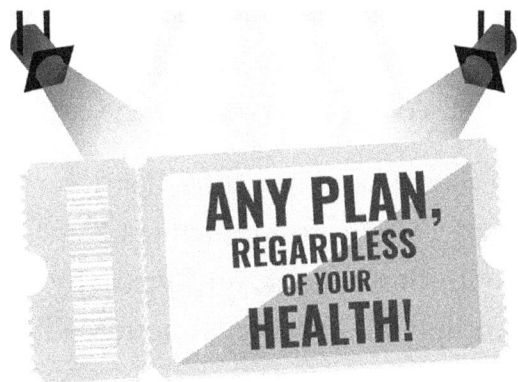

more or denied coverage because you are sick. The fact that you didn't have prior coverage doesn't matter. There is no waiting period and your benefits start on day 1. That is why it is crucial not to miss your once in a lifetime opportunity to use your "Golden Ticket."

Remember, Medicare supplements don't include drug coverage.

You'll buy a separate Part D drug plan. You can mix and match insurance companies so you can buy the supplement and drug plan from the same insurance company *if that best fits your needs*, or mix and match with different insurance companies. There is no discount or other benefit for buying them both from the same company. (Read more about Part D in Chapter 14).

HOW IT WORKS

When you go to the doctor you will present *both your government Medicare card and your Medicare Supplement insurance card*. Your doctor will send the bill to the government to pay its share and then the rest to your insurance plan to pay its share. If you've met your annual deductible already, you won't pay anything. If you haven't met your deductible, your doctor's office may either collect fees the day of your visit or send you a bill.

If the government pays your claim, your Medicare Supplement will always pay its part. If there was some confusion with your bill not being paid it's *almost always an error on the part of the medical billing person in your doctor's office*. Call them and ask them to resend the bill or check their coding. They know the drill.

You will have very little, if any, service issues with government Medicare and a Medicare Supplement Plan G. We have tens of thousands of clients with these plans, and virtually no complaints! Well, we get a lot of complaints, but that's about Medicare Part D and Medicare Advantage. Not Plan G.

SUPPLEMENTAL INSURANCE PREMIUMS

Unlike Parts A, B, and D, Medicare Supplement premiums are NOT paid out of your Social Security check. But you do have options! You can pay your supplement plans monthly — but only by bank draft — quarterly, semi-annually, or annually.

Most, but not all, Medicare Supplement plans now allow you to put your monthly premiums on a credit card. (I like to put everything on a credit card to earn airline miles.) The vast majority of people set up a monthly bank draft from their checking account. Some companies give you a small discount if you sign up for the monthly automatic payments.

I have a lot of clients who do not trust automatic payments and insist on paying by personal check. No insurance company will allow you to pay monthly by check. If you want to pay by check, you'll have to pay quarterly, semi-annually or annually. **Paying by check is dangerous.** If you are more than 30 days late on a payment, your insurance will be terminated. Yes, even if your spouse was in a car accident and you have never paid late in 10 years.

If you want the peace of mind of knowing that your coverage will never be terminated, you should set up automatic payments. I've had many clients lose their plans and were unable to re-enroll due to their health. As you'll see, only a few states allow you to enroll at any time of year and without asking health questions.

💡 *If your parents have Medicare Supplement plans, please check to see if they are set up on automatic payments!*

TRACKING YOUR CLAIMS

Medicare Summary Notices (MSN) is a letter that the government will send you every 3 months. Four times a year you can see all your Medicare claims and check for any errors. This letter will show you what Medicare paid, what your insurance plan paid, and how much you may still owe.

These notices are not bills!

See the sample summary below.

Medicare Summary Notice
for Part B (Medical Insurance)

The Official Summary of Your Medicare Claims from the Centers for Medicare & Medicaid Services

FACILITY NAME
JENNIFER WASHINGTON
STREET ADDRESS
CITY, ST 12345-6789

THIS IS NOT A BILL

Notice for Jennifer Washington

Medicare Number	**XXX-XX-1234A**
Date of This Notice	**September 16, 2011**
Claims Processed Between	**June 15 - September 15, 2011**

Your Deductible Status

Your deductible is what you must pay for most health services before Medicare begins to pay.

Part B Deductible: You have now met **$85** of your **$162** deductible for 2011.

Your Claims & Costs This Period

Did Medicare Approve All Services?	**NO**
Number of Services Medicare Denied	**2**

See claims starting on page 3. Look for NO in the "Service Approved?" column. See the last page for how to handle a denied claim.

Total You May Be Billed	**$150.86**

Providers with Claims This Period

June 18, 2011
Susan Jones, M.D.

What you owe is the **Patient Balance.** Most doctor offices collect the copays at time of service.

Your bill should never be higher than the Patient Balance. If it is, call your doctor's billing department.

So, 99.9% of the time you will just get your MSN (it is called Explanation of Benefits (EOB) if you are on Medicare Advantage) and see how little your doctor was paid, shake your head in amazement and throw it away. If you do have a question, you can use your **Client Portal** on our website to explain your problem and let us sort it out for you.

If you prefer to get these notices electronically, sign into your **MEDICARE.GOV** account and go to My Account Settings to sign up. If you have Medicare Advantage, you'll create an account with your insurance company and sign up there for an electronic EOB.

FRAUD ON MY ACCOUNT

In the past few years, thousands of people have notified Medicare they see urinary catheters billed on their behalf, which they never received. This is a known and ongoing scam. It has taken years, but this scam was finally shut down. But when the government stops one scam, another pops up.

You should alert the government if your doctor is billing for fraudulent items.

If you do see fraud, report it to 1-800-MEDICARE.

PRICING MEDICARE SUPPLEMENT PLANS

Supplement plan prices are based on a variety of factors. Here are the basics.

Attained-age rating is the most common pricing method. The monthly premiums for these policies will be based on your age when you enroll into your policy. The rates will increase every year. We can give you an estimate of upcoming rate increases. For example, for 2025 we see a 9% to 15% rate increase and expect similar increases for 2026.

Community-rated policies base rates on geographical factors, such as which zip code you live in or whether you use tobacco. They don't base rates on just your age. One company has managed to maintain the most stable rates over the past 2 decades using this pricing method.

Issue-age-rated policies have rates that are much higher than other plans when you first enroll. Your rate is based on your age at the time you purchased the policy. The insurance company cannot raise rates *as you get older*, but they can raise rates for other reasons. We do not sell plans like this at **THEMEDICAREFAMILY.COM** because they are misleading.

All the marketing material these companies use make it seem like these plans will never increase in price. But they will! No one escapes medical inflation.

Since all Medicare Supplement rates go up each year, our goal is to position you into a plan that has stable, predictable rate increases. We can see the rate increase history of the plans. That helps us see a trend in their pricing.

HOUSEHOLD DISCOUNTS

Household discounts look good on paper, but we rarely sell the same company's plan to both spouses or household members. Typically, this is because you and your spouse are enrolling into Medicare in different years and prices change each year. If you and your spouse DO both enroll into Medicare in the same year, this type of discount can save you a lot of money!

First, let me explain the discount.

Most Medicare Supplement plans offer discounts if more than one person in the same household has a Medicare Supplement plan *with the same insurance company.* Some companies only give the discounts to spouses, but other companies have expanded the discount to include domestic partners or even a friend or relative, as long as they are residing at the same address for a year.

> 💡 *I once got a discount for a client because her nephew had been sleeping on her couch for over a year! Not all states allow discounts for nephews; the exact terms will vary by state.*

These discounts can range from around 5% to 12%. In some cases, both people need to have a Medicare Supplement plan from the same company, but other times, *just living together is enough to qualify.* This is a good option for couples or people living together who want to save on their monthly premiums.

So why do we not use it very often?

Let's look at Ron and Donna. Ron is 5 years older than his wife. The most competitive Plan G in his state when he turned 65 was Pretend Company. Five years later when Donna turned 65, Pretend Company was not as competitive as Example Company. Even with a 5% discount, Donna was better to forgo Pretend and enroll with Example.

Now sometimes couples want to be in the same plan for simplicity, and I respect that, but if you are stretching your budget, you should search for the most competitive plan the year you enroll.

If you are both the same age, then a household discount can be a very attractive reason to choose the same insurance company!

INSURANCE "BLOCKS"

Most Medicare Supplement companies open a new block of business every 3 to 5 years. Then they close that block and the members on it start to take higher-than-expected rate increases. The healthy member will jump ship to a new plan at a lower rate, but those who can't move are stuck forever — unless they decided to abandon Medicare Supplements for a Medicare Advantage plan.

A few notable companies do not do this — yet.

We pay for subscriptions to actuarial services that allow us to see when a new block opens and how long it has been open. We can also see patterns in how different insurance companies operate.

To the untrained eye, the cheapest Plan G is an easy choice, but that may be with a company in its last year of a block of business. If you are sick, you made a poor decision.

There is much more to choosing a plan than going with the lowest rate!

💡 *Sometimes our clients ask for the bargain basement plan (that we know will skyrocket its price in about 3 years) because they are healthy, and plan to change companies and chase rates. A true gambling mentality! I'm OK with it.*

SOME STATES CHARGE HIGHER PRICES

Your state laws greatly impact what you'll pay for a Medicare Supplement. Some states charge more for Medicare Supplement plans because healthcare is more expensive there, or they have different rules. The states that usually have the highest prices include **New York, Massachusetts, Connecticut, Florida, and California.** These states just cost more overall, so the insurance prices are higher too.

LARGE VS. SMALL INSURANCE COMPANIES

In general, the small companies that you have not heard of are not able to maintain their rates as well as the large national companies. This is because the larger companies can spread their risk out over more subscribers.

Think of it like a boat. If you are on a huge cruise ship, you can feel the waves (the price increase) but not as much as if you are in a small boat where the waves are really crashing. I don't recommend that you get into a small boat unless you are healthy and feel comfortable that you can move when big rate increases come.

At The Medicare Family, we can see how many people are enrolled into each plan in your state and how long that plan has been selling in your state, among other things. But I don't need to look at it to know that a new company that has never sold Medicare Supplement plans before will have the lowest prices in your state (since they are not paying claims on anyone yet) and they are unlikely to maintain those rates.

Insurance is all about money.

The insurance companies are trying to make a profit. They'd love to enroll only healthy people, but by law, they have to take everyone at age 65. Many larger companies often offer very attractive rates for those who are aged 68 to 70 hoping to attract healthy people who were on a small boat and are dealing with large rate increases. The small boats can't just raise rates as they wish because each state has to approve their rates, so these small companies have to plead that they have holes in their boat (losses) that can only be plugged with rate increases. Some states are stricter than others when it comes to allowing big rate increases.

We have a for-profit healthcare system that you already have a love/hate relationship with. That relationship will intensify in retirement as healthcare spending takes on a much larger part of your life and percentage of your budget!

WHY GENDER MATTERS IN PRICING

Men are my toughest clients. They hate Medicare because they hate the thought of being sick. The majority of my clients who decided that Medicare A and B was enough, *were men*. Women are more insurance-friendly. Men often get hostile when I suggest they may be hospitalized at some point in the future. Women accept the fact that illness is lurking right around the corner.

Not that women love running to the doctor, but if we see something suspicious on our arm, we book an appointment the next day! Men may wait years to get the same spot checked out.

If you are nodding, then you'll understand why insurance companies charge men more for the same Medicare Supplement Plan G. Women tend to catch cancer earlier — when it is easier (and cheaper) to treat — which saves the insurance companies money.

THE BEST COMPANY

If there was a runaway winner — one with the best rates, service, rate stability, household discounts, and plan extras — we could save a lot of time by only representing that one insurance company. My life would be much easier.

But there isn't.

There are many good companies to choose from in each state, and not all companies sell in all states. AARP sells in all 50, but Cigna and Humana sell in 48 states, and State Farm sells in 45 states. Many smaller companies might only sell in a handful of states. That is why you may be disappointed if you call us from Florida to enroll in the same plan your sister has in Nebraska. It may not be available in your state.

State insurance laws prevent me from disparaging an insurance company *even if what I say is true and publicly documented!* Company Z has by far the worst customer service in the nation. Most agents know it, *but we can't tell you.* That seems ridiculous, but it's the law. We can gently try to tell you we've had great service with a different company, and you can read between the lines.

We can't even use superlative adjectives like "best" when talking about Medicare Advantage or Drug plans. But we can when referring to Medicare Supplement plans. It's a strange world to work in!

The "best" Medicare Supplement plan in your state is the one with the lowest price and *the stability to retain its rates into the future.* Often the very cheapest plan is a new company that will have terrible rate increases to make up for pricing that was too cheap to begin with.

None of this will matter while you are *healthy*. If your plan consistently takes higher rate increases than all your friends' plans, *you can just change to a different plan at any time*. If you are not healthy, then you may have locked yourself into that plan for the rest of your life. You can always bail out and move to private Medicare Advantages plans, but you will not be able to get a lower priced Supplement.

PREPARE FOR RATES TO GO UP EVERY YEAR

Ignore the company that boasts that their plan will NEVER go up when you get a year older. That's true, but what they are not telling you is that their plans — all plans — will go up due to regular inflation and medical inflation. *That plan won't increase due to you getting older, but it still goes up in price for other reasons.* Which only makes sense. Healthcare costs rise every year. It's never level for a few years, *and it never goes down*. Some plans go up like a rocket, and those are the plans we help you avoid.

Some people say, "Give me the lowest priced Plan G and I'll worry about the future later." The lowest plan usually can't hold its rates. Our job is to explain all of this to you and let you decide how much of a gamble you want to take. If you remain healthy, you'll be able to switch plans in the future.

Some gambles pay off. Some don't.

HELP IS AVAILABLE

There are several reasons thousands of people have sought our advice instead of trying to choose a Medicare Supplement policy on their own:

1. Our services are free.

2. We are independent contractors — not employed by insurance companies — and don't push you toward any particular plans.

3. We have decades of experience helping people all over the country.

4. You don't save any money going it alone.

5. We will be here to help you with service issues for the rest of your life.

6. Plus, we have decades of experience working with these companies.

Some plans are cheap today but have built-in explosive rate increases, while others are a bit more expensive today, but have a rate history of stability that you will treasure in the future. Some companies have terrible customer service. Sometimes we sell those plans, *but we try to warn you how to navigate their service issues.*

You pay a lot for the luxury of a Medicare Supplement plan. Just like grocery stores offer "Loss Leaders" to get you in the store, some insurance companies put out a plan that is priced below market so they can get all the business. They know they are underpriced, and once they get the number of clients they need to be profitable, they start jacking up the rates.

POINTS TO REMEMBER

- A Medicare Supplement is a private insurance plan from A to N to fill the holes in government Medicare.

- When you first enroll into Medicare Part B, you can get any Medicare Supplement plan from any insurance company, regardless of your health, and without a waiting period.

- You are not penalized if you don't have health insurance prior to enrolling into Medicare Part B.

- Medicare Supplements cost more than private Medicare Advantage plans because you can see any doctor and go to any hospital. No networks!

- Prices are based on your age, gender, location, and the plan you choose.

- There are several ways insurance companies rate their plans, but they all go up in price annually!

- Some plans go up much faster than others. We can help you navigate this.

- In general, the small companies that you have not heard of are not able to maintain their rates as well as the large national companies.

CHAPTER 10

SWITCHING MEDICARE SUPPLEMENT PLANS

Medicare Supplement plans are great when you first sign up, but over time, rates go up. If it's been a few years since you picked your plan, now might be a good time to see if you can find the same coverage for a better price. Switching plans can feel like a hassle, but it doesn't have to be. Whether you're just starting to see rate increases or it's been a while, it's always worth exploring your options at least every 4-5 years. Depending on where you live and your health, you might be able to save big!

Let's dive into how and when you can make the switch — and why it's important to keep an eye on those rate changes. Remember, your options will depend on the state you live in and your health.

Three main ways to change your Medicare Supplement plan:

1. **At any time of year if you are healthy** enough to answer the health underwriting questions.

2. If you **move states** at any time of year and your plan is not available in your new state.

3. If your **state has special rules**, you can change during that specific window, usually around your birthday.

4. When you qualify due to **special circumstances** in Illinois and California.

Unlike Medicare Advantage and Part D, there is no special time of year when you can change your Medicare Supplement plan. If you are healthy enough, you can change anytime.

💡 *Most Medicare Supplement companies send their rate increase notices in the fall, but a few wait until January. They can do it any time of the year but must give a 30-day notice. Whenever you get an increase that you don't like, call us to see if you can change to the same Plan G or N with another insurance company.*

DEFINING "HEALTHY ENOUGH"

Health underwriting is when an insurance company asks about your health. They might ask if you've been recently hospitalized, which medications you take and if you have any serious health problems. It helps them decide if they want to risk selling you a plan and how much they'll charge you for it.

Sometimes, if you're really sick — like if your kidneys don't work well or you've had cancer — they won't allow you to enroll in their plan. But remember, **when you first sign up for Medicare, they can't ask these questions**, so everyone gets approved!

When it comes to switching Medicare Supplement plans, every insurance company has its own set of **health underwriting** questions. These questions can be strict or lenient, and they can change over time. So, it's not always easy to know whether you'll be accepted for a new plan without some help. That's where we come in. We can compare dozens of companies and their questions for you at once — something that's impossible to do on your own unless you feel like calling each company individually.

Sure, you can use Medicare's plan finder tool to compare options, but it doesn't show you important details like how often rates go up or if there are any hidden fees.

Now, you might be thinking, "I've got some health issues, there's no way I can switch plans." But don't worry! If your conditions are well-managed with medication — like high blood pressure, high cholesterol, or type 2 diabetes — you can usually still get approved for a new plan (and often at a lower price if you've been on the same plan for 4-5 years).

However, if you have a more serious condition, it's tougher. Some health issues are what we call "knockout conditions," meaning no company will accept you unless you're in a special enrollment period where health questions don't apply. In that case, you'll have to stick with your current plan or consider moving to a Medicare Advantage plan, which doesn't require health questions at all.

COMMON KNOCKOUT CONDITIONS

Chronic Renal Disease

Chronic renal diseases result in gradual loss of kidney functions like End-Stage Renal Disease (ESRD), and Polycystic Kidney Disease (PKD).

In most cases, any chronic renal disease will result in denial because the final step in treatment often includes kidney transplants.

Auto-Immune Disorders

AIDS, HIV, Rheumatoid Arthritis, Psoriatic Arthritis, and Systemic Lupus are always knock outs.

Diabetes

Diabetes isn't a declinable condition if you meet certain criteria. Typically, if you take less than 50 units of insulin a day and have *no complications* other than diabetes, many plans will accept you! Some may charge you a bit more each month.

Cancer

If you currently have cancer, it is a knockout. But once you have been clear for more than 2 years, carriers will start to consider approving you for coverage. Some want to see you clear for 3 to 5 years. Nonmelanoma skin cancer is often not a problem.

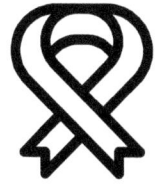

Nervous System and Neuromuscular Diseases

ALS, MS, epilepsy, fibromyalgia, and myasthenia gravis are knockout conditions.

Other Conditions

Heart disease, COPD, stroke, or heart attack within the last 5 years may cost you coverage. Again, some companies may accept you if the heart attack or stroke was 5 years ago, some make you wait longer.

Severe depression, schizophrenia, or bipolar disorder within the last 2 years, or being advised by a physician to have surgery, medical tests, treatments, that you have not completed can be problematic.

If a doctor has told you that you *need to get a treatment and you haven't had it yet*, that is a knockout question. No insurance company wants to take you on knowing you'll immediately schedule a hysterectomy or knee replacement. Finish your treatments before you apply to move companies.

Most companies start by asking these questions:

- Age
- Alcohol use
- Chronic health conditions
- Circulatory system
- Drug use (prescription, over-the-counter, and drug abuse)
- Gender

- Family health history
- Medical history
- Mental health history
- Tobacco use
- Weight (if you are very thin or very heavy)

> Depending on how you answer, you may be approved but have to pay more, or you may be denied.

Unlike life insurance, when you apply for a Medicare Supplement plan during a period where you have to answer the health questions, they do not ask for an EKG, blood work, a urine sample, or check your medical records. You do give the insurance company permission to do a *prescription drug check.*

Many people are not intentionally leaving drugs off their application, they often simply forget all the medications they are taking. Or they forget they had been prescribed a drug *in the past,* but they never filled that prescription and didn't take that drug. The insurance company needs to know the details before they can approve your application.

Just like there are conditions that are knockouts, there are also prescriptions that will automatically disqualify you!

Lying On Your Application

It's easy to lie on your application. The Medicare Supplement companies do not go to the expense of checking your medical records — until you have a claim. Let's say you said you were perfectly healthy on your application, but you ignored your doctor's order for an EKG. When you have a heart attack, they can see that you lied on your application. The insurance company will refund the premiums you paid and your policy is terminated. You must pay for all your hospital bills.

Be truthful on your application, but don't volunteer information.

The insurance company will ask you a series of questions. Answer them honestly, but do not volunteer information that was not requested. Your legal obligation is to answer what is asked. I had a client once say that she gets a little dizzy in the mornings before she drinks any water. Her application was declined.

The insurance company doesn't know if she suffered from an undiagnosed medical problem or if she, like me, just has low blood pressure and is perfectly normal (after I drink some water in the mornings).

PRE-EXISTING CONDITIONS

A Medicare Supplement plan can charge more for pre-existing conditions because your health issues increase the amount the company will have to pay. It's not common, but Medicare Supplement companies can even implement a pre-existing condition *waiting period*. **Medicare Supplement companies cannot have a pre-existing condition waiting period longer than 6 months.** This is period only comes into play if you are enrolling during a time when you are **not** guaranteed coverage regardless of your health.

Even if you have cancer, MS, or Parkinson's right now, you may still be able to change plans regardless of your health, *in certain states*.

Many states have certain times throughout the year during which you can change your Medicare supplement *without medical underwriting*. It's important to know the options and the laws in your state.

SPECIAL STATE RULES

1. **Birthday Rules** – California, Idaho, Illinois, Kentucky, Maine, Nevada, Oregon, Rhode Island.

2. **Anniversary Rules** – Missouri.

3. **Year-Round Enrollment Rules** – Connecticut, New York, Washington, Vermont.

If you live in one of these states, your state law allows you to change Medicare Supplement plans during special enrollment windows *without underwriting.*

These states provide guaranteed issue protections at least once per year to switch from Medicare Advantage to a Medicare Supplement plan, or to move from one Medicare Supplement plan to another Medicare Supplement plan.

IDAHO allows you to switch Medicare Supplement plans within 63 days beginning on your birthday each year. But you must move to the same or lower benefits. For example, moving from Plan G to Plan N is OK, but if you want to move from Plan N to Plan G, you'll have to pass health underwriting.

ILLINOIS gives you 45 days from your birthday to make a change. Illinois limits changes to plans offered by *your current insurer company.* If you have a Plan F with Mutual of Omaha, you can move to any other plan Mutual of Omaha offers. Note: if you are past age 75, you can't take advantage of this rule.

KENTUCKY lets you switch plans for up to 60 days starting the day after your birthday. You must choose a plan with equal or lesser benefits.

LOUISIANA gives you a 2-month window and only allows you to move to *lesser coverage.* You could move from a Plan G to a Plan N, but not the other way around (unless you can answer the health questions).

MARYLAND allows you to switch plans within 30 days, starting on your birthday. You must choose a plan with equal or lesser benefits.

NEVADA and **OKLAHOMA** both allow you to switch plans during the 60 days *after your birthday.* You must choose a plan with equal or lesser benefits.

OREGON lets you change plans starting *30 days before and ending 30 days after* your birthday. You must choose a plan with equal or lesser benefits.

MISSOURI is the only state with an **Anniversary Rule.** You can change your plan without answering health questions *within 30 days before and after the insurance policy's anniversary date* (the date you bought the plan).

CONNECTICUT, MAINE, NEW YORK, and **VERMONT** offer you **year-round enrollment**. This means you can change plans any time. You can move up to better coverage or move down to lesser coverage. You won't have a waiting period, and your pre-existing conditions will be covered.

Washington State allows you to change at any time of year but only in these configurations:

- Plan A may only move to another Plan A.
- Plan B, C, D, E, F, G, M, or N may move to any other.
- Plan B, C, D, F (including high deductible), G, M, or N regardless of benefits compared to your current plan.
- Old standardized Plans H, I, or J may move to another.
- less comprehensive Plan B, C, D, F, G, M, or N.
- Old Plan J will qualify for the state's Plan J Guaranteed Issue Conversion rule.

MORE UNUSUAL STATE RULES

MAINE lets you change to the same or lesser benefits at any time of year. Maine won't allow you to use this rule if you had a lapse in coverage of 60 days or more.

MASSACHUSETTS allows you to switch your Medicare Supplement plan without health questions from February 1 through March 31. Your new plan coverage will begin the following June 1.

Massachusetts handles Medicare very differently from the rest of the country! For example, you won't find Medicare Supplement plans named the same letters A through N like most of the country. You can still get the benefits of the plans A through N, but your plans are named differently. The Bay State also doesn't allow Medicare excess charges if you want a Plan N.

Before you petition your state to change its laws and adopt more lenient rules, you need to know that prices in these states are higher. You will find the lowest rates in the states that only allow you to change your plan when you can pass the health questions.

🔦 If you don't see your state on this list, just wait. Many of these states adopted these rules in the past 4 years. It is a trend moving across the country and your state may soon change its laws.

AFTER APPROVAL

If you have been approved to switch plans, be very careful not to jump the gun and cancel your current Medicare Supplement policy yet. Keep your current plan until you have proof in writing of acceptance from the new insurance company.

And as soon as you get your written proof, don't forget to cancel your old policy. Having 2 plans doesn't give you any additional benefit. Many people assume that enrolling into their new plan will automatically disenroll them from their old plan because that is how smoothly Medicare Advantage and Part D plans work. Not so with Medicare Supplements.

At your next doctor's appointment, give your new ID cards to the staff to replace your old policy. If you have already met your Part B deductible for the year, that carries over and you won't start paying your deductible again until the start of the new year.

Many people mistakenly assume that the insurance agent who enrolled them into a **new** Medicare Supplement plan canceled their **old** plan.

Only you can cancel your plan (for your protection).

The insurance company requires that you call them or notify them in writing if you want to cancel your plan.

💡 Once you have your new ID cards, throw out your old cards. I can tell you that many of my clients keep all the ID cards they've ever had in their wallet. This causes confusion! While you are still 100% sure that your new card is the one you want to keep, throw the old ones away. Adult children, this is a reminder to ask your parents how many old insurance cards they are carrying and help simplify things for them too!

POINTS TO REMEMBER

- Federal law guarantees you any Medicare Supplement regardless of your health when you first enroll into Medicare Part B.

- After that, state laws vary, and most states require you to go through health underwriting to change your insurance plan.

- You need to purchase a separate drug plan.

- Medicare Supplement plans are rated 3 different ways, but they all go up in price every year.

- Medicare Supplement plans are standardized. A Plan G is a Plan G from every company.

- You can change your plan at any time of year if you qualify.

- If your plan becomes too expensive, you can move to Medicare Advantage during the AEP each fall.

- Only YOU can cancel your old insurance plan.

CHAPTER 11

MEDICARE SUPPLEMENT PLAN G

The pros of Medicare Supplement Plans are ease of use and the cons are price. Really! In my opinion, there are no other drawbacks. It doesn't matter how good your insurance is if you can't afford it. In this chapter, I will focus on the most popular plan sold today, Medicare Supplement Plan G.

This is the plan I will purchase when I turn 65. By law, I'm never allowed to state what I feel the "Best Medicare Advantage Plan" is, but I can say that I believe Medicare Supplement Plan G is the "Best Medicare Supplement Plan *when you can afford it.*" It is simple to understand, and your costs are very predictable.

As you can see from the chart, Plan G has the lowest out-of-pocket expenses. Other than your monthly premium, your only other cost is your one-time annual Part B deductible. Plan G is very easy to understand and plan a budget around.

IT'S SIMPLE

- Pay your monthly premium.
- Pay your annual deductible.
- Don't worry about any other costs the rest of the year!

MEDIGAP BENEFITS
Plan G vs Plan N

A SIDE-BY-SIDE COMPARISON OF TWO OF THE MOST POPULAR MEDIGAP PLANS.

MEDIGAP BENEFITS	PLAN G	PLAN N
MEDICARE **PART A** COINSURANCE & HOSPITAL COSTS	100%	100%
MEDICARE **PART B** COINSURANCE/COPAYMENT	100%	100%
BLOOD (FIRST 3 PINTS)	100%	100%
PART A HOSPICE CARE COINSURANCE/COPAYMENT	100%	100%
SKILLED NURSING FACILITY COINSURANCE	100%	100%
PART A DEDUCTIBLE	100%	100%
PART B DEDUCTIBLE	✗	✗
PART B EXCESS CHARGES	100%	✗

> If your doctor accepts Medicare (and over 90% of doctors do) your doctor also accepts your Supplemental plan.

When you go to your doctor, present your government Medicare card and your insurance card. If you've met your annual deductible, then the doctor's office will bill Medicare for 80% of your visit and your insurance company for the other 20%. You don't pay anything. If Plan G sounds cheap, easy, and stress-free, it is!

For a few years.

Then the rates go up. Maybe not the first 4 or 5 years, but one day you will call and say, "How am I supposed to afford another 10% rate increase? Don't you know I'm on a FIXED INCOME?"

I then remind you that I told you this would happen back when you were 65.

> That was the honeymoon phase!

Plan G is very affordable at age 65, but it will go up every year, **for the rest of your life**, no matter if you use your insurance or not. Your rates never increase based on your health, the rates will only increase on an entire block of business. You are never singled out.

Medicare Supplements are loved by all providers. Doctors and hospitals get paid *more* when you have this type of insurance.

With Plan G, you will almost never have to search to find a specialist that accepts your insurance. You won't have to wait for your doctor to get approval from the insurance company before you can get your surgery.

We have tens of thousands of clients happily enrolled into Advantage plans, but you paid good money for this book and want the unvarnished truth. The good and the bad. Supplement plans are great, except price. They get expensive fast.

But other than price, they are far superior to Advantage plans because of these three reasons:

1. **The benefits never change.** When you buy a Medicare Supplement plan, it will remain the same for the rest of your life. As long as you pay your monthly premium, you can keep it. They can't get rid of you. They can't charge you more when you get sick.

2. **No network.** You can see almost any doctor and hospital in the nation. Mayo Clinic? Yes. Johns Hopkins? Yes. **Any hospital in the nation**. There is no network. Every doctor wants your insurance! Travel anywhere in the country without worrying if you are in or out of the network.

3. **No Prior Authorizations required.** If your doctor orders a surgery,

just go book it. You don't have to ask the insurance company for permission and wait to see if it's approved.

4. **Very few to no service issues.** If Medicare pays its portion, your supplement will pay its portion. There is rarely ever an issue with Medicare Supplement claims. When there is, it is usually because your doctor's office filed something incorrectly.

Plan G really is easy.

Go to any doctor, show both Medicare and Plan G cards, and BOOM! The front desk person at your doctor's office makes me look like a liar. He says he is sorry, but they don't accept Aetna, Cigna, Humana, or whatever Plan G you own. Immediately you feel deceived by me and proceed to burn this book.

Let me warn you, the front office in many doctor's offices do NOT understand all the insurance options. I don't blame them for being uninformed. This stuff changes annually and office staff have to deal with hundreds of types of insurance every day.

> So let me reassure you. If your doctor accepts Medicare, she also accepts your Plan G, regardless of which insurance company you bought it from.

Your doctor's front office staff is confusing Aetna, Cigna, and Humana's Medicare Advantage plans which do have a network, with Medicare Supplement Plan G, which does not have a network.

If the person at the front desk insists he is correct, please ask him to confirm with the billing office. Or just ask to call billing yourself while you are still in the doctor's office.

With Plan G, when your doctor schedules a surgery, you can go to any hospital. Your doctor may have hospital privileges at several hospitals and ask you if you have a preference, but you can choose whichever you'd like, knowing that your insurance will pay the same wherever you go.

When you have an inpatient surgery, you have $0 additional cost. Your Medicare Supplement picks up the hospital deductible.

When you are discharged, you may have weeks of therapy. Again, if you've met your annual Part B deductible already, you pay $0 for each therapy.

What if you get an infection and are back in the ER? Plan G covers it.

WHAT PLAN G DOES NOT COVER

1. **Part D Drugs**. You need a separate plan for your prescriptions. It does give you coverage for Part B drugs!

2. **Dental**. You need a separate plan for dental benefits.

3. **Hearing exams and hearing aids**.

4. **Annual vision exams** if you are healthy. If you already have macular degeneration, glaucoma or diabetes, then Medicare provides eye exams. But if you are healthy, Medicare won't cover an annual exam to see if things are still good.

5. **Long-term care in a nursing home**. This is the biggest financial risk to your retirement, and beyond the scope of this book. Just note that your Medicare Supplement is NOT the protection from an extended Nursing Home stay that you may need.

FILLING HOLES AND SPLITTING PLANS

You can fill the holes with private insurance depending on your health and wealth. Buy as much or as little extra insurance as you feel you need. It's also not uncommon to spend more of the family budget on the sicker spouse and strip down the coverage on the healthier spouse. Sure, it's a gamble, *but insurance is all a gamble.*

For example, Bob and Mary are a married couple both turning 65 this year. They have a tight budget. While they would love to both purchase a Medicare Supplement Plan G, they also need to save money, so they choose to split up and put better coverage on Bob and save money on Mary.

Bob is a diabetic who has had 2 heart attacks and takes 6 prescriptions daily. Since he may need to see more doctors and specialists in the future, a Plan G allows him more flexibility to see the best doctors without worrying about who is in the network. This also reduces the hassle of having to get prior authorizations.

Mary is very healthy and takes no medications. She's willing to get the "cheaper" insurance to free up money to keep Bob on a Medicare Supplement Plan G. The women in her family typically have good health into their late 80s. She chooses a Medicare Advantage PPO with $0 monthly premium.

Her PPO includes drug coverage. She is excited because her plan offers some dental coverage and she gets $100 each quarter to buy over-the-counter health items. She's happy that her family doctor accepts her PPO plan and her preferred hospital is also in-network.

Both are happy.

Then Mary gets cancer, and they panic. Now it's often too late for Mary to move over to a Medicare Supplement Plan G (although there are instances where she might be able to do that). Will her care be substandard? Will she suffer with long waits for care and will her out-of-pocket costs bankrupt the family? NO!

Mary's Medicare Advantage plan has a maximum amount she will have to pay each year. If she only had government Medicare A and B, she would have no protection.

If Mary got cancer on Medicare A and B only, without private insurance, she would have to pay 20% of the cost of her chemotherapy and radiation treatments. This can cost her tens of thousands of dollars, especially if she needs several rounds of treatment. Since she has a PPO plan, she will pay copays, but they stop after she meets the annual max (MOOP).

Here is another example where a couple split up and went different ways with their Medicare choices, **my own parents.**

Dick and Margaret Gordon took separate routes with Medicare even though their budget was not tight, and they are both licensed insurance specialists.

Who did my mom choose at age 65? Mutual of Omaha Plan G for about $80 per month (the price reflects this was years ago).

You'd think that my dad would also go with a Plan G and also with Mutual of Omaha to get a spousal premium discount, *but you'd be wrong.*

Dad chose a Medicare Advantage PPO plan. He paid $0 per month and loved his plan. "Why pay monthly for a plan that I know I'll not need?" Turns out he was right. Dad is now 89 and between age 65 to 88 he had no major health issues. No surgeries, no outpatient treatments. Nothing.

Mom, on the other hand, had 4 joint replacement surgeries in that same 13-year span. Her supplement plan went up about 7% every year. She pays about $300 per month and is very happy with her insurance.

Dad *was* on his PPO (and would probably still be on that plan), but I insisted that he move to a Medicare Supplement Plan G in 2023 at age 88. He pays about $400 per month and complains about the wasted monthly cost.

Why did I insist Dad change plans?

He could easily afford the cost of Plan G and the odds are good that he will eventually need expensive healthcare. If he gets sick, he would hate to deal with the waits and frustration that Medicare Advantage Prior Authorization creates. If he gets a rare illness and his doctor refers him to the Mayo Clinic or Cleveland Clinic, he would have had to pay for it out-of-pocket if his old plan wasn't accepted. Every hospital will accept his Medicare Supplement Plan G.

He now has complete flexibility to get the best care, anywhere in the country. He saved tens of thousands of dollars over the past 13 years, but if he gets something major and needs to see an out-of-network doctor, that could easily eat up the money he saved.

Many 88-year-olds are not healthy enough to make this jump from Medicare Advantage PPO to Plan G. You have to be healthy enough to pass the health questions, and each company asks different questions. Since Dad is now a Type 2 diabetic, he is charged extra on his Plan G. He is otherwise very healthy and was able to pass health underwriting.

This has worked for my parents but doesn't mean it will work for you. *It's all a gamble.*

Most couples do go the same route when choosing Medicare plans. It's much easier that way. But keep in mind that down the road, as things change, going your own way may be the best way to stretch the family budget.

PLAN TO SWAP

I urge you to consider a Medicare Supplement plan when you first join Medicare. It's affordable at age 65 and an easy way into retirement. As it goes up in price, you can plan to jump over to a Medicare Advantage plan any year, regardless of your health, during the Annual Election Period (AEP), October 15th through December 7th. You will know it's AEP time because the TV ads about it are non-stop and your mailbox will overflow with solicitations!

A current client of mine, I'll call her Martha, had a great corporate career and felt pretty well-off at age 65. She wanted "the best" coverage and went with a Plan G. At age 70 she called me. "I'm still really healthy, why am I paying $200 a month for something I never use? I want to try a Medicare Advantage plan for $0 per month like my friend has."

We discussed her options and I moved her to a PPO and she loved the cost and the extra benefits (those change every year, but she enjoyed them) for a few years.

Then at age 75 she called me back. "A lot of my friends are getting cancer now and my out-of-pocket maximum on my PPO plan is $8,000 if I get cancer. I think I'd rather go back to a Medicare Supplement."

She was healthy enough to pass the health underwriting and today is happily on a Plan G at age 81, and still healthy.

This kind of moving around is not uncommon. Most people expect to make these decisions once. File it away. And be done. Alas, only the ultra-rich have that luxury.

> The rest of us are chasing rates and benefits our whole lives.

If we can get the same plan at a better price, we move. If our budget gets tighter, we move from Plan G to a PPO. And later, if it gets even tighter, we move from a PPO to an HMO. In other words, you are never done with your Medicare decisions.

DIFFERENT INSURANCE COMPANIES

If you think a Medicare Supplement Plan G looks like a great way to start your retirement, your next choice is which insurance company to choose.

> You have at least 20 to 30 Medicare Supplement companies to choose from in most states.

Many are household names like Blue Cross Blue Shield, United Healthcare, and Allstate. Others you've never heard of. You may want a plan that your sister raves about in Oregon, but it's not available in your state. Remember, your location matters.

Our company is an independent contractor for dozens and dozens of insurance companies. I am personally contracted with over 150 different insurance companies to offer a wide variety of products. You don't want to hear the pros and cons of each company. Ain't no one got the time for that! **You just want me to tell you what to buy, and why. I can do that.**

First, I need to know some personal information about you.

1. **How is your health?** Legally I can't ask you that at age 65 or if you are enrolling into a Medicare Advantage plan *at any age.* So, make it easy on me to follow the law and just volunteer your health information. I'm not judging you or your life choices, I'm trying to gauge which plans to recommend to you. None of the prescriptions you are on are new to me. I've seen it all. The more you tell me the better advice I can offer.

2. **What drugs and dosages are you taking?** I mean prescription drugs, but you can tell me the other drugs too. Sometimes it's relevant info that I can use (like marijuana).

3. **How tight is your budget?** I've asked thousands of people and all but about 10 said, "tight." The cardiologist in whose mansion I was sitting when I posed this question also told me his budget was tight. Once you are on a fixed income, everyone stresses about money. But I need to know HOW TIGHT your budget is.

   Can you comfortably afford the out-of-pocket maximum on a PPO plan? Everyone is attracted to the $0 monthly premium, but if you get cancer, can you come up with $6,000 to $14,000? If you get cancer at the end of a calendar year and are still in treatment into the next year, you could hit that maximum again in the new year.

4. **How much do you travel?** This question catches people off guard, but it matters. If you spend a few weeks each year out of your home area, visiting your kids or travelling, you are not a great candidate for a Medicare Advantage HMO plan with a small network. You might benefit from a PPO with a nationwide network or a Medicare Supplement that gives you complete coverage to go

anywhere. If your budget is tight, you are healthy, you don't travel, a PPO or HMO might be a great fit.

5. **What are your genes like?** This is the easiest and hardest question to answer. Unless you are adopted, most people have a good idea how long people live in their families. In my family, everyone has arthritis and needs new hips and knees. (Shoulders are good, thankfully.) There is no cancer in my family tree, but heart disease is prevalent on one side. Based on this information, I'd recommend a Medicare Supplement and no additional cancer insurance.

Once I have your information, I can advise several plans with several different companies, in many budgets. But trust me, you really don't want to hear about all 150 options.

PAYMENT OPTIONS

A quick reminder on payment options. You can't choose to have your Medicare Supplement plan premiums deducted from your Social Security check like you can Medicare Advantage and Part D drug plans. Many people prefer to write a check and are leery of automatic bank drafts (ACH). **Please, please sign up for bank drafts.**

I've seen too many people get distracted with an illness or death of a loved one and neglect to pay for their Medicare Supplement. If you are 1 day past the 30-day grace period your coverage is terminated. It won't be a problem to re-enroll, and you'll have a month without coverage in many cases, but many people are not healthy enough to pass the health questions and are left without coverage. Forever.

🔆 *If you have elderly parents, now is the time to help them convert to ACH! Do it right now. I've heard the following sentence too many times, "Sylvia, I've paid my premiums on time or early for over 15 years, I'm sure they'll make an exception because I'm only 1 day late." They won't.*

Some companies offer a small discount if you sign up for ACH. As my mom says, "That's better than a kick in the butt." If you insist on writing a check, and I have many clients who do, no company will allow you to pay monthly by check. You'll have to pay quarterly, semi-annually, or annually. Some give you a decent discount for paying annually (as they should). Personally, I put everything on a credit card to accrue airline miles. Not all Medicare Supplement companies currently allow payment with credit cards.

Note that your old company is not going to refund your unused premiums quickly. I can't make them speed it up, so you have been warned. If you paid annually, you will be waiting on a large refund and may have cash flow issues when you change plan mid-year.

To wrap things up, Medicare Supplement Plan G is a strong choice for those looking to minimize out-of-pocket costs and avoid surprises. Just be sure to review your plan every 3 to 5 years, compare rates, and stay flexible to get the most value from your Medicare insurance coverage.

POINTS TO REMEMBER

- Plans are standardized so A through N have the same benefits regardless of which company you enroll with.

- Three states don't alphabetize their plans, but you can still get the same benefits by a different name, in all states.

- Rates go up annually on all plans, but some companies go up faster than others!

- When you are healthy, you can change Medicare Supplement plans at any time of year.

- If you are not healthy enough to pass health underwriting, you may still be able to change plans based on your state's law.

- There is no "best company." The company with the best rates, service, and most likely to hold their rate changes all the time.

- You can keep your Medicare Supplement forever, as long as you continue to pay your premiums. Your plan benefits will never change.

- It's smart to set up your payment by automatic bank draft so your plan doesn't get cancelled if you forget or neglect to pay your premiums.

- Household discounts can save you a lot of money if you and your spouse enroll into the same plan at the same time. But they aren't always the best way to go.

CHAPTER 12

MEDICARE SUPPLEMENT PLAN N

Medicare Supplement Plan N is a nice middle ground between Plan G and a PPO plan. It has doctor copays, similar to a PPO plan, but no network, similar to Plan G.

Medicare Supplement Plan N is a good plan when you are very healthy and don't want the network limits of a Medicare Advantage plan, but do want to save some money over the monthly cost of Plan G.

1. Like Plan G, you must pay the annual Part B deductible before your insurance plan pays anything.

2. You are responsible for up to $20 copays for doctor visits and up to $50 copays for ER visits.

3. Only specific doctor visits apply to the $20 copay. For example, you don't pay a copay for each physical therapy session.

4. If you see a doctor who doesn't accept what Medicare pays, you can be charged up to 15% more. This is called **Medicare Excess** charges, and you can avoid them.

MEDICARE EXCESS CHARGES

Plan N is usually about $30–$40 cheaper per month than Plan G. The vast majority of people buy Plan G (no copays or excess charges to contend with), but people who need to save some money might start with Plan N with the intention of moving to a Medicare Advantage plan down the road if they start incurring a lot of copays.

The big risk with Plan N — and the reason more people don't buy it — is it has the *potential* to cost you more in **Medicare Excess** charges. You could be billed an additional 15% above what Medicare pays the doctor if your doctor doesn't accept Medicare assignment (the amount Medicare approves for a covered service). For most people the conversation stops there, but **Medicare Excess** charges are not as big a risk as you might think. Any doctor who does NOT accept Medicare assignment must have it conspicuously posted in the waiting room by law.

> Over 85% of doctors accept what Medicare pays,
> but begrudgingly.

The risk of **Medicare Excess** charges is usually associated with seeing a specialist. Before you call to book that appointment, ask if the doctor accepts Medicare assignment. If the answer is no, you can ask for a different doctor. If this is the best doctor for your procedure, you can still get the procedure and potentially be billed up to 15% above what Medicare pays.

Will that 15% extra bankrupt you? Not likely. It's usually $200 or less.

Doctors who do not accept Medicare assignment receive 95% of the Medicare fee and can add 15% to that. Medicare punishes doctors who don't accept Medicare assignment by paying them less and delaying those payments. This hassle is why the vast majority of doctors accept Medicare's fee structure, even though it is low.

Let's look at a scenario.

Phyllis goes to a doctor who does not accept Medicare assignment. The doctor performs a test for which Medicare's rate is $500.

In this case, Phyllis will pay $71 excess charges.

95% of $500 = $475
$475 × 1.15 = $546.25 (rounded to $546)
$546 − $475 = $71

Medicare pays the doctor $475. Phyllis pays the doctor $71.

Excess charges are easy to avoid by simply asking your doctor if she accepts Medicare assignment. If she does, she cannot charge over the Medicare-approved amount.

With Medicare Supplement Plan G, you'll never have to worry about excess charges because your plan pays them. Plan N is different. That's part of the reason it is cheaper.

Another reason Plan N is gaining popularity is because healthy people buy it. Because of this, the rates have historically increased about half as fast as Plan G rates. But this trend has changed in the past few years. In some states, rate increases on Plan N are not much lower than Plan G.

FAVORABLE PLAN N STATES

It's illegal for doctors to charge Medicare Excess charges in these eight states:

- Connecticut
- New York
- Rhode Island
- Massachusetts
- Ohio
- Vermont
- Minnesota
- Pennsylvania

If you live in one of these states, you'll never have to worry about excess charges *unless you see a doctor in a different state.* That other state may charge excess, so just ask before you schedule your doctor appointment.

If you live in one of the listed states, Plan N looks almost the same as

Plan G. With both plans you must meet your annual Part B deductible before your insurance kicks in. With a Plan G, after the deductible, you are done. No other out-of-pocket costs. With Plan N you pay a $20 copay to see a doctor and $50 to go to the emergency room.

Since you can see any doctor and are not limited to a network — like you are on Medicare Advantage PPO and HMO plans — many people think of Medicare Supplement Plan N as the middle ground between the "best" coverage with Medicare Supplement Plan G and the "not the best but still pretty good" Medicare Advantage plans.

As long as you are healthy, you can ride out Plan N for a few years and lock in some savings on monthly premiums. Then duck back into a Plan G as you get older. Remember, you can change your Medicare Supplement plans at any time of year, *if you are healthy enough to answer the health questions.*

The confusion about what you must pay out-of-pocket with Plan N usually follows a visit to the doctor's office or emergency room.

DOCTOR VISITS

You will pay **up to** a $20 copay with Plan N. Sometimes it's less than $20. But it's never more than $20.

The Plan N copay is not required for physical therapy, lab work, or X-rays.

You could pay this copay several times in one day if you schedule several doctor visits on the same day.

EMERGENCY ROOM VS. URGENT CARE

Medicare wants you to use Urgent Care, which is much, much cheaper than the emergency room. You will not likely have a copay at an Urgent Care. The $50 ER copay is meant to dissuade you from using the ER, which costs Medicare much more than your urgent care visit.

If you must go to the ER and your visit results in you being admitted as an inpatient, the hospital waives your $50 copay.

When you're in the emergency room, your care is covered under Part B, but when you are admitted as an inpatient Part A covers your inpatient stay. Therefore, if you are an inpatient in the hospital after an ER visit and Part A covers your care, your Plan N copay will be waived.

Plan N provides comprehensive coverage for Medicare beneficiaries who prefer lower premiums and don't visit the doctor often. *If you see the doctor often, the copays can add up and eat into any savings you had over a Plan G.*

I like Plan N if you live in one of the states without excess charges, but I still prefer Plan G overall for myself, my family, and my friends.

POINTS TO REMEMBER

- Plan N is the second most popular Medicare Supplement plan sold.

- Plan N has a lower monthly premium than Plan G.

- Plan N has no network, but you'll pay up to $20 for each doctor visit.

- Plan N has no network, but you'll pay $50 for a visit to the ER (waived if you are admitted to the hospital).

- Plan N may subject you to Medicare Excess charges if you see a doctor who doesn't accept Medicare assignment.

- If your doctor doesn't accept Medicare assignment, it must be conspicuously posted in the waiting room. If this is the case, then you can only be charged up to 15% more than the Medicare payment schedule.

- Many people forget to ask if their anesthesiologist accepts Medicare assignment because they typically don't see them until they are in the operating room! Anesthesiologists often hit you with excess charges.

- Some states do not allow excess charges by state law!

CHAPTER 13

PLAN G VS. PLAN N

Since most people will choose either a Medicare Supplement Plan G or N, let's compare those plans side by side.

If you are healthy and rarely see the doctor, you could save some money with a Plan N, but everyone feels differently about their long-term health. Here's a comparison to help you decide.

1. COVERAGE DIFFERENCES

Plan G covers nearly all the gaps left by government Medicare A and B, including Part A and B coinsurance, hospital costs, and excess charges. The only out-of-pocket costs you're responsible for is the annual Medicare Part B deductible.

Plan N has similar coverage to Plan G, but with some big differences. It doesn't cover Medicare Part B excess charges, which means if a doctor charges more than what Medicare pays, you'll have to pay the difference. Additionally, Plan N requires copayments for some office visits (up to $20) and emergency room visits (up to $50, waived if you are admitted).

2. COST OF MONTHLY PREMIUMS

Plan G typically has higher premiums than Plan N because it covers more expenses, like Part B excess charges and copayments.

MEDIGAP BENEFITS
Plan G vs Plan N

A SIDE-BY-SIDE COMPARISON OF TWO OF THE MOST POPULAR MEDIGAP PLANS.

MEDIGAP BENEFITS	PLAN G	PLAN N
MEDICARE **PART A** COINSURANCE & HOSPITAL COSTS	100%	100%
MEDICARE **PART B** COINSURANCE/COPAYMENT	100%	100%
BLOOD (FIRST 3 PINTS)	100%	100%
PART A HOSPICE CARE COINSURANCE/COPAYMENT	100%	100%
SKILLED NURSING FACILITY COINSURANCE	100%	100%
PART A DEDUCTIBLE	100%	100%
PART B DEDUCTIBLE	✕	✕
PART B EXCESS CHARGES	100%	✕

Plan N usually has lower premiums, but the trade-off is paying copays and the potential for out-of-pocket costs if you run into doctors who do not accept Medicare assignment.

3. OUT-OF-POCKET COSTS

Plan G provides more predictable out-of-pocket costs since it covers nearly everything except the Part B deductible. This is particularly beneficial if you visit doctors frequently or live in an area where doctors often charge Medicare excess fees.

Plan N can be more cost effective for those who don't mind paying small copays for office and ER visits and are less likely to face excess charges. It can save money on premiums but may come with slightly higher out-of-pocket costs during the year.

4. DOCTOR FLEXIBILITY

With Plan G, you're fully protected from excess charges, so you have more flexibility when choosing doctors, even those who charge above Medicare's rates.

Plan N might lead to unexpected expenses if you see doctors who bill excess charges since it doesn't cover these.

WHY WOULD I CHOOSE PLAN G OVER PLAN N?

1. **Predictability** – Plan G provides more predictable expenses. I want to avoid surprise bills.

2. **Comprehensive Coverage** – Plan G covers almost all Medicare gaps, offering me peace of mind.

3. **Potential Savings** – I expect to see the doctor more frequently in the future and I do not want to pay $20 for every visit.

4. **Fear of the Unknown** – I'm worried that more doctors may end up charging excess fees in the future. I hope I'm wrong, but this uncertainty keeps me from choosing Plan N over Plan G for myself.

You may feel differently, and these decisions are very personal. Plan N might be a better choice for you.

> If you want hassle-free healthcare, you want government Medicare + Medicare Supplement Plan G.

Let's use a knee replacement as an example.

With **Plan G**, you're in the driver's seat. Once your doctor says you need a knee replacement, you can go ahead and schedule it whenever it works best for you and your doctor. The best part is you can choose any doctor or hospital that takes Medicare, no questions asked. No extra hurdles.

With **Plan N**, it's almost as smooth as Plan G, but you need to double-check that both your doctor and anesthesiologist accept Medicare assignment. If they don't it's still manageable — you just need to be a bit more aware that you'll pay more.

I won't cover Medicare Advantage plans until the next chapter, but I'll throw them in here for comparison.

With a **PPO or HMO** (Medicare Advantage), things get a little trickier. Before you can have the surgery, your doctor has to get **prior authorization** from the Medicare Advantage company. This means they need approval before going ahead and there's a chance the company might deny the request without giving a clear reason. That could cause delays as your doctor appeals.

With Medicare Supplement plans like Plan G or N, you don't usually run into these kinds of issues. You'll need to make sure your doctor and hospital are in your plan's network, to keep your costs down *when you are on an Advantage plan.*

POINTS TO REMEMBER

- Medicare Supplement Plans G and N are very similar.

- Plan N typically costs $30–$40 less per month than Plan G.

- Plan G is the most popular because it has the least out-of-pocket costs.

- Plan N is more popular in a few states because their state laws prohibit doctors from charging Medicare Excess charges, which you are normally responsible for on Plan N.

- You will usually pay a $20 copay to see a doctor on Plan N but you can see any doctor in the nation, there is no network.

- Medicare Excess charges may be illegal in your state, but if you travel out of state and get sick, it could cause you to have surprise bills.

- If you do incur Medicare Excess charges, it is not thousands of dollars. The government limits how much more a doctor can charge than government Medicare's fee schedule and you can only be charged up to 15% more.

- Since Medicare's fee schedule is very low, an additional 15% charge usually is only a few hundred dollars.

CHAPTER 14
MEDICARE ADVANTAGE PART C

Medicare Advantage was created to bring private insurance companies into Medicare. The idea was that these companies would compete by offering lower prices and better services, *which would save money for both the government and people on Medicare.* Oops! Medicare Advantage actually costs the government more than if people just used regular government Medicare.

Even though it's more expensive, some plans are keeping people healthier, which could save money in the future. It's hard to know exactly how much this helps, since not all plans are the same.

Medicare Advantage costs are also tough to control because these plans are popular with both political parties. This is partly because people who use these plans are often very satisfied with the service.

Medicare Advantage is a solid option for many people, but it's not the choice I'd make when I hit 65. I prefer the stability and coverage of a Medicare Supplement G plan.

But at the end of the day, it's all about finding *what works best for you.* Whether you choose Medicare Advantage or a Medicare Supplement plan, it's important to compare the options and make the choice that fits *your health and financial needs.*

CONFUSING TERMINOLOGY CLARIFIED (A LITTLE)

Medicare Part C is a combination of Medicare Parts A and B — and often Part D — into one plan called a Medicare Advantage plan. Many in Congress feel that the name Advantage is misleading. I make a point of distinguishing *government* Medicare from *private* Medicare Advantage.

As a reminder, when you read about Medicare on the internet, Original Medicare is the official term for government Medicare.

> There are many types of Part C plans, with many names including: Medicare Advantage, Managed Care, PPO, HMO, PFFS, Cost Plans, D-SNP, C-SNP, and more.

Medicare Advantage plans are administered by private insurance companies and must include all the benefits in government Medicare. It is not stripped down. In fact, the government requires Medicare Advantage plans *to offer extra benefits*. These extras are very enticing but vary dramatically from plan to plan and year to year.

To have Medicare Advantage, you must continue to have Medicare Parts A and B.

Besides continuing to pay your Medicare Part B premium, you may also have to pay a premium for your plan. *Medicare Advantage quickly spread in popularity because plans often have a $0 monthly premium.* About 25% of people are on an Advantage plan that does charge a monthly premium. Most plans still have a very low monthly premium compared to Medicare Supplement plans.

💡 *When you see a doctor, you do NOT show your red, white, and blue Medicare ID card because government Medicare is not paying any of your claims. You only show your private insurance card. If you are on Medicare Advantage, leave your government Medicare ID card at home.*

A QUICK COMPARISON

- Medicare Advantage may charge you $0 or a very low monthly cost but charges you a fee *when you get care.*

- Medicare Supplement Plan G charges you a high monthly premium, *whether you need care or not. But when you need care, you don't pay more than your annual deductible.*

If you see a doctor and find out you have cancer, you may need to see a cancer specialist many times, get a biopsy, inpatient surgery to have your tumor removed, followed by weeks of chemotherapy and radiation.

How would your cost look with each type of plan?

1. Medicare Supplement Plan G

If you get cancer you'll pay your annual Part B deductible which is only $257 in 2025. That's it. You have NO other medical expenses for Medicare approved care after you pay $257. You can see any doctor and go to the best cancer centers in the nation. No matter how extensive your treatment is and how many rounds of chemo you undergo, you will not pay more than $257 out-of-pocket.

2. Medicare Advantage PPO

If you get cancer you'll pay a copay per doctor visit, coinsurance (usually about 20%) for each chemo treatment, a copay for labs, X-rays, MRIs etc. If you are hospitalized, you'll pay between $300–$400 per day while you are an inpatient. Your plan has a maximum out-of-pocket (MOOP) limit. The government sets the maximum MOOP each year. Let's say your plan has the 2025 in-network limit which is $9,350 (plans can charge less than max). Once all the copays and coinsurance you have paid totals this amount, you stop paying! You'll only pay your monthly premium, if you have one. *For the rest of your care in this calendar year, you pay nothing else out-of-pocket.*

💡 *All amounts listed above are hypothetical. An accurate price estimate would require your zip code and actual treatment details. Remember that experimental treatments not covered by Medicare will not be covered by private Medicare Advantage plans either.*

MEDICARE ADVANTAGE NETWORKS

Like many insurance plans, Medicare Advantage works within doctor networks. You probably have experience with networks if you had insurance through your work.

Being in a network means the doctor contracted with certain insurance companies to accept their pay structure. Doctors in a network expect to receive more clients and in return they accept less money from the insurance company. Doctors are always negotiating for higher pay and insurance companies are trying to lower the amount doctors earn. When a contract expires, your doctor may not renew it. Then your doctor is out-of-network.

Why would your doctor choose to be out of network? Because he can earn more money taking only clients on Medicare Supplements. He doesn't have to agree to accept any Medicare Advantage plans. Or he might only accept one Medicare Advantage plan, because they offered to pay him more than other plans.

Don't blame doctors. They are working harder and getting paid less each year. Some doctors accept all Medicare Advantage plans in their area, while other doctors refuse to accept any. To make this more convoluted, networks are always in flux. Your doctor may be in your insurance plan's network when you enrolled into Medicare at age 65, But then shortly after you enrolled, your doctor's contract was up and she declined to re-enroll into your plan's network.

Now you are out-of-network after only a few months. You can't change insurance plans until the AEP so basically, you are now stuck paying more to see your doctor or in many cases, you'll pay his whole bill if he won't agree to see you in an out-of-network arrangement.

"Why did Sylvia's team enroll me in that plan if my doctor's contract was about to expire?" Agents are not privy to the terms of the doctor contracts. We have no idea when contracts will expire. We don't know how likely a doctor or hospital is to break down negotiations with a particular insurance company.

All we can confirm is what doctors and hospitals *are in a plan's network today*. While this sounds murky, the reality is that the vast majority of doctors and hospitals do renew their contracts and remain in network. But I want to warn you that it is a possibility looming ahead of you.

You must stay in-network to get the biggest benefit.

Let's use Dr. Sandy Rudd as an example:

If you want to see Dr. Rudd, you must verify that she accepts your private insurance plan. If she accepts your insurance and is accepting new patients, you'll pay a copay for every visit. A typical primary care visit can cost you between $0 to $60 per visit. (Remember, every Medicare Advantage plan has different copays and coinsurance amounts). The insurance company sets the copay amount and you pay it to Dr. Rudd.

If she does not accept your insurance (out-of-network), you may have to pay 100% of the cost out of your own pocket or, in a best-case scenario, you'll be able to see her out-of-network if she allows it. If she is out-of-network, but accepts your insurance plan, you will pay her a higher copay.

I stressed in the prior sections about Medicare Supplements that you can see *any doctor*. Medicare Advantage companies make money by negotiating to pay doctors and hospitals less than government Medicare. Doctors do not like this. Hospitals hate this. But most can't afford not to be in a large company's network since their patients would have to see other doctors.

> The government surveys Medicare members and they consistently give their Medicare Advantage plan very high reviews. Patients like the plans, doctors and hospitals do not.

A few doctors — mostly it seems in California — love these plans because they are in a profit-sharing arrangement with an insurance company. Yes, this is legal. If your doctor really pushes you to join a certain insurance plan, you can be suspicious that doctor has a financial incentive.

Recall that my dad loved his PPO plan for 13 years. He paid $0 per month. He, conservatively, saved over $25,000 in Medicare Supplement premiums over that span of time. You can see why he would rave about his plan. He stayed in network and rarely had to see a doctor. It worked for him. He was very healthy. Medicare Advantage gets more complicated when you have major health issues.

MEDICARE ADVANTAGE SERVICE AREA

Anyone who has Medicare Parts A and B is eligible to enroll into a Medicare Advantage plan *as long as you live within the service area* of that plan.

> Your Service Area = Your Zip Code

Your Service Area is the county where the plan accepts members. What plans are available to you are based on your address. *If you move out of that area, you have to leave that plan.* I've had clients move to be nearer to their children specifically because there were better Medicare Advantage plans at the new address than offered at their home address.

Dale and Louise live in Indiana, zip code 46060. They love their Medicare Advantage plan and told their neighbors across the street to give us a call so they can enroll too. But the county line divides their neighborhood. Their neighbor is not able to purchase the

same plan because they are in a different county. Plans available in their county may offer less or more benefits than they offer in other counties. Or the insurance company may not offer any plans in their county, even though they live right across the street from Dale and Louise.

Why would this happen? It's all about $.

- Insurance companies know which zip codes are profitable. Doctors and hospitals charge more in some areas.
- They are not required to file a plan in an area that isn't profitable.
- Rural areas where there is only one hospital are often unprofitable so you'll typically find less options for Medicare Advantage plans in rural areas.

FUNDING MEDICARE ADVANTAGE

The government gives insurance companies a set amount of money each year to cover your care. In 2025, most plans receive about $12,000 per member enrolled. The exact amount depends on things like the type of plan, how sick you are, where you live, and your plan's government **Star Rating.**

If your insurance plan spends more than what the government gives it, it loses money on your care. But don't worry — the plan can't drop you or refuse to enroll someone just because they're sick. Medicare Advantage plans have to accept everyone, no matter their health, there's no waiting period and they can't cancel your coverage unless they cancel the entire plan and everyone on it.

Medicare Advantage plans have been very successful because most people don't need a lot of medical care. Many people see the doctor one time a year or less. Healthy people are very profitable for Medicare Advantage plans!

But here's the twist: insurance companies make even more if you fall into a special group, like if you have both Medicaid and Medicare, or if you have chronic health conditions.

You can tell how much money is involved by watching the changes in available plans. When the government didn't pay much for Medicaid-Medicare patients, plans for them barely existed. But as soon as the government started paying more, these plans popped up all over the place. All money flows from the government down to the insurance plans down to the providers.

> Roughly half of all people eligible for government Medicare now choose to enroll into private Medicare Advantage plans.

HOW TO ENROLL

Medicare Advantage is getting more popular as Medicare Supplement prices keep going up and people hear about all the extra perks these plans offer.

To sign up, you first need to have Medicare Parts A and B. Once you do, Medicare Advantage will cover all your healthcare and the government will not pay for any of your care anymore. That is why I recommend you leave your government Medicare ID card at home. When you give it to a doctor's office along with your Medicare Advantage plan, you can seriously confuse them!

The government still makes the rules that govern Medicare Advantage plans. **Uncle Sam requires that Medicare Advantage plans offer you the same, or even better, benefits than regular Medicare.** But each insurance company gets to decide what extra perks to add to their plan, like vision, dental, cash back or gym memberships!

There are almost 4,000 different Medicare plans in 2025. Most people have a choice of 30–40 plans to choose from in their zip code.

Can you research and compare plans alone? Sure, good luck. Have fun throwing a dart at the wall. Go to **MEDICARE.GOV** to compare plans. You'll have access to some but not all the data you'll need to make an informed decision. For example, you can't check to see if your doctor is in the plan's network without going to the website of EACH insurance company. Since our services are free, please use professional help to see all the plan details before choosing a plan. If you don't like us, choose one of the 40,000 other insurance agents that sell Medicare Advantage. But don't go it alone.

COSTS AND BENEFITS

It's easy to think a $0 premium insurance plan must be junk. I've heard this from a lot of people who believe "you get what you pay for" so a $0 plan can't be good. But Medicare Advantage plans aren't cheap. Actually, they cost the government *more than if you stayed on government Medicare*. Your plan isn't free, it's just that taxpayers are covering your monthly premium. You still pay your Medicare Part B premium too.

The insurance itself is really good. The coverage is solid because it has to be as good as government Medicare by law.

Think of it like comparing a buffet restaurant to ordering off a menu. You're still getting a full meal, but how you pay changes.

Buffet $30

Eat as much as you want for one price. Similarly, with a Medicare Supplement Plan G, you'll pay up front monthly for as much healthcare as you need (after you've met your annual deductible).

A La Carte Cafeteria

You only pay for what you eat. Similarly, with a $0 monthly premium Medicare Advantage plan, you'll pay a copay every time you get a service (preventative care is free). If you are not using your plan, you won't be paying anything above your Medicare Part B costs. Just like an à la carte cafeteria, you'll only have to pay for the turkey, slaw, and pecan pie that you order.

> Some areas of the country have more than 70 different Medicare Advantage plans available each year.

You might pay $30 to see a doctor in your PPO network, but $60 if your doctor is out-of-network. You might also pay $400 per day, up to 5 days, if you are hospitalized, and $150 for an ambulance. These prices are different with every company and will change every year.

Even if the plan costs $0, there is still a lot to understand about this mammoth and controversial program. Remember, if you do get sick, really sick, you could pay much more on private Medicare than had you been on government Medicare and a Medicare Supplement. It doesn't always happen, but an expert can help you gauge which of the dozens of $0 premium plans could cost you the least in the event of (insert ANY medical diagnosis here).

CRITICAL POINTS

You can't have both a Medicare Advantage plan *and* a Medicare Supplement plan. Medicare Supplement Plans are available only if you enroll in government Medicare A and B. Medicare Advantage plans are in lieu of government Medicare.

Plans are only available in certain areas. If you move out of state, you'll have to enroll into a new plan. Sometimes, if you just move to a new county in the same state, you may have to change plans too.

People buy a Medicare Supplement Plan G and a stand-alone drug plan because they don't want Medicare Advantage's annual changes, limited networks, prior authorizations or other red tape.

An extra warning:

Bob chose to enroll into a Medicare Supplement Plan G and a Part D drug plan at 65. When Bob turned 66, he walked into a grocery store, pharmacy or big retail store and an insurance agent enticed him to enroll on the spot into a "free" plan with a food card, help with utilities and more.

Bob was excited.

Think of the savings!

He enrolled right there in the grocery store. How convenient! This automatically kicked out his Medicare Part D plan. Fine, he won't need it now because the new Medicare Advantage plan includes drug benefits.

The problem — and there are many, many more than this:

Bob's on-the-spot enrollment in the grocery store terminated his Medicare Part D plan, but it doesn't terminate his Medicare Supplement plan. Bob would have to personally call and terminate it by phone or mail the company a letter. *Many people forget this step.*

Bob erroneously assumed it was terminated automatically, like his drug plan — only to find out it wasn't terminated until after January's bank draft went through and he paid $200 or more for a Medicare Supplement plan that he could no longer use.

Will he ever get that money back? No. It was Bob's mistake.

But Bob's biggest mistake was still ahead of him.

He had to *use* his insurance to find out that he could no longer see his urologist. Bob wasn't comfortable in a grocery store setting (with no privacy) to tell the agent about all his health conditions and list off all his doctors and specialists. He skipped disclosing his prostate situation. It was a little embarrassing, so he didn't mention his urologist to the agent.

The agent chose a plan that covered only the doctors and medications that Bob mentioned. Many people carry around a list of the medications and dosages, and a list of their doctors, but most do not have that information handy.

Bob made a rush decision based on a great sales pitch and promised benefits. This is not a decision to be rushed. Insurance companies place agents in pharmacies, malls, and anywhere they think they'll find retirees during the busy AEP season. There is a lot of money to be made. Unfortunately for Bob, this decision turned out to be a very expensive one.

MEDICARE ADVANTAGE FOOD CARDS

Is the Medicare Advantage Food Card a scam?

I get asked this question daily. It looks like a scam because it's rather new, and the way some agents market make it look like a scam. For example, I was at my mom's house, and she got two cold calls from different agencies letting her know that she "needed to claim her free food card." She said that she gets several calls every day about this and wanted to know if it was real. Cold calling retirees about Medicare Advantage plans is illegal, *but the food card benefit itself is not a scam.*

$150 **per month** to spend on healthy food and over-the-counter wellness items.

This benefit is not widely available and ads about this benefit are likely to reach people where there is no actual benefit. They lure you in and then switch you to a plan that is available in your zip code — but without the food card.

A food card benefit can be a helpful and a legitimate perk of certain Medicare Advantage plans, but you should consider this benefit *after* you have determined that the plan best covers your doctors and prescriptions.

How the Medicare Advantage Food Card Benefit Works:

1. **Eligibility** – Not all Medicare Advantage plans offer this benefit and eligibility is often determined based on participation in Medicaid.

2. **Prepaid Card** – If you qualify, your plan might give you a prepaid card with a set amount of money that can be used for purchasing food items, often at specific retailers. The card might reload monthly or quarterly with a certain dollar amount, which varies depending on the plan.

3. **Eligible Purchases** – Generally, the card can be used to buy foods like fruits, vegetables, whole grains, dairy, and lean proteins. Some plans may restrict purchases to specific categories or stores, so it's essential to know the rules of your plan.

4. **Limits** – The amount loaded on the card isn't unlimited. Depending on the plan, it might be anywhere from $25 to $200 per month, and unspent amounts may or may not roll over to the next period.

But wait, there's more!

OTHER MEDICARE ADVANTAGE BENEFITS

Since I've been involved from the start of Medicare Advantage in 2003 and I'm licensed in all 50 states, I've seen the strange history of Extra Benefits evolve over the past 20 years. One plan used to give 2 Viagra pills per month to each member. Another plan offered a pet food allowance for service animals. Extra Benefits keep expanding and contracting based on cost and what is likely to attract new members. Here are some of the most common Extra Benefits you are likely to see offered:

1. Dental Coverage

Most Medicare Advantage plans offer dental benefits, which typically include preventive services like cleanings, exams, and X-rays.

Some plans also provide coverage for more extensive dental work, such as fillings, crowns, root canals, implants, and dentures. Since there is no waiting period, this is by far the most popular benefit.

There are a few plans that allow you to *purchase additional dental benefits*, but most include it in the plan's premium.

2. Vision Care

Many plans offer vision benefits, which can include annual eye exams, coverage for eyeglasses or contact lenses, and even discounts on corrective vision surgery like LASIK. Vision benefits are especially valuable since government Medicare does not cover routine vision care.

3. Hearing Services

Medicare Advantage plans often provide hearing exams and coverage for hearing aids, which government Medicare doesn't cover. Hearing aid coverage can vary significantly between plans, so it's important to check the specifics.

4. Over-the-Counter Benefits

Some plans provide an allowance for over-the-counter items like vitamins, pain relievers, first aid supplies, and other health-related items. This benefit typically comes in the form of a quarterly or monthly stipend that can be used at participating pharmacies or retailers.

5. Fitness Programs

Many plans include memberships to fitness programs such as **SilverSneakers** or similar gym and wellness programs. Some plans reimburse you for buying new running shoes. It really is all over the board what type of fitness benefit is available.

6. Transportation

Transportation to and from medical appointments is another common benefit. Some plans offer a set number of rides to doctor's appointments, pharmacies, or even grocery stores, which can be particularly useful for people who lack reliable transportation. This benefit is common if you are on Medicare and Medicaid.

7. Meal Delivery After Surgery

After a hospital stay, some Medicare Advantage plans offer a limited number of home-delivered meals. This benefit is designed to help with recovery by ensuring you have access to nutritious meals during critical times.

8. Telehealth

While telehealth expanded dramatically during the COVID-19 pandemic, *it is being scaled back again in 2025*. Many Medicare Advantage plans cover virtual visits for both primary and specialty care but this is usually for people in rural areas or for people who have a hard time finding a mental health provider near them.

9. Home Modification and Safety Devices

Some plans are beginning to offer benefits for home modifications, such as the installation of grab bars, ramps, or other devices that improve safety and accessibility in the home for older adults or those with mobility challenges.

10. In-Home Support Services

Certain plans may provide in-home support services, like help with light housekeeping, laundry, or personal care for those recovering from an illness or managing chronic health conditions. This is particularly aimed at keeping beneficiaries in their homes and out of nursing facilities. Very few plans offer this!

11. Emergency Response Devices

Some Medicare Advantage plans offer personal emergency response systems, which allow beneficiaries to call for help in case of an emergency, such as a fall, with just the push of a button.

12. Part B Givebacks

The Medicare Advantage Part B giveback is a benefit some Medicare Advantage plans offer where the plan reduces the amount you pay for your Medicare Part B premium. Normally, most people have the cost of Part B taken out of their Social Security check each month. With the giveback, your Medicare Advantage plan "gives back" a portion of that premium, *so you pay less or get more in your Social Security check.* I've seen plans range from a $2 monthly giveback up to the full cost of Medicare Part B!

> With cuts to Medicare Advantage plans, these Extra Benefits are quick to be slimmed down or eliminated.

Starting in 2025, insurance companies are required to send their members a mid-year notice of unused extra benefits. *This is because most people forget about them, and they go unused.* One year, I tried to call all my clients and remind them to use their extras before they ran out. Many told me it was too much hassle to register for them, shop online, or they just didn't want to mess with it. Benefits are easier to use now and with this mid-year notice, you'll be reminded not to let them expire.

A QUICK RECAP

- Medicare Advantage has many names — Part C, Medicare Advantage, and Private Medicare are just a few.

- It is administered by an insurance company that will pay all your claims.

- You will have a network of doctors and hospitals your plan has contracted with. Using in-network doctors is easier (and cheaper) than going out-of-network.

- If your plan allows you to go outside its network, you will pay a higher copay.

- There are many types of plans, with PPO and HMO being the most common.

- PPOs have a wider network and higher MOOP than HMOs.

- There is a very low (sometimes $0) monthly premium. The price is based on the plan you buy and what is available in your zip code. As of today, there are no Advantage plans in the state of Alaska, and about 30% of the nation doesn't have a $0 plan.

- Plans in your area may offer Extra Benefits such as dental, food cards, transportation, meal benefits, and money back to reimburse you for some of the cost you pay for Medicare Part B.

- You are always in-network in an emergency with ALL Medicare Advantage plans. Regardless of your network, if you end up having a heart attack while visiting Yellowstone National Park, you will pay in-network charges in the ER.

One of the reasons people complain about Medicare Advantage is because they *should never have bought that plan in the first place.* These people often purchased these plans because an aggressive agent pushed the Extra Benefits instead of the core health benefits.

> Extra Benefits will get your attention because they are attractive!

In 2024 a plan offered "Unlimited Dental Coverage, including implants, on day #1 with no waiting period!" That company is — you guessed it — no longer offering that benefit in 2025. Remember, Medicare Advantage plans can change their extra benefits each year. Don't get sucked in by flashy benefits.

People often buy a Medicare Advantage plan because they need immediate dental benefits but they don't make sure their doctors are in-network. That is a big mistake.

If you buy a plan that doesn't include your doctor, you'll eventually be angry. Complaints to Medicare are tallied and we know that people are mad, overwhelmingly complaining that their doctor wasn't in the plan network and/or their medication wasn't covered. This can happen for a variety of reasons (your doctor left the network) but it can also happen because you only cared about getting a root canal and didn't choose the health plan your doctor accepted.

In other words, never let Extra Benefits distract you from choosing a plan that first and foremost covers your doctors and preferred hospitals. We check core health benefits before we even look at the available Extra Benefits. Buy the steak, not the sizzle!

> Last year our clients chose a Medicare Advantage plan about 30% of the time. Meaning most of our clients chose a Medicare Supplement plan.

A lot of people do choose Medicare Advantage plans for the same reason my dad did 13 years ago — they are very healthy, rarely go to the doctor, and don't want to spend $200 or more per month for a Medicare Supplement Plan G and Part D plan. Fair enough. It's your choice and your money! But we want you to have all the information so you can make the right decision for you.

PRIOR AUTHORIZATION DELAYS

Medicare Advantage Prior Authorization means that before you can get certain medical treatments or tests, your doctor has to ask your insurance company for permission. The insurance company checks to see if you really need the procedure before it gives permission. If the insurance company says NO to your request, your doctor can appeal. This back-and-forth appeals process drives doctors crazy and delays your treatment.

All Medicare Advantage companies use the Prior Authorization process to save costs. Their thinking is too many doctors order tests unnecessarily, wasting money and time. After all, what does your doctor care if he orders 5 different tests at the same time? It doesn't cost him anything.

Since Medicare Advantage companies are tasked with managing the Medicare dollar better, they put up barriers to stop doctors from wasting money. Sometimes this means before you can get approval for a surgery, you must try a less invasive treatment first, like therapy or cortisone shots. This can be frustrating for you because it means you have to wait longer or try different options before getting the treatment you originally wanted.

💡 *A new law starts in 2026 requiring Medicare Advantage companies to respond to a request for Prior Authorization from your doctor within 7 calendar days, and within 72 hours if it is an urgent request. Insurance companies must give a REASON for the denial. This will make it much easier for your doctor to appeal a denial. There is still no guarantee you'll ever get an approval for your procedure.*

THERAPY IS CONTROVERSIAL

If you need therapy in your home, a hospital or in a nursing home, Medicare covers some physical, occupational, and speech therapy. But approval can be difficult to get.

If you have a Medicare Advantage plan, your nursing home will not like it. They prefer you to have a Medicare Supplement plan because it is more lenient when it comes to getting you any type of therapy. All types of therapy are approved by government Medicare for *as long as you continue to improve.* This is a gray area that can be exploited for…money.

I have a friend who was a nursing home administrator. She confirmed what I'd assumed all along: if you have only government Medicare A and B, or a Medicare Supplement, the nursing home *can bill for more therapies than are medically necessary.* No one is watching. Private Medicare Advantage watches how the money is spent. They stop therapy when you fail to improve. They follow the letter of the law.

I've had clients who called me to complain their spouse who had a stroke was being given therapy *that was completely useless.*

My own family member, a 92-year-old woman with a broken hip, was given the maximum amount of speech therapy allowed. She had no trouble speaking or with cognition. She had no medical justification for speech therapy. She couldn't understand why she was getting it. The answer is usually money. The hospital could bill Medicare for it, so they did.

The flip side is NOT getting the therapy you actually need and want!

If you justifiably need a lot of therapy, Medicare Advantage could cut you off before you or your doctor are ready. Don't take my word for it, it is easy to google this hot topic.

This is a real problem that doesn't have a solution, for now.

Medicare Advantage companies want to save money by getting you off therapy as soon as possible. Are there times when you are not improving, but you want therapy anyway? Yes. Are there times that you desperately need to continue therapy but your insurance cuts you off? Also, yes.

💡 *Getting any form of therapy is easier when you do not have a Medicare Advantage plan. That's a risk that you take when you opt for Medicare Advantage.*

SOME DISADVANTAGES TO NOTE:

1. Once you buy a plan, you are usually "locked in" for one year. You can always change next fall during the AEP, but if you buy a plan and a few months later realize you can't see your rheumatologist, you can't change insurance plans. You'll have to find a new doctor who accepts your insurance. If you've been seeing the same doctor for years, *this is not a pleasant situation to find yourself in.*

2. Prices change annually. Well, Medicare Supplement prices go up annually too, so why is this worth noting? Because Medicare Advantage has a bevy of prices, and they can *all* change annually. It's a lot to compare and contrast annually.

3. Even if your doctors are in-network, they can drop out by giving you a 30-day notice.

4. Some plans lack out-of-network coverage completely! This, of course, varies by plan.

5. Your rare condition may be best treated by a specialist across the country — or even just in a different county — but that doctor is likely out-of-network. The charges will be higher to see him.

6. Advantage plans have limited coverage outside of the USA while traveling. Most plans don't cover you outside the country, but a few do offer this benefit.

7. Prior Authorization delays can be a pain! Sometimes they can even be harmful.

8. Therapy options may be limited.

WHO LIKES MEDICARE ADVANTAGE?

Most people who have a Medicare Advantage plan like it a lot! Government surveys show that people are overwhelmingly in favor of this type of plan — even with the drawbacks.[1]

💡 Milliman is a consulting firm that provides analysis in the healthcare industry. One of their key contributions to the Medicare industry is their analysis of Medicare Advantage plans, including studies on star ratings, plan costs, and member satisfaction.

---

1   Milliman, "The future is now: 2024 Star Ratings release," available at **US.MILLIMAN.COM**. This is a great resource! Use it.

Many people like the Medicare Advantage plans because of the price! Even if they have to deal with some extra steps like **Prior Authorization,** people like the potential to save money. And because many Medicare Advantage plans don't make you pay a monthly fee, which sounds cool if you're healthy and don't go to the doctor a lot, these plans can save you money compared to other types of Medicare plans.

But here's the thing. Even though you don't pay monthly, *you still have to pay every time you use the plan.*

For example, if you go to the doctor, you'll need to pay a copay. Going to a specialist or having surgery can cost even more. Sometimes, a surgery might cost you up to 20% of the total price! These plans save you money, but only if you stay healthy and don't need to see the doctor much. If you get sick, the costs can pile up quickly.

A serious illness may eat up all your savings fast. If you get cancer, you'll likely hit the **Maximum Out-of-Pocket** (MOOP). And maybe the following year too. Your MOOP is a critical feature of all Medicare Advantage plans. In my opinion, this is the single most important feature!

You can't spend more in a calendar year than your plan's MOOP. **Government Medicare doesn't offer you this protection.** Even with the negatives that come with Medicare Advantage, the fact that you won't face a bill for $50,000+ is a great benefit.

A deductible is the opposite of a MOOP. Your deductible is the amount you pay *first,* before your insurance pays. The MOOP is what you pay *last.* Once all your copays, coinsurance, and deductibles have reached the annual maximum limit, you pay $0 for in-network healthcare for the rest of the calendar year. This can work in your favor, or it can cause financial hardship if you haven't banked those savings from not having a high monthly payment.

> There is NO maximum you may be charged if you only have government Medicare A and B. Every Medicare Advantage plan has a limit to protect you.

The government sets the MOOP. Each insurance plan may then choose to charge you less, but never more than the annual MOOP. In 2025, the max in-network cap is $9,350 for all plans. Some plans have a higher cap for out-of-network services. Some plans cover you at all if you go out-of-network. In 2025, the combined in and out-of-network charge cannot be higher than $14,000 for any plan.

HMO PLANS

A Health Maintenance Organization (HMO) typically only allows you to go to in-network doctors and hospitals. HMO plans must follow the same annual out-of-pocket cap rules. The big difference is that most HMO plans have NO out-of-network benefits. No cap. No coverage (unless it's an emergency).

If your rare condition requires you see a specialist at the Mayo Clinic and you have an HMO plan, you will likely have to pay 100% of your bill.

You read that right.

All of it!

Even if you have a Preferred Provider Organization (PPO) plan, most of the top tier hospitals in the nation do not contract with Medicare Advantage plans. Why would they agree to take a lower payment when they have a list of patients who are willing to pay the full price!

Be careful buying a plan because the Mayo Clinic is in-network. Don't let that be your deciding factor because I'm warning you, *network contracts can and do change!*

Let's look at Jim's case.

Jim heard a doctor on the internet saying to steer clear of Medicare Advantage. He didn't like the price of a Medicare Supplement Plan G and decided government Medicare was fine for him.

I've had a lot of clients like Jim in my career. It almost always goes like this.

Jim eventually has a heart attack, gets MS, needs dialysis or cancer treatments. The big-dollar items.

He is shocked to learn that he has to pay $50,000 or more out of his pocket.

Jim hates to call our office. He knows I'll say, "I told you so," and I do. OK, I actually do not rub it in that I was right, but he knows that he made a mistake. In most states it's then too late to ever get a Medicare Supplement Plan. He can get a Medicare Advantage plan during the fall AEP, but even with that type of plan, he will still most likely pay 20% of the total bill for his cancer or dialysis treatments up to his MOOP.

Remember with government Medicare, Jim has no limit to what he can be charged. With an Advantage plan, he will have MOOP protection each year for in-network care — or out-of-network if his plan allows that.

That is why I cringe when nursing homes try to disenroll patients from Medicare Advantage and tell them that government Medicare is better. "No network! No prior authorization! No red tape." All of which is true. But they fail to mention there is a huge financial risk.

I won't go into it further here. We have a lot of information on our website, **THEMEDICAREFAMILY.COM**, that discusses the bias nursing homes have against Medicare Advantage and their reasons (hint: they make more money when you don't have Medicare Advantage).

UNDERSTANDING PLAN NETWORKS

There are actually more than 4 types of Medicare Advantage networks, but these (in the following chart) are the most popular types.

You may already be familiar with networks.

If you had health insurance through your work, it had a plan network. Medicare Advantage is the same. Insurance companies negotiate with each doctor and hospital to agree on a price to treat their members.

4 Types of Medicare Advantage Networks

	HMO	LOCAL PPO	Regional PPO	PFFS
Network Size	One or more counties	One or more counties	Larger network area, such as statewide	Varies
Plan Availability	Most common type of MA plan	Most common type of PPO plan	Least common type of PPO plan	Only available in areas with less than 2 MA plans
Do you have to specify your PCP?	Yes	No	No	No
Are referrals required?	Yes	No	No	No
Is there a maximum out-of-pocket?	Yes, in-network only (no out-of-network benefits)	Yes, in-network and out-of-network	Yes, in-network and out-of-network	Yes, in-network and out-of-network

If you see a doctor in the plan's network, you pay less than if you see a doctor outside the network.

Insurance companies count on being able to pay doctors less than what they would be paid on government Medicare because the insurance company will drive people to the doctor's office. If the doctor refuses to be in-network, people may leave the doctor to find a doctor that is in the plan's network.

> Doctors who accept Medicare Advantage make less money, but it's better than nothing.

For some doctors, they'd rather fill their roster with patients who have other types of insurance and do not participate in any plan networks. Then you'll have a random doctor who only accepts *one* Medicare Advantage plan. Why is that? Either that doctor negotiated a contract that is agreeable to him, or he is on a type of contract called Value-Based Enrollment where he can participate in the profits and share in the losses with the Medicare Advantage company.

If all your doctors and preferred hospitals are in the plan's network when you enroll, you may have a lovely honeymoon phase. Then, in a few months, you may receive a notice that your doctor or hospital will no longer be in-network. This fills you with anger! You feel misled. Now you will face a higher copay to see your doctor, or if you don't have out-of-network coverage, you may have to pay 100% to see that same doctor.

This is not your fault or the fault of your insurance agent.

We relied on the plan's network at the time you enrolled. You relied on our advice. We have no way of knowing when the contract expires or if the doctor will renew his contract with your insurance company.

If this happens to you, be mad. I'd be mad too.

Remember, I can't make it make sense.

> Congress should act to lock in managed care doctor networks the same way Medicare members are locked into a plan for a year.

THE MOST POPULAR NETWORK

The most popular type of Medicare Advantage network is an HMO. This type of plan has the lowest costs, often the highest Extra Benefits, and a smaller network. You give up access to a wide variety of doctors in order to get much lower prices. Copays, coinsurance, and your MOOP will be lower on an HMO than a PPO.

Some areas have an HMO Point-of-Service plan (POS) where you can go out-of-network. With an HMO-POS plan, you may be able to see an out-of-network doctor if she agrees to accept you. These types of plans are not widely available.

I PREFER PPO PLANS WHERE AVAILABLE.

PPOs cost more, but it's worth it to have a wider network. The PPO plans in your area may have the same $0 monthly premium as HMO plans. You'll have to compare all the copays in the **Summary of Benefits** to see if it's worth the extra risk to enroll into a PPO.

As you know, insurance is for the unknowns. You may be very happy with a limited HMO network now, while you are healthy. But I've had too many clients get rare cancers that were best treated by doctors in other states, outside of the HMO's network.

When someone tells me, "I need the very lowest cost plan due to my budget."

And, "I agree to be treated in-network and understand in most cases, if I have to go out-of-network, I will have to pay 100% of my health-care costs."

And, "I don't travel. All my family lives nearby or if they live in other states, they come to visit me, I don't leave my area."

I'll happily help her enroll into a Medicare Advantage HMO plan. But I always mention I, personally, would prefer a PPO for the out-of-network flexibility.

If you live in southern California, most plans available are HMOs. They offer some of the lowest priced and highest benefits available in the nation, but they are HMOs. For those clients, I have no problem recommending an HMO. But in the rest of the nation, I'd talk to you first about a PPO. Sure, you'll pay more to go out-of-network, and I hope you try to stay in network, *but this flexibility is important when you get sick.*

I think we can all agree that:

1. We don't want to get sick.

2. But if we do, we want to get the best healthcare available.

3. If the doctor most likely to save our life is out of our plan's network, we all want the ability to see that specialist anyway!

If you are nodding along, you'll want to be on a PPO plan, not an HMO. But our job is not to convince you to go this way or that way. We want to explain your options, tell you the pros and cons and let you choose what is best for you.

PFFS PLANS ARE RARE

There is another type of Medicare Advantage network called Private Fee-for-Service (PFFS). These plans are rare now.

On a PFFS plan, you can see almost any Medicare-approved provider you choose, as long as he accepts the terms and conditions of your plan. You won't need a referral with a PFFS plan. But this type of plan is unpredictable. *Just because the doctor accepted your insurance the last time you saw him doesn't mean he has to accept it again.* He hasn't agreed to formally be in-network.

Generally, it's safer to choose a PPO or HMO over a PFFS — if they are even available.

NETWORK CONFUSION

As you have learned, this stuff is complicated and confusing. So don't be surprised when your doctor's office staff is also confused, and you have to educate them yourself.

Let's say you purchase a Medicare Advantage plan from Q company. That company invariably has a Medicare Supplement, PPO, HMO, and Part D drug plan all branded with the same Q name.

When you have a Q PPO plan, you must make sure your doctor accepts the specific Q PPO plan, not Q the insurance company. Most people give a quick call and ask the doctor's office, "Do you accept Q insurance?" That type of VAGUE question leads to problems.

> You must ask each provider you see if they accept your specific insurance plan.

You may have Q HMO and assume your doctor's office would naturally also accept the Q PPO. But they often do not!

As a general rule when dealing with anything Medicare, make no assumptions.

Remember, every office accepts a Medicare Supplement, fewer are in-network for a PPO plan, and even fewer accept an HMO plan. To top it off, networks change. Just because your doctor accepted your plan last year, doesn't mean he will next year. Which leads us to our next topic: Plan Exits.

MEDICARE ADVANTAGE PLAN EXITS

In 2024, about 1 million people were notified their Medicare Advantage plans would end on December 31st. Those insurance companies felt they were not making enough profit to remain in those counties, so they exited those markets.

It was a hard year for Medicare Advantage companies. Government reimbursement was down, medical costs were up, and people were using their insurance more. It was easy to make money when COVID-19 had all elective surgeries canceled, but now, times are tough. Some companies folded up shop. Others just pared down their benefits.

> Every year a handful of Medicare Advantage
> plans exit areas. It's not unusual.

So, what do you do if your Medicare Advantage plan chooses to close shop and leave your county or state? You'll be **notified in writing** to choose a new plan during the Annual Election Period. If you missed this notice, you will revert back to government Medicare A and B. You won't be left without any insurance, but it's only A and B. *You'll have no drug coverage, and you carry all the financial risks I mentioned earlier.*

This is just another reason why you need to build a relationship with an insurance agency you can rely on to help you through the crazy ups and downs ahead.

It's not always bad news when you find out your Medicare Advantage plan is exiting your county. You may be sick and would have preferred to move to a Medicare Supplement plan but were not able to move due to your health. In this case, **a Medicare Advantage plan exit allows you to move to a Medicare Supplement plan without answering health questions!**

When your Medicare Advantage plan exits your service area or discontinues coverage, you typically have 123 days to make a switch — 60 days before your plan ends and 63 days after your coverage ends. This gives you a total of 123 days to exercise your **Guaranteed Issue** right to enroll in a Medicare Supplement plan — such as Plan G — without facing health underwriting. Regardless of your health, they have to accept you in this situation.

If your Medicare Advantage plan exited, no Medicare Supplement company can't require a waiting period before covering your pre-existing health conditions or charge you a higher premium than what is paid by other people your age.

The Advantage plan exit isn't always a bad thing.

ANNUAL NOTICE OF CHANGE LETTERS

Medicare Advantage plans will change every year. Please read this notice!

Every Medicare Advantage and Part D drug plan must notify you of their plan changes for the upcoming year. You must receive this notice by September 30th. *If you signed up to receive it electronically, be sure to look for and read that email.* Most people ignore this information and that can be very dangerous.

The **Annual Notice of Change** letter (ANOC) isn't easy to understand. At the end of a day, no one wants to see a large booklet in the mail, so they typically ignore it or briefly glance at it. These people are happy with their Medicare Advantage or Part D plan and don't plan to change.

So why spend time reading this notice?

Because the plan you have now, that you love, may be changing dramatically for the upcoming year. It may even be leaving your area, forcing you to choose a new plan or revert to government Medicare A and B on January 1. It may even be offering new benefits or changing prices and copays. Everything you need to know about the upcoming year is in this notice.

For the past 15 years, it seems like plan benefits have gotten richer each year. Sure, prices went up, but not a lot. The copays have gone up a bit but still, not dramatic increases.

> The largest increases have come in the form of inpatient hospital copays and your maximum out-of-pocket, not in increased monthly premiums!

Now that insurance companies are getting less money from the government and medical costs continue to rise, companies have pared back benefits for 2025.

You must read your ANOC to see if you can live with the changes or if you want to shop around to see what else is available during the next Annual Election Period.

If you don't receive your ANOC by September 30th each year, call your insurance company to request it immediately.

We post notices on **THEMEDICAREFAMILY.COM** and on our private Facebook group to remind you to read your ANOC. Invariably people wait till after the holidays to pick it up — which is after the AEP ends. Call our office immediately if you need to change plans and missed the AEP, we might still be able to help you if you have a special exception!

MEDICARE ADVANTAGE "TRIAL RIGHTS"

Hands down, the most interesting feature of Medicare Advantage is the Trial Rights protection.

Under normal circumstances, you can only change from a Medicare Advantage plan to a Medicare Supplement policy during a qualifying enrollment period such as the Annual Enrollment Period, Medicare Advantage Open Enrollment Period, or Special Enrollment Period.

Luckily, the government helps people "sample" Medicare Advantage to make sure they like it. Many non-insurance companies offer a 30-day free look when you buy their product. Medicare offers something similar.

Medicare Advantage offers a one-year free look. It's a trial period lasting no more than one year, called Trial Rights. This allows you to move from Medicare Supplement to

TRIAL RIGHTS
1-YEAR FREE LOOK

YOU CAN ONLY USE TRIAL RIGHTS ONCE IN YOUR LIFETIME.

Medicare Advantage and back to Medicare Supplement, even with pre-existing conditions!

There are 2 situations where you can use Medicare Advantage Trial Rights:

1. **First Time Trying Medicare Advantage** – If you joined a Medicare Advantage plan when you first became eligible for Medicare at 65, you have a 12-month window to switch back to government Medicare and pick up a drug plan.

2. **Switching from Medicare Advantage to Medicare Supplement plan** – If you left a Medicare Supplement plan to try a Medicare Advantage plan for the first time, you have up to 12 months to switch back to your Medicare Supplement plan *if you're not satisfied for any reason.*

Many people want to stay on their Medicare Supplement, but it gets too expensive. They are desperate to save some money and want to try a Medicare Advantage plan but are scared.

It is a big move, and it terrifies many people.

Let's look at Sharon's case.

Sharon could no longer comfortably afford her $400 per month Medicare Supplement Plan G. She wanted to try a PPO plan with the understanding that she had a one-year Trial Right. Unfortunately, she was diagnosed with Parkinson's Disease 3 months later. She called me to move back to her prior Medicare Supplement plan.

I explained I could move her back to her Medicare Supplement plan, but I knew she was struggling to afford it. We talked about her prognosis. Her doctor put her on a drug and said he'd see her again in a year. She thought it over and decided to keep her PPO plan. Dollar to dollar is looked to be more affordable to her.

Sharon's story is just her story. Everyone is different. You have options, you have a budget you'd like to stay within. We educate you and then you roll the dice.

When money is not an issue, you'll enroll into a Medicare Supplement Plan G and never flinch at the future of rate increases or need to explore more affordable options. For most people on a fixed income, we take it one year at a time.

STAR RATINGS

★★★★★

When we present a Medicare Advantage or Part D plan, we are required to tell you the plan's annual star rating. You can also go to **MEDICARE.GOV** and see how highly rated your Medicare Advantage or Part D drug plan is on a scale of 1 to 5 stars, with 5 stars being the highest.

Star ratings are important because the higher the rating the more money the government gives that insurance plan, the richer the extra benefits are, and the lower the prices can be.

Medicare Supplement plans are rated by independent financial organizations, but these ratings are not based on the same criteria as the Medicare Advantage and Drug plan ratings.

Here are some of the key criteria used to determine the 5-star rating for Medicare Advantage and Part D:

1. Staying Healthy

Screening tests and vaccines: How well the plan ensures members are getting important preventive services like flu shots, mammograms, and colon cancer screenings. This is why these plans push preventive care!

Health maintenance: Encouraging healthy behaviors like managing blood pressure and cholesterol.

2. Managing Chronic Conditions

Chronic disease management: How well the plan help members manage chronic conditions such as diabetes, hypertension, and heart disease.

Medication adherence: Ensuring that members take their prescribed medications, particularly for conditions like high blood pressure, diabetes, and cholesterol.

3. Member Experience

Customer satisfaction: Member feedback on their overall experience with the health plan, including ease of getting care, handling claims, and overall satisfaction with the healthcare providers.

Timely access to care: How quickly members are able to see doctors or specialists when needed.

4. Member Complaints

Complaints and appeals: Tracking the number of complaints filed by members and the number of times they've needed to appeal a decision made by the health plan.

Plan improvement: Whether the plan's performance has improved or worsened over time.

5. Customer Service

Call center performance: How well the plan handles customer inquiries and resolves issues, including providing accurate information and timely assistance when you call the health plan.

Processing appeals and grievances: Efficiency and fairness in handling member appeals and grievances regarding coverage decisions.

6. Prescription Drug Services (for plans with a drug benefit)

Drug plan member experience: Evaluating how easy it is for members to fill prescriptions and the availability of needed medications.

Drug safety and accuracy: Ensuring safe use of high-risk medications and adherence to prescription drug regimens.

Ultimately, your voice matters! When you are sent a client satisfaction survey, take the time to fill it out. If you like your plan, a good rating from you can help that insurance company a lot. And if you complain to 1-800 Medicare about your plan, that can hurt them too.

> If a Medicare Advantage plan is below average for three years, the government makes them stop selling the plan!

In 2024, one of the largest Medicare Advantage companies had to pull their plan from an entire state. That's frustrating for those 100,000 or more members, but it actually acts as a protection. This way a company can't just ignore complaints from its members, doctors, and the government. *Poor performers will no longer be allowed to do business.*

That company may still be able to offer plans in the other 49 states because their star rating is high enough in other locations. Each plan in each state will have its own star rating. You might be on an X Plan with 5 stars (which is great) and your sister in New York is with the same company, but her X Plan has only 3 stars (not great).

Each year, J.D. Power publishes its list of Best and Worst Medicare Advantage plans by state. I encourage you to check it out before enrolling into a plan. You still may want to enroll in that plan, but you should discuss the survey results with your agent to understand the reasons for the ratings.

The average star rating for Medicare Advantage plans with drug benefits in 2025 is 3.92. Only 7 plans in the nation received a 5-star rating this year. Because of this, it is unlikely you will be able to find a 5-star plan in your zip code, but it's worth asking. If there is a 5-star plan in your area, you can move into it at any time of year! This is a special exception.

💡 High star ratings reward plans that perform well (they get more money from the government) and penalize those plan that don't do well (by giving them less money from the government). I've seen 5-star plans that were not, in my opinion, better than 4-star plans. Ratings help but are not definitive.

POINTS TO REMEMBER

- Medicare Advantage is private Medicare through an insurance company.

- You must have government Medicare A and B to enroll into private Medicare Advantage plans.

- You can enroll regardless of your health with no waiting periods.

- Many plans include the Part D drug benefit.

- All plans have some type of Extra Benefit not found in government Medicare, most commonly dental, vision, hearing, money back, and transportation.

- All plans have an annual out-of-pocket maximum (MOOP) you can pay in a calendar year. This is great financial protection you won't find in government Medicare A and B alone.

- There is no best plan or best company, you must find the plan that covers your specific doctors, hospital and medications. This may change from year to year.

- Medicare Advantage benefits and prices change annually.

- You are able to change your plan every year during the AEP, which is Oct. 15th to Dec. 7th, or at any time of year if you have a special reason.

- Plans available to you are based on your county of legal residence.

- Trial Rights allow you a one-year free look to try Medicare Advantage. You can use this once in your lifetime.

- Many people eventually switch from a Medicare Supplement to Medicare Advantage due to price.

CHAPTER 15

THE MEDICARE PART D DRUG PROGRAM

We finally get to the most complex and frustrating part of the book: drugs.

A Part D plan's national average cost per month for 2025 is $36.78. This is NOT the actual average cost that all people on Part D will pay; that amount is around $46.[1] So why are there two separate numbers? The first number is the amount the government uses to calculate late Part D penalties. The second number is the *actual average cost if you tally up what people are really paying for their drug plans this year.*

Why the difference? It's too long to explain, but the gist is that it helps those who are late, pay a lower late penalty.

Hands down, everyone gets frustrated with their drug plan for these reasons:

1. They are healthy and never use their drug insurance. "Why am I paying for something I don't use?"

2. They are moderately healthy, but still don't use their drug insurance because they can get their prescriptions at a lower price with a drug discount card like GoodRx, or SingleCare, or at Mark Cuban's Cost Plus Pharmacy, or Amazon Prime.

---

1   Centers for Medicare and Medicaid

3. They are taking a lot of medications but can't find a drug plan that covers all their drugs. Their plan covers some, but they still have to pay out-of-pocket for the rest of their prescriptions. It's frustrating!

Who is happy with Medicare Part D?

- **Not the insurance companies.** It is not a great money-maker for them, but they must have it to remain competitive with their Medicare Advantage plans, where they do make money.

- **Not insurance agents.** In general, we don't get paid to help you with basic stand-alone drug plans, so most agents will refer you to **MEDICARE.GOV** so you can enroll into a drug plan on your own.

To find a happy player in this game, look for the retiree who is taking a lot of brand name drugs. He is happy! He is even happier now that the total drug costs are capped at $2,000 per year.

HOW ARE PART D PLANS STRUCTURED?

First, you need to understand these key terms:

1. **Monthly Premium** – The cost you pay each month. The most popular drug plan in the nation in 2025 has a $0 to very low monthly cost, in most states.

2. **Deductible** is the amount you pay BEFORE your Part D plan begins to cover costs. In 2025, this cannot be higher than $590. Not all plans require you to pay the deductible for all drugs. Many plans only apply the deductible on expensive drugs, but not on generics.

3. **Catastrophic Coverage** – After reaching the $2,000 out-of-pocket drug MOOP, your plan covers 100% of the costs for your covered medications *for the rest of the year.*

4. **Coinsurance** – This is the percentage of the cost you pay for your medications during the initial coverage phase, after the deductible is met. It's 25% for 2025.

5. **Copayment** – A fixed amount you pay for each prescription after meeting your deductible during the initial coverage phase. Some drugs have a $0 copay.

6. **Formulary** – The list of prescription drugs covered by your Medicare Part D plan, categorized into tiers based on cost. This is important and often overlooked. If you take a drug that is NOT on your plan's formulary, it is not covered by the $2,000 cap.

7. **Initial Coverage Phase** – The phase after you meet your deductible where your plan shares the cost of your medications through copayments or coinsurance.

8. **Out-of-Pocket Maximum (MOOP)** – The most you will pay out-of-pocket for covered drugs in a year. For 2025, this amount is capped at $2,000 and will increase annually.

9. There is no **"Donut Hole"** any longer! No need to explain it since it stopped in 2025.

HOW PART D WORKS

You'll usually (but not always, depending on the drug) need to meet an annual deductible before your insurance starts covering costs. After that, you'll move into the initial coverage phase where your plan covers a portion of your drug expenses. Once your out-of-pocket costs hit $2,000, your plan takes over for the rest of the year.

DRUG PRICING TIERS

Every plan creates its own list of covered drugs (**formulary**) and decides how much to charge you for each drug. Drugs are priced in tiers with cheap drugs being on tier 1 and the most expensive ones being tier 5.

One plan may cover a drug that another plan doesn't offer. The same drug may be tier 2 in one plan's formulary and on tier 3 in a different plan's formulary. A drug that has been on tier 1 for years could be on tier 2 next year!

Medicare Part D has five tiers for prescription drugs.

- **Tier 1:** Preferred generic drugs (cheapest)
- **Tier 2:** Generic drugs
- **Tier 3:** Preferred brand drugs
- **Tier 4:** Non-preferred brand drugs
- **Tier 5:** Specialty drugs (most expensive)

BIOLOGIC AND BIOSIMILAR DRUGS

Most people know about generic drugs. These drugs are exact copies of brand-name meds, made from chemicals that can be perfectly replicated. Generic drugs are inexpensive.

But biologic drugs are a whole different game. They come from living systems, so you can't copy them exactly.

Enter biosimilars. These are nearly identical to biologics in all the important ways but are not quite the same. Think of it like a fraternal twin, not an identical one.

Starting in 2025, your insurance plan can switch you to a biosimilar drug in the middle of the year. This could confuse folks who've been on something like Humira and suddenly get switched to a biosimilar version. Biosimilars will save you money, but not as much as generics do.

So, keep an eye out for these changes. They're becoming more common and might affect your prescriptions.

SEARCHING FOR A DRUG PLAN

You can search drug plans on **MEDICARE.GOV** or call us for help.

1. **MEDICARE.GOV** allows you to shop for drug plans that cover your specific drugs. You'll need to shop your drug plan every year!

2. You will choose a drug plan that covers all your drugs at the lowest annual price.

3. You must pay your deductible before the plan pays anything.

4. After your deductible, you'll pay 25% of the drug costs.

5. You won't pay more than $2,000 out-of-pocket in 2025 for Medicare Part D drugs that are covered by your insurance plan.

6. Your plan can change the drugs that it covers after the first 2 months of the year, but you are locked into your plan for the rest of the year unless you have a special exception (such as moving to a new state).

7. If you move, and there is no plan available that covers your drugs, you can get a **Transition Refill**, which is a one-time 30-day supply of your drug from your new drug company. You can then appeal to be allowed to continue to get that drug, but they can deny your request. Remember, every drug plan has a list of drugs that it covers called a formulary.

Keep in mind, there is a lot of movement in the drug sphere. New drugs are approved, drug patents expire and go from brand name to generic and other drugs are removed from the market for safety reasons.

Insurance companies can stop covering a drug after the first 2 months of the year as long as they give you a 60-day notice.

You won't be able to change plans at that time (unless you have a special exception) but you might be able to ask your doctor to prescribe an alternative medication. People hate this back and forth with the insurance company and their doctor, but this is the system we have.

For over 40 years, there was NO Medicare Part D drug benefit. When we finally got one in 2003, people were elated! But the cost of drugs have now gone up astronomically.

Let's use Betty as an example:

Betty has a rare melanoma of the eye. Her drug, Kimmtrak, costs about $1,000,000 per year. If you are shocked, there are drugs that cost more!

Betty gets her chemo drug infused in the hospital. There are oral chemo drugs now, which fall under Medicare Part D, but she is getting a traditional liquid infusion of her chemo because her condition is not a candidate for oral drugs.

Depending on her insurance, here is what the Kimmtrak will cost her per year.

Option #1

If she only has **Medicare Parts A and B**, she will pay 20% of the cost of her drug. Remember, there is no MOOP on her Part B spending on government Medicare alone. She will pay $200,000. If she is at or below 600% of the federal poverty level, she's eligible for assistance for this drug from the manufacturer. It varies, but it could be free to her. Or if she is middle class, she might not qualify for any type of assistance. (More on **Patient Assistance Programs** at the end of this Chapter.)

Option #2

If Betty has a **Medicare Advantage PPO** plan, prices will vary, but a large majority of plans across the country will charge her 20% of Part B drug costs. Her PPO has a MOOP as her protection for costs from Medicare Parts A and B services only. Her drug falls under Part B, not Part D! This matters.

Her plan may have a $9,350 MOOP, which is the most any plan could charge in 2025 if she stays in the plan's network.

But, since she's already had cancer surgery and radiation, she's likely already met her out-of-pocket for the year. *She pays $0 for Kimmtrak for the rest of this calendar year.* Every year the MOOP goes up, and she restarts a new benefit period. Still, this is vastly better than if she only had Medicare A and B!

A worst-case scenario for Betty would be if she had to go to the Mayo Clinic, Cleveland Clinic or Johns Hopkins (which usually are not in-network for any Medicare Advantage plans). She would have to pay the out-of-network MOOP cap for the year, which is $14,000 in 2025. A worst-case scenario would be if she had an HMO plan without out-of-network options. In that case, she would have to pay for the full cost of care at the cancer centers.

💡 *The government raises the maximum protection in Medicare Advantage plans (in and out-of-network MOOP) each year. Twenty years ago, the maximum was only $2,000 and we are closing in on $10,000 soon. Each insurance company can choose to set their own plan maximum lower than the annual limit, and many do. You'll find the lowest max on HMO plans, but they often only cover in-network charges.*

Option #3

In addition to Parts A and B, Betty enrolled into **Medicare Supplement Plan G.** There are a lot of price variables here based on her age and location. Let's say she is from Indiana (call out to all Hoosiers) and is 65 years old. Her plan G costs her about $125 per month. She's already met her annual deductible, so she pays $0 for Kimmtrak. Because she's on Plan G, she has no network to contend with and can pick her own doctors and hospitals.

Obviously, Option #3 is the best one. She pays more per month but has less to pay when she gets really, really sick.

PRESCRIPTION PAYMENT PLAN

The Medicare Part D Prescription Payment Plan is commonly referred to as **M3P.** This program *doesn't save you money*. It just allows you to pay for your drugs in equal monthly payments instead of a large upfront payment. You can enroll at any time of year by calling your Part D drug insurance company or your Medicare Advantage company. Find their customer service number on your ID card. Starting in 2026, you'll be able to enroll in this program at the pharmacy on the spot.

Let's say I'm prescribed Stelara, one of the most expensive and commonly prescribed medications. It has a retail cost of about $25,000 per year. My drug plan covers it. Since my out-of-pocket spending cap is $2,000 (including the deductible of $590) the insurance company can't charge me more than that for *all my covered Part D drugs in a calendar year.* In fact, due to the M3P payment plan, I can only be charged $181 per month for a total of $2,000 spread out over 11 months.

Sounds too good to be true? It gets even better.

If you are enrolled in the M3P with your insurance company, you pay nothing upfront when you fill your prescription at the pharmacy. Instead, your insurance company will bill you in monthly installments. It may take the insurance company a month to get your billing information to you. You will then make equal payments for the rest of the year.

If you change drug plans *during* the year (for example, if you moved to a new state) you must pay off the balance owed to your old Part D drug plan *before* you can enroll into the M3P with your new Part D drug plan.

If you have some financial problem that prevents you from paying your monthly installments under the M3P, *you can't be dropped from the insurance company or charged late penalties or interest, but you can be dropped from the M3P.* This means that you'll have to pay your copay at the pharmacy if you go in to fill any new prescriptions.

Sometimes Stelara is covered under **Part B** because your doctor infuses it in his office. In this case, your costs might be different than if it were covered under **Part D**. For instance, under Part B, after you meet your deductible, Medicare will usually cover 80% of the cost, and you'll be responsible for the remaining 20%. If you have a **Medicare Supplement Plan G,** it will help cover that 20%, potentially leaving you with little to no out-of-pocket cost!

It gets a lot more complicated if you take Stelara and have a Medicare Advantage Plan with drug benefits. The way you pay for it will depend on the details of your specific Advantage plan. Here's what happens:

1. **Coverage Under Part B** – Since Stelara would be classified as a Part B drug, your Medicare Advantage plan will follow the rules for Part B coverage. Typically, under Part B, after you meet your **Part B deductible**, you would pay **20%** of the medication cost. However, Medicare Advantage plans often set their own copayment, or coinsurance amounts for Part B drugs, so this will differ based on your plan.

2. **Out-of-Pocket Maximum** – One of the key benefits of a Medicare Advantage plan is that it has a **MOOP** which government Medicare doesn't have. This means once your total out-of-pocket costs (including your copays and coinsurance) reach this limit, your plan will cover **100% of covered services** for the rest of the year. If Stelara is a recurring treatment, this could help limit your yearly expenses.

3. **Prior Authorization** – Most stand-alone drug plans and Medicare Advantage plans require prior authorization for expensive drugs like Stelara. This means your doctor will need to get approval from your plan before the treatment is covered, so it's important to check with your plan provider ahead of time and prepare for some possible delays getting approved.

4. **Network Rules** – Medicare Advantage plans often have network rules, so you may need to receive your Stelara infusions at an in-network facility for it to be covered under Part B. Out-of-network treatment could lead to higher costs or may not be covered at all, depending on your plan.

In summary, while Medicare Advantage plans must cover Part B drugs like Stelara, how much you pay depends on your plan's specific terms, including coinsurance, copayments, prior authorization requirements, and whether or not you've hit your MOOP. Always review your plan's formulary and network rules, and check with your provider to ensure you're prepared.

"WHAT WILL I PAY IN PART D PREMIUMS?"

That is an impossible question to answer without knowing all your prescription drugs, specific dosages, and your location.

I can tell you the average national cost of a plan, but that is meaningless. What you pay monthly in a plan premium could be $10. You stop there and think, "That's a great price!" But the monthly price is misleading. You could have one drug where your coinsurance could cost you $7,000.

Since there is an annual cap of $2,000, and you can spread that out over 12 months, your monthly prescription costs will be around $200. For now, you have the security of knowing that you won't pay more than $2,000 (they will index this for inflation so it will go up slightly each year) + the cost of your plan's monthly premium (which definitely will go up).

Unfortunately, the $2,000 cap on your drug costs doesn't cover drugs that don't fall under Medicare Part D. Drugs that are administered in a healthcare professional's office fall under Medicare Part B. *Part B has no cap on how much you could pay in a year!*

This is a sleeper threat because no one expects to get a serious diagnosis like cancer. (If cancer does run in your family, please talk to our family about separate cancer insurance.)

> Part D is funded mainly by general tax revenues and monthly beneficiary premiums. Like Part B, you will also pay the IRMAA surcharge on Part D monthly if you are a high earner.

With so many Americans battling diabetes, the cost of insulin has become a political hot button the past few years. Both parties claim credit for lowering the cost of insulin, and in reality, both parties did, in different ways. The bottom line is that insulin is still not free.

Insulin could be $35, if *your* plan covers *your* insulin brand.

While the cost of some insulins has come down dramatically, your Part D drug plan may not cover your prescription. It's imperative that we know your specific drugs and dosages to recommend a plan for you.

I threw that Insulin bit in there because it truly is a bit of good news on the Part D drug topic. But when the government mandates that one drug get cheaper, *the drug companies rebound by raising the prices on other drugs!* This burden is carried by work insurance plans now that Medicare Part D costs are capped at $2,000 annually.

The price on some inhalers is now at $35. But it is not a government-mandated price like certain insulins. The $35 cap on out-of-pocket costs for inhalers has been voluntarily implemented by pharmaceutical companies like GSK, AstraZeneca, and Boehringer Ingelheim. Before you applaud them too loudly, *these same inhalers cost around $9 in most of Europe and retail for $500 in the USA.*

DRUG FORMULARY

Part D drug plans don't have to cover every drug.

Each insurance company has a list of drugs they cover, called a **formulary.** Typically, the cheaper the monthly premium, the smaller the formulary. If your Part D drug plan has $0 monthly premium, it likely covers fewer drugs than the plan that costs $100 per month. If you take inexpensive drugs, they are likely covered on every plan's formulary. If several plans cover all your drugs, you'll choose to enroll in the Part D plan with the lowest annual out-of-pocket cost.

MEDICARE.GOV doesn't allow you to do a formulary comparison. If you want to know how many drugs each insurance plan has, you get the time-consuming job of going to each drug plan's website and tracking the information down! Not fun.

Let's say you didn't plan to get sick, and you gambled on the least expensive drug plan. I'd do the same thing. The worst-case scenario is you may have to pay for your newly needed drug for the rest of the year and enroll into a new plan that covers your drug during the next AEP. If you worry about a cheap plan's limited formulary, you can buy peace of mind with a slightly more expensive plan with a larger formulary.

> A drug that isn't covered by your plan's formulary is also not subject to the $2,000 spending cap.

Neither are drugs covered that are not Medicare approved. Ozempic, Wegovy, and Mounjaro are popular weight loss drugs. Medicare Part D specifically excludes drugs prescribed solely for weight loss. If your doctor prescribes these drugs for diabetes or to prevent a stroke, then they are covered by Medicare. *That doesn't mean that your Part D plan will offer those drugs on their formulary.* Why would a company want to offer such an expensive drug if they don't have to?

If you are prescribed a drug that isn't covered, you can always appeal it. But if you lose the appeal, you'll pay for it out-of-pocket.

Since there is an annual cap of $2,000, the drug companies have to make up their losses on the people who take the cheap drugs. They can also try to chase away business by not offering expensive drugs on their formulary.

BARRIERS TO PART D DRUGS

Just because your drugs are technically covered by your drug plan doesn't mean the drug companies don't have other tricks to keep you from accessing expensive drugs. When you read your drug plan's formulary and see these initialisms behind a drug, it is always a bad sign: PA, QL, ST.

1. **Prior Authorization (PA)** – Some drugs require prior approval from your drug plan before they'll be covered. Your doctor must justify

why you need the specific medication, and the plan must agree that it's medically necessary before you can fill your prescription. *Prepare for delays while your doctor and plan go back and forth.*

2. **Quantity Limits (QL)** – Plans may set limits on how much of a drug you can get at one time. For example, they may only cover a 30-day supply, even if your doctor prescribes more. This can require extra steps for refills and may delay access if you need more than what's allowed. Typical drugs with QLs are pain meds, sleep aids, antidepressants, and specialty tier 5 drugs.

3. **Step Therapy (ST)** – Even if your medication is on the formulary, some plans will require you to try less expensive medications before they will cover more expensive ones.

There are some formulary exceptions. One drug that commonly requires a formulary exception is **Adderall** or other ADHD medications like **Vyvanse**. These drugs are often placed on higher tiers or excluded entirely from some Medicare Part D formularies due to their classification as controlled substances. Another common example is **Xarelto**, a blood thinner, which may not be covered or might be placed in a high-cost tier.

MEDICARE PART D RULES

QUANTITY LIMITS	PRIOR AUTHORIZATION	STEP THERAPY
Plans can limit the amount of medications they cover over a period of time.	You and your provider may need to receive approval from your plan for certain medications.	Your plan may request that you take a less expensive medication first if possible.

Drugs for chronic conditions, such as **Enbrel** or **Humira** (used for autoimmune diseases), can also require exceptions due to their high cost and specialty drug status.

If you need one of these medications, there are ways to request an exception. Patients often need to show other drugs on the formulary didn't work for them or they've had adverse reactions to cheaper drugs first, before they can get these drugs covered through an exception. This is part of **Step Therapy.**

The first step in Step Therapy is to try a cheaper drug than the one your doctor prescribed. Doctors often complain they know you won't perform on the cheaper drug and don't want to waste time, *or risk your health,* waiting to prove the cheap one doesn't work, but if you don't go through the steps, you'll have to pay for the expensive drug out of your pocket!

PRICE NEGOTIATIONS

The Inflation Reduction Act allows Medicare to negotiate lower prices on 10 drugs starting in 2026, another 15 drugs in 2027, 15 more in 2028, and 20 in 2029.

Medicare will be allowed to negotiate *Part B drugs* in 2028 and 2029 as well as Part D drugs. This is great news as some of the most expensive drugs fall under Part B. These types of medications are usually injected or infused in a doctor's office or infusion center. Part B drugs are usually administered by physicians such as oncologists, rheumatologists, and urologists.

So, in 2026, we will have the first 10 drugs with enforced lower prices. Ten is a paltry amount, but something is always better than nothing. Luckily, the government chose some of the most popular and expensive drugs to be "negotiated." They spread the pain around to all the major drug manufacturers.

Eliquis is the nation's most popular blood thinner. About 4 million people will have the cost of this medication cut in half starting in 2026.

How much you'll pay will still depend on the prices set by your drug plan. But since the insurance company is getting Eliquis cheaper, you'll feel that savings too.

RATE STABILIZATION DEMONSTRATION

The impact of the new law capping Part D out-of-pocket costs at $2,000 was touted as revenue neutral. It wasn't going to cost the American taxpayers, and the money for the program would come from the drug manufacturers and the insurance companies. But when the insurance companies told the government how high they planned to price their plans for 2025, the government panicked.

Retirees would not like their Part D premiums to double or triple, especially so close to an election. So, the government announced a plan to subsidize the Part D insurance companies for 2025.

Companies that agreed not to raise their premiums more than $35 over the prior year could get up to a $145 subsidy, per member, per month. What this means is that the taxpayers are paying the majority of your Part D premium each month until this project ends (it's slated to last as long as three years but could end sooner).

You are likely fine with this arrangement, but eventually we have to pay the piper. The subsidy will run out. Your Part D monthly premium will skyrocket.

If your Medicare Part D premium went from $10 a month in 2024 to $100 a month in 2025, many people would have been priced out of their Medicare Supplement plans. They would have moved into a Medicare Advantage plan. An exodus of healthy people out of Medicare Supplements drives up the prices on those plans! It's a landslide of change we expected in 2025. It's still looming, but now we don't know for sure when it will hit.

HELP PAYING FOR PRESCRIPTIONS

You may qualify for help paying for your drug costs. The Extra Help program (also called the Part D Low-Income Subsidy or LIS) offers these benefits:

1. Pays for your Part D premium up to a state-specific amount.

2. Lowers the cost of your prescription drugs.

3. Gives you a Special Enrollment Period (SEP) once per calendar quarter during the first 9 months of the year to enroll in a Part D plan or to switch between plans. You cannot use the Extra Help SEP during the fourth calendar quarter of the year which is October through December. (You should use AEP each fall to make prescription drug coverage changes.)

4. Eliminates any Part D late enrollment penalty you may have incurred if you delayed Part D enrollment.

Depending on your *income and assets*, you may qualify for Extra Help. To receive this assistance, your prescriptions should be on your plan's formulary, and you should use pharmacies in your plan's network.

Remember that Extra Help is not a replacement for Part D or a plan on its own; it's just help paying for Part D. *You must still have a Part D plan to receive Extra Help.* If you do not choose a Part D drug plan on your own, you will be automatically enrolled in one.

Are you eligible?

1. If your monthly income is up to $1,943 in 2025 ($2,615 for couples) and your assets are below specified limits, you may be eligible for Extra Help.

2. Even if your income or assets are above the eligibility limits, you could still qualify for Extra Help because certain types of income and assets may not be counted!

3. If you are enrolled in Medicaid, Supplemental Security Income (SSI), or a Medicare Savings Program (MSP), you automatically qualify for Extra Help regardless of whether you meet Extra Help's eligibility requirements. Look for a letter on purple paper from the Centers for Medicare & Medicaid Services informing you that you do not need to apply for Extra Help.

If you are eligible for Extra Help and already have other creditable drug coverage, you should evaluate your costs and coverage when deciding whether to enroll in Part D and Extra Help or just keep your current drug coverage. Ask your former employer or union if you can get a Part D plan *without losing the retiree health benefits you want to keep.* Be careful that disenrolling from your retiree drug coverage doesn't kick you off your other retiree health benefits.

If you cannot have both Part D and your retiree health benefits, or if keeping both is not possible for you financially, think carefully about whether you should get a Part D plan.

POINTS TO REMEMBER

- Medicare Part D must be purchased from an insurance agent — like our company — or directly from the insurance company. You don't enroll with the government.

- Your Medicare Advantage plan may already include a drug benefit. It will follow the same rules as a stand-alone drug plan.

- You must have Medicare Parts A or B to be eligible to buy a Part D drug plan.

- Not every drug plan covers all drugs. Each plan has a list of drugs it covers each year, called a formulary.

- Typically, a cheaper plan has a smaller formulary.

- Your drug plan can drop a drug from its formulary or change its price with 60 days' notice!

- The most you can pay for your drugs is capped at $2,000 per year for 2025 and will increase each year with inflation.

- Your plan's maximum deductible in 2025 is $590.

- If you get your drugs from the VA, you likely won't need a drug plan.

- If you are considered low-income, you may qualify for Extra Help to pay for your drugs.

CHAPTER 16

HEALTH INSURANCE FOR THOSE UNDER 65: OBAMACARE

In 2010, President Obama signed the Affordable Care Act (ACA) into law and embraced the term 'Obamacare'. I struggle to call it the Affordable Care Act because for most of our clients, it is not affordable! You'll find some people who call it the Marketplace. This term was coined because you buy this type of insurance on the Federal Marketplace, **HEALTHCARE.GOV.** It has a lot of names. As discussed previously, I prefer to use the term Obamacare to keep things simple.

If you buy any private health insurance and you are under age 65, it is Obamacare. People tell me all the time they don't have this type of insurance because they don't realize their state rebranded it, but all health insurance for those under age 65 is Obamacare! Here are some of the names it's known by in different states:

- **Covered California** (California)
- **NY State of Health** (New York)
- **Connect for Health Colorado** (Colorado)

Why am I writing about this type of insurance in a book about Medicare? Many people are on Obamacare prior to age 65. If they qualify for a tax subsidy, chances are good they love their plan and do not want to move to Medicare. You need to know that all tax subsidies stop as soon as you are eligible for Medicare. Eligible is the key word.

Some people turn 65 *but are not yet eligible for premium free Medicare Part A.* That can happen when they or their spouse didn't work and pay into Medicare for at least 10 years. These people are allowed to stay on Obamacare and keep their tax subsidies until they are eligible for Medicare.

Some people who are eligible for Medicare just keep on keeping on with their Obamacare plan at 65. They are healthy, not really using it, and don't want to mess with figuring out how to move to Medicare. They will end up paying **Medicare Late Enrollment Penalties** that I covered in Chapter 6.

Most people, however, are not getting a tax subsidy and are not happy with the monthly cost and high deductibles of Obamacare. The average 60-year-old pays about $1,263 per month for a Silver Plan with an annual deductible of $4,000 to $5,000.

Plans are priced based on factors such as your age, location, and tobacco use. Premiums are lower for people with subsidies, which are based on income.

So, what happens when you are on Obamacare and one spouse is eligible for Medicare?

Let's look at Roger and Carol.

Roger is carrying the health insurance for his spouse, Carol. Roger retires and enrolls into Medicare. Carol is only 62 and does not qualify for Medicare. When she loses her insurance through Roger's job, she must enroll into Obamacare until she is 65 and can get Medicare on her own.

This is where Roger and Carol must do some research before Roger retires. If they see how much Obamacare will cost for Carol, and how high the deductible is, they may decide that Roger should work another year or 2 just for the insurance.

Before your spouse retires, you can do a quick price check to see how much Obamacare will cost by going to **HEALTHCARE.GOV** and providing some simple information. If your state sets up their own healthcare exchange, you'll have to search there. For example, if you live in California, you'll have to search on the Covered California website.

TAX SUBSIDY

If you don't make a lot of money, the government gives you money (via the tax subsidy, not cash) to help cover part of your monthly payment for Obamacare. The less you earn, the more help you get. When you sign up, they look at how much you expect to make that year and decide how much help you qualify for.

DO NOT LIE ON YOUR APPLICATIONS!

Some people try to game the system and purposefully underestimate their annual earnings when applying. This can cause them to have to pay back some of the subsidy at tax time.

We Can Help

Our office is here to help people enroll in Obamacare if they live in one of the 22 states that uses the **HEALTHCARE.GOV** website.

ENROLLMENT

You can enroll in Obamacare during the Open Enrollment Period, which usually runs from November 1 to January 15 each year. If you miss this window, you can only sign up during a **Special Enrollment Period** if you have a qualifying life event, like losing other health coverage, getting married or divorced, having a baby, or moving to a new area.

HOW TO SWITCH

If you and your spouse are both on an Obamacare plan and only ONE of you wants to move to Medicare, here's what you should do to not inadvertently cancel your spouse's insurance:

1. **Update the Obamacare account** – Instead of canceling everything, go to the website where you signed up (like **HealthCare.gov**) and tell them you're switching to Medicare, *but your spouse is staying on Obamacare.* This way, only your coverage stops, and your spouse keeps theirs.

2. **Don't cancel the whole plan** – If you just stop the whole plan, it might cancel for both of you. Be sure to update the plan correctly so only you leave it, keeping your spouse's plan active.

3. **Check with the insurance company** – After updating, it's a good idea to call the insurance company and make sure your spouse is still covered.

4. **Make sure timing is right** – Make sure your Medicare starts at the right time, so you're always covered and your spouse's coverage stays active.

This will keep your spouse covered and let you move to Medicare without any problems!

POINTS TO REMEMBER

- Private health insurance for those under 65 is called by many names, but it's all Obamacare.

- If you are getting a tax subsidy, it stops when you become eligible for Medicare.

- You could continue with Obamacare at 65 if you are not yet eligible for Premium Free Medicare Part A.

- If you are eligible for Part A without any costs, then you should move to Medicare or you'll have late penalties later when you do move over to Medicare.

- How much you pay for this type of plan depends on your expected income. Those with low incomes can qualify for tax subsidies.

- We can help you enroll if you live in one of the 22 states that use the federal enrollment website **HEALTHCARE.GOV**.

- Mind the timing of how you terminate your coverage if your spouse is also on the Obamacare plan, so you don't inadvertently leave your spouse without coverage when you move to Medicare.

CHAPTER 17

PATIENT ASSISTANCE PROGRAMS

Even with a good Medicare Part D drug plan, you still may need additional help paying for drugs that are not covered by your plan.

STATE PROGRAMS

State Pharmaceutical Assistance Programs (SPAPs) are programs some states have to help people pay for their prescription medicines. If your medicine costs a lot of money, and Medicare doesn't cover everything, SPAPs might give you some financial help. Each state has its own rules about who can join, and they usually help people who don't have a lot of money or who are older or disabled.

Not all states have these programs. If your state doesn't offer a program, you have to use other options such as Medicaid, federal **Extra Help, Patient Assistance Programs (PAPs)** or discount cards.

If your state offers assistance, they can help pay for things like your drug copays or they can help cover medicines that your Medicare plan doesn't pay for. Each state's program is a little different.

Here are 4 examples:

- **New York (EPIC):** The EPIC program is one of the most generous in the nation. To apply, you must be 65 or older. You can earn over $50,000 as a single person and $100,000 as a couple and still be eligible for help in NY! Go to the New York State Department of Health website or call 1-800-332-3742.

- **Ohio (Ohio's Best Rx):** Open to Ohio residents *of any age* who struggle to afford their medications. This program offers discounts on prescription drugs, and you don't need Medicare to use it. You can apply online at **OHIOBESTRX.ORG** or call 1-866-923-7879.

- **California Medicaid (Medi-Cal):** California doesn't have a specific pharmaceutical assistance program, but it does have Medi-Cal which helps low-income residents with prescriptions. You can apply through the Covered California website **COVEREDCA.COM** or call 1-800-300-1506.

- **Florida:** Florida does not have a dedicated program.

ASSISTANCE THROUGH DRUG COMPANIES

Most drug companies offer **Patient Assistance Programs (PAPs)** that can help lower, or even eliminate, the cost of certain brand-name drugs. These programs are designed for people who need financial help, and even if you're on Medicare, you can often (not always) still qualify.

Plans are called Pharmaceutical Assistance Programs or Patient Assistance Programs (PAPs) and they help people afford their medications, even if they're already on Medicare.

Even if you're on Medicare, you can still apply for these programs. The only catch is you might need to show your Medicare Part D plan doesn't fully cover the cost of your medication, or you can't afford your share of the costs — copays and deductibles.

Income eligibility varies by program, but many are available to middle- or low-income individuals.

What They Cover

These programs typically provide free or deeply discounted medications directly from the drug manufacturer.

You usually need to apply *directly to the drug company,* providing proof about your income and insurance coverage. If you're approved, you might get your medication mailed directly to you or sent to your doctor's office or pharmacy.

ASSISTANCE AND PART D

Some programs only offer help if your drug plan won't cover your specific drug, while other programs only help people without any insurance. If you have Medicare, regardless of your income, many programs won't help you.

How to Apply

Each drug manufacturer has its own application process, but the common steps usually include:

- Filling out an online or paper form.
- Providing proof of income and Medicare coverage.
- Getting your doctor to sign off on your need for the medication.

These programs are especially helpful for expensive specialty drugs, like those used to treat cancer, rheumatoid arthritis, or diabetes.

If your drug prices are crushing you, don't overlook **Patient Assistance Programs** from drug companies — even if you're already on Medicare. You might be surprised at how much help is available. Just be sure to check each program's specifics to see what you qualify for because every program varies and can change at any time.

Here are a few examples of Patient Assistance Programs (PAPs) offered by pharmaceutical companies:

Pfizer RxPathways

- Popular drugs covered: A wide range of Pfizer medications, including drugs for cholesterol, cardiovascular issues, mental health, and cancer.
- Call 1-844-989-7284 or go to **PFIZERRXPATHWAYS.COM**.
- Income limits apply, and they accept patients with Medicare, depending on the specific medication.

Merck Patient Assistance Program

- Popular drugs covered: Januvia (for diabetes), Keytruda (for cancer), and Zetia (for cholesterol).
- Call 1-800-727-5400 or go to **MERCKHELPS.COM**.
- Available to those with no prescription coverage or those with high out-of-pocket costs, *including some Medicare recipients.*

Lilly Cares

- Popular drugs covered: Trulicity (for diabetes), Cymbalta (for depression), and Humalog (for diabetes).
- Call 1-800-545-6962 or go to **LILLYCARES.COM**.
- Medicare Part D recipients can apply if they meet certain income limits.

Sanofi Patient Connection

- Popular drugs covered: Lantus (for diabetes), Aubagio (for multiple sclerosis), and Dupixent (for asthma and eczema).
- Call 1-888-847-4877 or go to **SANOFIPATIENTCONNECTION.COM**
- Medicare Part D recipients can apply if they meet certain income limits.

GSK (GlaxoSmithKline) Bridges to Access Program

- Popular drugs covered: Advair (for asthma/COPD) and Shingrix (for shingles).

- Call 1-866-728-4368 or go to **GSKFORYOU.COM**

- Medicare Part D recipients can apply if they meet certain income limits.

More Programs

Check out **NeedyMeds (NEEDYMEDS.ORG)** or **RxAssist (RXASSIST.ORG)** to search for additional Patient Assistance Programs.

Each program has its own application process and income requirements, but most offer great savings or even free medications if you qualify.

ASSISTANCE AND PART B

I always try to distinguish between **Part D** and **Part B** drugs. The new $2,000 out-of-pocket cap only applies to **Part D** drugs. You could still be out a lot more money if you are taking **Part B** drugs! Many people, especially those battling cancer, may be taking both Part D and Part B drugs.

Good news, some PAPs offer separate assistance programs for Part B drugs. There may be additional restrictions depending on the medication and treatment. Of the companies I listed earlier, only Lilly offers a Part B assistance program for *some* insulins administered through an insulin pump.

Here are some other drug manufacturers that do list Part B drugs on their PAP program:

AstraZeneca's AZ&ME Program provides assistance for many of their drugs, including some Part B medications, such as those used for cancer treatments and chronic conditions that require infusion or injection by healthcare professionals. Check them out at **AZANDMEAPP.COM**

Genentech Access Solutions offers help with certain Part B drugs, especially those used to treat serious illnesses like cancer. Check them out at GENENTECH-ACCESS.COM/PATIENT.HTML

Bristol Myers Squibb Patient Assistance Foundation also covers Part B medications, especially those used in oncology. Check them out at BMSPAF.ORG.

DRUG DISCOUNT CARDS

After the massive marketing blitz GoodRx has done, you'll likely see their cards at all your doctors' offices and pharmacies. It's become a household name.

GoodRx often offers the cheapest discount on generic drugs, but it's always good to compare and then compare again the next time you refill your prescription. You can get steeper discounts at different pharmacies, so use the GoodRx location feature to compare pharmacies near you. It may be worth the drive to save even more money by driving to a pharmacy a little farther away.

Here are some popular drug discount cards similar to GoodRx which may give you steeper discounts on brand name drugs.

1. **SingleCare – singlecare.com**

2. **RxSaver – rxsaver.com**

3. **Blink Health – blinkhealth.com**

   Blink Health is a little different. It allows you to get a discount on your medications by letting you pay for the prescription *through their platform and then pick it up at a participating pharmacy. They also offer home delivery for some medications.*

4. **WellRx – wellrx.com**

5. **NeedyMeds – needymeds.org**

These programs negotiate lower prices with pharmacies and pharmaceutical companies, passing those savings on to consumers. They are free to use, and there are no obligations or memberships required. You simply search for your medication on the website or app, choose a pharmacy, and show the discount card or coupon at the time of purchase to receive the discounted price.

These cards are often used by people without insurance, but many people who do have a Medicare Part D drug plan also use them. Why? Because some people don't want to pay the $590 annual deductible most drug plans charge in 2025. They enroll into a Part D drug plan and don't use it! It's there if they get prescribed expensive medications, but for their everyday, cheap drugs, they use drug discount cards instead.

> The discounts will vary between cards and pharmacies. It is worth comparing prices across multiple cards to get the best deal.

If you use a discount card like GoodRx instead of your Medicare Part D plan to pay for a prescription, it may allow you to get the best of both worlds.

1. Does not apply to your deductible or spending cap.

When you use a discount card to purchase medications, the amount you pay *won't count toward your Medicare Part D deductible or $2,000 spending cap*. This is because you're using an external discount and not billing the medication through your Part D insurance.

2. Part D plans won't track the purchase.

Your Part D insurer won't have a record of the transaction if you use a discount card, which means it won't affect your plan's spending limits or other cost-sharing structures. *Essentially, the insurer won't know you bought the drug.*

3. Best for medications not covered by Part D.

Using a discount card can be helpful if the medication you need is *not covered by your Part D plan* or if the out-of-pocket cost using the discount card is lower than the price through insurance.

4. Your pharmacist may be willing to guide you.

Some medications may be cheaper with a discount card than using Part D, but it's important to ask the pharmacist to compare the price through your insurance versus the discount card. You can then choose the cheaper option but remember that your Medicare Part D insurance plan won't track the discount card purchase.

💡 *You may find that at certain times of the year (like flu season) pharmacists are overwhelmed and don't proactively bring up discount cards like they do in the off-season. Be sure to ask for advice if you are not sure which way to proceed.*

POINTS TO REMEMBER

- Most drug manufacturers offer an assistance program based on financial need.

- Most, but not all, programs require you to not have other insurance to be eligible.

- If you are accepted into a PAP, your costs will not count toward your annual Medicare Part D cap.

- There are many drug discount cards that are free and may charge you a lower copay than using your drug insurance plan.

- Discounts can vary based on location, so also check surrounding pharmacies to get the lowest price.

- GoodRx often offers the lowest discount on generic drugs but check out other discount cards for brand name savings.

CHAPTER 18

HOSPICE CARE

Medicare Hospice is a program that provides care and support for terminally ill patients and their families. Your doctor must certify that you are terminally ill with a life expectancy of 6 months or less. You must sign to agree to hospice instead of standard treatment under Medicare Part A. In other words, no one can force you into hospice; it is your choice. The program focuses on comfort care as you pass away. The goal is not to cure your illness.

Once you start getting hospice care, government Medicare (Parts A and B) will cover everything you need related to your terminal illness, *even if you remain in a Medicare Advantage Plan or other Medicare health plan.*

Medicare-certified hospice care can be provided in many settings, including your home, a nursing home, a hospital, or a free-standing hospice facility. You can use the online search tool on **MEDICARE.GOV** to find Medicare-certified hospices in your area.

Hospice care usually includes nursing visits, symptom management medication, bathing and grooming.

It is not 24/7 medical care.

WHAT'S NOT INCLUDED?

While hospice care does not usually include primary care, some basic primary care is still offered. Hospice care is focused on providing physical and emotional comfort for pain and other symptoms. This typically includes spiritual support, bereavement counseling, and guidance on making end-of-life decisions.

Other parts of primary care not included in hospice are medical equipment like feeding tubes, ventilators, and oxygen tanks, unless this medical equipment is used to give patients comfort.

Curative Treatments

Hospice care intends to allow the patient to have a dignified passing, *not to try and cure* a terminal illness.

Certain Durable Medical Equipment

Hospice does provide some medical equipment, which is known as durable medical equipment (DME).

DME includes equipment that can help improve a patient's quality of life, like wheelchairs, oxygen tanks, walkers, and hospital beds. Most hospices have this type of medical equipment. *However, expensive equipment like motorized scooters, patient lifts, and sleep apnea machines are typically not covered by some hospice care facilities or may be deemed unnecessary by your medical insurance provider.*

Caregiver

If you want around-the-clock care, you will need to provide your own caregiver. This person can be a close family member or a friend, or you can hire your own aide. But if you don't have someone to care for you at home, you will have to move into and pay for a hospice facility.

The medical professionals may pop in a few times a day or only a few times a week for hospice at home. They are typically not there very long. The majority of your time in hospice care is with your caregivers, not medical professionals.

Emergency Room Visits

The goal for many hospice care providers is to reduce hospitalizations as much as possible, so *they do not include trips to the emergency room.* But there are situations where a trip to the emergency room will be covered.

WHAT IS INCLUDED IN HOSPICE?

There are many different types of hospices available. Most include:

Nursing Visits

Because hospice care comforts patients in their final days, nursing visits provide pain and symptom management rather than treatment. Nurses also provide basic training for your caregiver on how to administer medication and use medical supplies so she can do it on her own.

Medication to Reduce Symptoms

Patients are provided with medication to try to alleviate pain to keep them comfortable. Your other doctors will no longer handle your medication. Hospice will order it for you.

Basic Medical Equipment

Hospice care does not usually include durable medical equipment (DME). Some exceptions are made for canes, walkers, adult diapers, latex gloves, catheters, and hospital beds. It depends on each hospice program.

TIME LIMITS

If you live longer than 6 months, you can still get hospice care as long as the hospice medical director or other hospice doctor recertifies that you're terminally ill. People are often hesitant to use hospice because they are afraid they can't later change their mind (revoking hospice) and still have their Medicare benefits. You can always go back to your Medicare coverage.

A quick note on revoking hospice.

What if you change your mind?

You can choose to stop receiving hospice at any time, without a doctor's consent. It is called revoking hospice. Sometimes patients choose to discontinue hospice services because they want to give curative treatments another try.

Respite for Caregivers

To help your caregivers, Medicare offers Respite Care. This allows a family caregiver to get a break of up to 5 consecutive days and nights from caregiving duties while you are cared for in a Medicare-certified inpatient facility. This benefit allows caregivers to avoid burnout. If you are a caregiver, I encourage you to use this! Cut yourself some slack.

💡 *Palliative care is similar to hospice but for people with illnesses that won't result in death within 6 months. Many people living with terminal conditions receive this type of care to help manage their symptoms. They also may receive curative treatments, unlike hospice.*

POINTS TO REMEMBER

- Hospice is covered under Medicare Part A even if you have Medicare Advantage or other health plans.

- Hospice is voluntary and you can revoke it at any time.

- You can get Medicare-certified hospice at home, in a hospital, nursing home or other facility.

- Your doctor must certify you are terminally ill and recertify every 6 months.

- Hospice is not meant to cure your illness but to keep you comfortable.

- Medicare will not provide 24/7 medical care; you'll have to have a family member or friend at home to care for you.

- Healthcare professionals might not come frequently.

- Caregivers can get some rest through the Respite Program.

CHAPTER 19

INTERNATIONAL TRAVEL

If you are planning to travel out of the country during your retirement, make sure you're covered should you need healthcare away from home.

MEDICARE A AND B

Your Medicare Parts A and B coverage follows you if you travel to another state in the U.S., or one of the 5 major territories: Puerto Rico, U.S. Virgin Islands, Guam, Commonwealth of the Northern Mariana Islands, and American Samoa.

In most situations, Medicare Parts A and B won't pay for healthcare or medical supplies outside of the U.S.

When your vacation, work, or mission trip takes you to another country, then you'll need to know how to use Medicare.

Here are some exceptions that would allow you to get coverage outside the U.S. under Medicare Parts A and B.

- You're in the U.S. when you have a medical emergency, and the foreign hospital is closer than the nearest U.S. hospital that can treat you.

- You're traveling through Canada without unreasonable delay by the most direct route between Alaska and another state when a medical emergency occurs, and the Canadian hospital is closer than the nearest U.S. hospital that can treat you. Medicare determines on a case-by-case basis what qualifies as "without unreasonable delay." If you were on a camping trip working your way to Alaska, it's likely you wouldn't be covered because of the "unreasonable delay" clause. But it's a risk.

Medicare **does not** pay for prescriptions outside of the U.S., but you'll usually find prescription drugs are *dramatically* cheaper in other countries anyway. Many people travel for the sole purpose of stocking up on medications that are cheaper in other countries.

Medicare *may* cover medically necessary healthcare services on a **cruise ship** if:

- The doctor is allowed under certain laws to provide medical services on the cruise ship.

- The ship is in a U.S. port, or *no more than 6 hours* away from a U.S. port, when you get the services, regardless of whether it's an emergency.

If you like cruises, please note that Medicare doesn't cover healthcare services when the ship is *more than 6 hours away from a U.S. port.* This is why I always recommend that you purchase private travel health insurance.

🔆 *Medicare will only reimburse you for Medicare-covered services. You can't get services that are not approved in the U.S.*

Although U.S. hospitals must submit claims to Medicare for you, foreign hospitals aren't required to file Medicare claims. If you're admitted to a foreign hospital, then you pay the full cost to the healthcare provider. I've heard from many travelers that the hospital wouldn't admit them without putting a $5,000 hold on their credit card. Some required cash up front. It's not something you think about when planning your vacation, but you should!

When you get back to the U.S., you must submit an itemized bill to Medicare. If your bill is in a foreign language, you must get it translated. It's a mess. Which is why I recommend you purchase a travel health plan when leaving the country, even if only for a week. (I buy travel health insurance when I travel.)

MEDICARE SUPPLEMENTS

Your Medicare Supplement plan may cover services that government Medicare A and B do not, such as emergency medical care that you get outside the U.S.

Medicare Supplement Plans C, D, E, F, G, H, I, J, M, and N provide foreign travel emergency healthcare with *a lifetime limit of $50,000.*

Currently, only Medicare Supplement plans C, D, E, F, G, M, and N offer coverage outside the U.S. These plans:

1. Will pay 80% of the billed charges for certain medically necessary emergency care outside the U.S. You will pay the other 20% out-of-pocket.

2. Require you to meet *your $250 deductible* for the year.

3. Cover foreign travel emergency care if it begins during the *first 60 days of your trip,* and if Medicare doesn't otherwise cover the care.

4. Have a foreign travel emergency coverage *lifetime limit of $50,000.*

💡 If you have Plan E, H, I, or J – which are no longer sold – you may keep it if you bought one of these plans before June 1, 2010. They still cover foreign travel emergency care.

EMERGENCIES WHILE ABROAD

If you have a medical emergency while traveling outside the U.S., go to the nearest hospital right away to get help. After you're treated, make sure you keep all the bills and paperwork. If you have a Medicare Supplement plan that covers emergencies outside the U.S., you'll need to send these bills to your insurance company when you get back home (if you want to potentially get some money back). If you bought travel insurance, follow their steps for making a claim.

MEDICATIONS

Medicare Part D doesn't pay for medicines you purchase in other countries, but your medicine may be cheaper in another country. I still recommend that you take enough medicine with you for your whole trip, and check if your medicine is available where you're going.

TRICARE

Good news! **TRICARE for Life (TFL)** members do not need a Medicare Supplement and TFL offers coverage worldwide.

If you're a military retiree, you may have healthcare coverage through TRICARE for Life *after you enroll in Medicare*. TFL typically covers Medicare's deductibles, copayments, and coinsurance, but it also provides additional benefits, *such as healthcare outside of the U.S.* It's the same foreign travel insurance military retirees and their dependents have before enrolling in Medicare. You pay any deductibles and copayments for that coverage.

TFL acts like a private Medicare Supplement. Medicare pays first and TFL pays second.

RETIRING ABROAD

If you plan to live abroad, or travel back and forth regularly, you can enroll in Medicare. It won't work outside the country (except in the emergency exceptions above), so your day-to-day healthcare won't be Medicare. If you want to keep Part B while you are gone, you won't have coverage, but you must continue to pay for it. A few people may also have to pay Part A premiums if you or your spouse haven't paid Medicare taxes long enough to get it premium-free.

Let's assume you turned 65 while living in Thailand. You don't want to pay $200 a month for Medicare Part B. Care in Thailand is cheap. But, as often happens, you get diagnosed with something major and you want to come back to the U.S. for care. Now you may have to pay a late enrollment penalty if you didn't enroll into Medicare Part B during your initial opportunity.

If you work abroad and receive health insurance from your employer, live in a country with a national health system, or volunteer and have health coverage through a sponsor organization, *you may have some exemptions to avoid late penalties!*

This includes eligibility for an 8-month special enrollment period after you stop working or lose your insurance, 6-months if you're volunteering. It's a good idea to research your options before making any decisions about healthcare insurance while traveling.

If you plan to move back to the U.S. or travel back frequently, you might consider delaying or dropping Part B if:

- You or your spouse currently work outside the U.S. for a company that provides you with health insurance, or you or your spouse works in a country with a national health system. You will qualify for a Special Enrollment Period to enroll in Part B without penalty. This SEP begins at any time while you (or your spouse) are still working and for up to 8 months after you lose your health coverage or stop working.

- You volunteer internationally for at least 12 months for a tax-exempt non-profit organization and have health insurance during that time. You will have a 6-month Special Enrollment Period to enroll in Medicare without gaps or penalties. This SEP begins once your volunteer work stops or your health insurance outside of the U.S. ends, whichever comes first.

(Shout out to Catherine B. who volunteers in an orphanage in Malawi. I learned this while helping her navigate Medicare years ago.)

When Is My Special Enrollment Period?

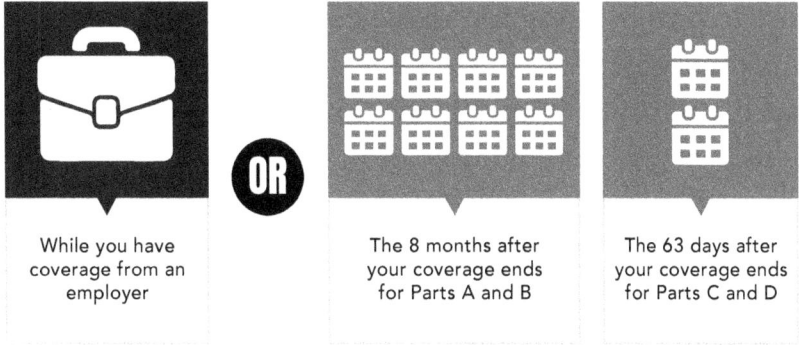

| While you have coverage from an employer | OR | The 8 months after your coverage ends for Parts A and B | The 63 days after your coverage ends for Parts C and D |

If you live in a foreign country when you turn 65 and first qualify for Medicare, you can sign up by requesting enrollment forms from the United States Embassy or Consulate in the country where you currently live.

The Social Security Administration should also send you a letter explaining that you have entered your Initial Enrollment Period, along with a form to request an enrollment packet. Be sure to keep copies of any forms that you complete.

🔆 *Be sure to send paperwork via certified mail to ensure delivery so you are not frustrated if it gets lost in the regular mail.*

If you are collecting benefits from SSA or from the Railroad Retirement Board while abroad, *you may be automatically enrolled* in Part A and B when you become eligible at age 65.

If you are not drawing Social Security at age 65, you won't be automatically enrolled, so be sure to understand your options. If you make an error and don't enroll on time, you'll be able to enroll later, but you will have to wait, and while you are waiting, the late penalties are growing.

If you do not enroll in Medicare Part B when you are first eligible, you have to wait until the General Enrollment Period, which runs January 1 through March 31 each year. Your coverage will start the first of the month after the month in which you enrolled.

Is it better to pay monthly for Medicare Part B while living abroad so you can always go back to the U.S. for care at any time? Or should you drop Part B to save that monthly cost knowing that if you had to come back to the U.S. you could enroll and get back into the system with a delay (depending on what month you return) and a 10% late Part B penalty for every year you were late? It's easy for wealthy people to continue to pay for Part B. Those who are not wealthy usually drop Part B and hope to stay healthy.

It's all a gamble. Most retirees who move abroad tell me they are NEVER coming back. But many do.

SOCIAL SECURITY WHILE LIVING ABROAD

In most cases, you can receive Social Security benefits while living overseas. As long as you're eligible, the SSA can send payments to many countries around the world. The country you're living in must be one that allows the SSA to send payments. *Most countries are on that list, but a few exceptions exist — like North Korea and Cuba.*

To keep your benefits flowing, be sure to keep your address and banking information up-to-date on your SSA online account.

Some rules may affect the way payments work, depending on your citizenship and residency status. If you're a U.S. citizen, your benefits will generally continue as usual. However, if you're not a U.S. citizen, you may need to meet additional criteria to keep receiving payments. It's a good idea to check with the SSA to see what specific rules apply based on your situation and location.

> There might be some tax issues if you're living abroad and receiving Social Security benefits.

Depending on the country you're in, you could be subject to U.S. taxes or even local taxes on your benefits. The U.S. has tax treaties with many countries, so your tax situation will vary based on where you live. It's a good idea to consult with a tax professional familiar with both U.S. and international tax laws to ensure you're following the rules and don't get caught by surprise when tax season rolls around.

POINTS TO REMEMBER

- In general, Medicare stops at the U.S. border.

- Your Medicare Supplement may provide some coverage but it's best to buy private international coverage when you leave the country.

- Some Medicare Advantage plans offer limited international coverage, but it's not common.

- You may want to continue to pay for Medicare Part B while living overseas to avoid a late penalty when you return and re-enroll into Medicare.

- Or you may want to terminate Medicare Part B.

- You cannot be enrolled in a Medicare Advantage, Part D, or Medicare Supplement plan if you live outside the country.

- If you are working overseas with creditable coverage, you have the same rights and enrollment periods when you stop working to enroll into Medicare without a penalty.

- If you are a volunteer overseas, you may be able to avoid late Medicare penalties if you meet the requirements.

- You can continue to receive your Social Security benefits in most, but not all, countries.

CHAPTER 20
ALTERNATIVE MEDICINE

I've had a holistic doctor since my 40s *when several clients warned me not to go to a regular doctor for menopause.* To the many women who pointed me in the right direction, I am forever grateful. Three traditional doctors told me I was fine, even though I absolutely could not sleep from the hot flashes, had trouble in my job because my memory disappeared, my hair was falling out in clumps, and I'd gained 15 pounds after being the same weight my entire adult life. Suddenly, without injury, I had the most painful sensation of my life: a frozen shoulder.

I knew something was broken. After 4 hellish years, a holistic doctor changed me overnight (estrogen, progesterone, thyroid medicine, D3, K2, and iron that the other doctors all said I didn't need). In a few months the hot flashes stopped, and I could sleep. The hair and nails came back in a year. So, yes if this feels like I'm pro holistic doctors, I heartily am!

All my symptoms were classic symptoms of menopause, but my traditional doctors never offered me an ounce of helpful advice.

The alternative medicine industry is growing and it's important to understand if Medicare covers holistic, functional, or alternative medicine.[1]

---

1   It is very important to note that I am not advocating for dangerous treatments and you MUST do your research before seeing a holistic or naturopathic practitioner. Just like there are bad doctors out there, there are also many bad holistic practitioners. Be careful. Be smart.

Naturopathic medicine, acupuncture, massage therapy, and other forms of alternative medicine are not covered by government Medicare. However, some Medicare Advantage Plans provide extra benefits to cover a variety of health and wellness services that are considered holistic or alternative therapies. Plans vary by your location and benefits can vary from year to year.

CHIROPRACTIC AND OSTEOPATHIC SERVICES

People either hate chiropractors or swear by them. I love mine. He cured my sciatica, stopped the lightning pain down my neck, and stopped the numbness in my pinky finger.[2]

But chiropractic isn't one and done. It takes a course of treatments and can be expensive. Medicare offers some coverage.

Part B typically only helps pay for one type of chiropractic service: spinal manipulation. Here are some important facts to know:

- The treatment must be deemed medically necessary by a medical professional to correct a subluxation (a condition when the vertebrae are out of position) by a chiropractor or other qualified provider.

- Medicare will only cover manual manipulation, not other services offered at a chiropractor, such as X-rays, tests, acupuncture, or massage. (Note: make sure your chiropractor takes X-rays before doing any manipulation.)

- You must pay your Part B deductible before Medicare pays its share.

- Once your deductible is met, Part B will pay 80% of the Medicare-approved treatment amount — you will still owe the other 20%. If you have Medicare Supplement Plan G, it pays 20% (after you've met the annual deductible).

- Part B does not cover spinal manipulations *as maintenance or preventive services.*

---

2   Shout out to Dr. Todd McDougal in Fishers, Indiana **INCHIROPRACTIC.COM.**

- There is no limit on the number of visits as long as they are deemed medically necessary to correct an existing problem.

Medicare does not cover spinal decompression therapy *as a stand-alone treatment*. There are some circumstances in which Medicare will cover part of the cost of spinal decompression treatments for certain conditions such as herniated discs, degenerative disc disease, and radiculopathy.

NUTRITIONAL CARE

If you require access to nutritional services due to your diabetes or kidney disease, you can usually get coverage for nutritional care under Medicare Part B.

CUPPING

When cupping is performed by a licensed massage therapist or acupuncturist who is *within a* Medicare Advantage *network*, your plan may provide some coverage. Cupping is not covered by government Medicare. I used this with great success for my frozen shoulder.

HOMEOPATHY

Homeopathy is very different from naturopathy. In general, Medicare won't cover homeopathy. These practitioners work for cash.

FUNCTIONAL MEDICINE

Functional medicine is a type of alternative care that's based on your body's biochemistry and your lifestyle, as well as evidence-based solutions. Treatment is performed by a physician with holistic training, or it may be performed by a naturopathic doctor or another alternative care practitioner. Like homeopathy, in general, Medicare won't cover this type of care. These doctors work for cash.

ACUPUNCTURE

Medicare Part B covers up to 12 acupuncture treatments for **chronic low back pain** within a 90-day period. There are conditions to getting acupuncture covered.

If you show improvement, Medicare may cover an additional 8 sessions, *for a maximum of 20 treatments in a 12-month* period. However, Medicare does not cover acupuncture for any other condition such as neck pain, knee pain, or migraines.

The reality is that very few acupuncturists accept Medicare because most can't get approved as a Medicare provider. Search here to see if any acupuncturists near you accept **MEDICARE MEDICARE.GOV/ CARE-COMPARE.**

The long and short of it is that alternative treatments are not likely covered by your Medicare plan, but it's always worth it to check!

POINTS TO REMEMBER

- Government Medicare covers very few holistic or alternative treatments.

- Some Medicare Advantage plans provide extra benefits for alternative therapies like acupuncture, massage, or nutritional care, but coverage varies by plan and location.

- Medicare Part B covers nutritional counseling if you have diabetes or kidney disease, but it doesn't generally cover other holistic or dietary treatments.

- Many holistic treatments, such as homeopathy, cupping, and functional medicine, are not covered by Medicare and must be paid for out-of-pocket.

- Always confirm with your healthcare provider if they accept Medicare and explore Medicare's provider directory to find Medicare-approved practitioners for services like acupuncture.

CHAPTER 21

HEALTH SAVINGS ACCOUNTS

Tax avoidance is very complicated, but Health Savings Accounts (HSAs) are easy to understand and use. If you are fortunate enough to have the ability to participate in an HSA at work, you must understand when to stop contributions *prior to enrolling into Medicare*. Not understanding the rules can cause you a lot of frustration and tax penalties.

But first let's look at why you should be taking advantage of an HSA.

> Your contributions to an HSA are either pre-tax or tax deductible!

The amount you contribute will lower your taxable income for the year in which you make the contribution. For example, if you contribute $3,000 to your HSA and your taxable income is $60,000, you can deduct the $3,000 from your taxable income, bringing it down to $57,000. Depending on your tax rate, you might have an immediate tax savings.[1]

There is no problem if you have an HSA *and are planning to retire at age 65*. You can continue to make contributions up till age 65. The problem arises when you work *past age 65, continue to contribute to your HSA, and plan to enroll into Medicare.*

---

1   Talk with your accountant or other professional to get individual financial advice about tax withholdings and liabilities. These laws change every year, just like Medicare coverages. Remember, I can't make it make sense.

Timing of Medicare is critical!

An HSA is a triple winner for tax savings.

1. If you make contributions via payroll, **you won't be subject to Social Security, Medicare, or income taxes on that amount.**

2. Your investment within your HSA grows **tax-free**.

3. You can withdraw your funds **tax-free,** when you use them for approved medical expenses.

If you have an HSA, be aware that once you enroll *in any part of Medicare,* you cannot continue to make contributions to your HSA — I'm not talking about a *dormant* account that you haven't contributed to in years. As long as neither you nor your employer are contributing to your HSA, having this type of account and enrolling into Medicare will not create a problem.

> When you plan to retire, be sure to stop all contributions to your HSA at least 6 months before starting Medicare after age 65.

What's up with this random 6-month rule? When you enroll into Part A past age 65, the government wants to help you in case you forgot to enroll earlier. Maybe you've had hospital claims and didn't realize you were eligible for Medicare Part A, so to help you out, the government makes your Part A start-date *retroactive 6 months.* A bizarre consequence of the government trying to help people but actually hurting people.

It is unlikely most people would know this rule unless their plan administrator alerted them. Many insurance agents do not know this rule either. You may only find out about it after you retire.

> If you contribute to your HSA during the 6 months BEFORE enrolling in Medicare Part A, you may face a 6% excise tax and income tax on those contributions.

Remember, if you are not yet age 65 and eligible for Medicare none of this applies to you. This problem only arises if you are eligible for Medicare and have an HSA that you want to keep making contributions to after the age of 65.

Many people enroll into Social Security but delay taking Medicare. If they are OVER age 65, then Medicare Part A is automatic when starting any Social Security benefit. Your Part A will conflict with your HSA.

No, there is no way to only take Social Security after age 65 without getting Part A. Choose Social Security or contributions to your HSA.

If you find yourself in the situation where you should have stopped HSA contributions but didn't, call your HSA plan administrator immediately. You may be able to reverse the last 6 months of excess contributions so you can avoid tax penalties.

But you must do this *before you file your income taxes* for the year in which you made those excess contributions. If you waited past tax-time to find out you could reverse contributions, you still have the opportunity to file an amended tax return.

If your employer has already issued your year-end W-2 showing your HSA contributions, you will have to ask your employer to issue an amended W-2. Technically your employer can request that money back.

You can imagine what a mess this can be!

Or your employer could recharacterize those amounts and treat them as if they were post-tax bonus payments, which is what most employers in this situation usually do. Either way, your employer will have some record-keeping to rectify. I say we blame your employer for this mess. He was in the position to educate his employees about these rules and failed to do so!

It's a lot of hassle to try to back out of those HSA excess contributions and avoid the penalty and taxes. It's better to plan ahead and avoid this chaos by **stopping all contributions to your HSA 6 months before** you enroll into Medicare after the age of 65.

WHAT IF YOU GET LAID OFF?

You can't control that, yet the painful penalties hit you all the same if you were contributing to your HSA within 6 months of taking Medicare. You could try to get another job with health benefits to run out the clock in those 6 months, but most people just retire and pay the penalties.

> If you want to work past age 65,
> you should plan a firm date to retire.

A firm retirement date allows you to do some advanced planning and make your transition into retirement smoother. I've had many people over my career tell me they like their job and plan to work *indefinitely.* That is a flexible way to look at retirement *unless you have an HSA.*

If you have an HSA, please do not wing your retirement date!

HSAS AFTER DEATH

What happens to your HSA when you die? Are the withdrawals still tax-free?

The rules differ based on whom you leave your account to.

1. **Surviving spouse** – If you transfer your remaining HSA funds directly to your surviving spouse, she becomes the account holder and can make tax-free withdrawals for qualified medical expenses just like you could have.

2. **Non-spouse beneficiary** – If all of the funds are distributed to your named beneficiary. She will be taxed on the amount as ordinary income. The HSA is no longer an HSA and must be emptied.

3. **Your estate** – If the remaining funds are transferred to your estate because you didn't list a beneficiary, or your beneficiary is also dead, then the amount of money in your HSA fund is taxed as income on the final estate tax return.

Now is a good time to check with your plan administrator to see who you chose as your plan's beneficiary. You may want to update that now.

Note: If you die with outstanding medical expenses, the remaining funds can be used to pay for those expenses tax-free for up to 1 year after your death.

HSAs, when available, are a great investment option. You can use that money down the road to pay for qualified medical expenses. There are over 200 qualified health expenses you can use your HSA funds for and there is *no deadline to spend the money.*

Here are a few tips:

1. Write a check each month to reimburse yourself for the cost of Medicare Part B (if the premium is automatically deducted from your Social Security check).

2. Pay for your Medicare Part D premiums and deductibles.

3. Pay for your Medicare Advantage premiums, copays, or coinsurance.

4. **But note that you cannot use HSA funds to pay for Medicare Supplement premiums.**

If you want to keep working, enroll into Medicare, and stop contributing to your HSA, you can continue to use the funds for qualified medical expenses *while you are working.*

"I'm still working past 65 and my wife is on my health plan. She is over 65 and on Medicare. Can I still contribute the family maximum to my HSA?" Yes, you can.

If your spouse is retired and on Medicare, you can still contribute to your HSA. Your account is tied to you, not your spouse.

A GREAT RETIREMENT VEHICLE

Instead of retiring and using your HSA funds, you can tie them to an index fund and let them grow in the stock market.

You can save all your qualified medical receipts and wait to file for reimbursement for 5 to 10 years while your account grows. Your receipts do not expire. There is no deadline to spend the money. You'll need to work with a financial advisor to get those HSA funds growing in an index fund instead of sitting dormant.

💡 *You cannot use HSA money to pay for your Medicare Supplement's monthly plan premium but you can use it to pay for your Medicare prescription plan or a Medicare Advantage plan! I dare you to make that make sense!*

FLEXIBLE SPENDING ACCOUNTS ARE DIFFERENT

You'll have none of these issues if you have a different type of employee benefit at work known as a Flexible Spending Account (FSA).

> If you have an FSA, your employer controls that money.
> If you leave, you can't take it with you,
> unlike an HSA where your money follows you.

POINTS TO REMEMBER

- You cannot take any part of Medicare and continue to contribute to your HSA at work past age 65.

- If your spouse is on your work insurance but she has Medicare, you can still contribute the family maximum.

- Once you draw Social Security, you are required to enroll into Medicare Part A. You can't make any further HSA contributions once you have any part of Medicare.

- You must stop all contributions to an HSA 6 months prior to the date you plan to enroll into Medicare when you continue to work past age 65.

- If you violate the previous rule, it is possible to back your contributions out and avoid the tax penalties, but it's difficult.

- When you change jobs or retire, your HSA goes with you (unlike a FSA which is owned by the employer).

- You can use HSA money to pay for many healthcare expenses BUT NOT to pay for your Medicare Supplement premiums.

- Your HSA funds don't expire.

- How your HSA funds can be used after your death varies depending on whom you leave the funds to.

CHAPTER 22

MEDICAID ESTATE RECOVERY

For most retirees, our home is our biggest asset. We plan to pass it along to our family, but a prolonged stay in a nursing home can basically take the house. Not literally, but your state government can place a lien on your house so that Medicaid is paid back for the cost of your nursing home stay. This is called **Medicaid Estate Recovery**.

Don't confuse Medicaid with Medicare — Medicare is health insurance and doesn't place claims on your home.

If you're worried about losing your home due to a nursing home stay, you're not alone. Your home is usually exempt while you're living in it or if your spouse or disabled child still lives there.

The good news is, there are ways to protect your home and other assets from being eaten up by a nursing home stay.

5-YEAR LOOK-BACK PERIOD

First, you must understand Medicaid's 5-year look-back period. This will impact almost every option you have to avoid Medicaid Estate Recovery. When you apply for Medicaid to pay for your nursing home stay, the state looks back over the past 5 years to see if you transferred your assets, including your home, to someone else. If you gave your house to your son or daughter during this 5-year period, Medicaid will penalize you by delaying when they will pay for your care.

The thought process here is logical. If you have the money to pay for your nursing home stay, you should pay for your care on your own and not expect taxpayers to pay for you.

Let's look at an example:

Your house is worth $200,000. You transfer it to your son for $1. That's legal. But the next year you end up with dementia in a nursing home. You must pay for your care, but you only have Social Security and a small pension. It won't begin to cover the $10,000 per month your nursing home care costs. You apply for help from your state's Medicaid program. Medicaid sees that you gave your $200,000 house to your son last year.

$200,000 would cover 1 year and 8 months in a nursing home that costs $10,000 per month. Therefore, Medicaid will not pay for your care for 1 year and 8 months. They want your son to pay for the first $200,000 of your care before Medicaid will cover any of the cost of your care.

If your son won't give your house back and he isn't able to pay for your nursing home care for 1.8 years, you may be able to get a **Hardship Waiver** from your state's Medicaid program. If denial of care would cause you a severe hardship, you can apply for a waiver (but approval is rare).

Key points about the look-back period:

1. **It applies in all states.** This is a federal rule. New York is trying to introduce a 2.5-year look-back for home care or community-based Medicaid. It was supposed to start a few years ago but has been delayed. It's likely to start at some point in the future.

2. **It impacts all types of transfers** including gifts, transferring ownership for less than fair market value, and setting up trusts to shield assets from Medicaid.

3. **The penalty period** is based on the amount that you gave away during the look-back period. The length of the penalty is calculated

by dividing the value of the asset you gave away by the average monthly cost of a nursing home stay in your state.

YOU HAVE OPTIONS TO PROTECT YOUR ASSETS

Let's walk through some options to protect your assets from a nursing home stay. Remember they all need to be in place 5 years *before* you go into a nursing home. If you want to really understand all your options, consult with an elder law attorney near you.

If you are married, you can transfer the home to your spouse **without penalty and without the 5-year look-back**. If your spouse is still living in the home, it is considered an **exempt asset** and does not count toward Medicaid's asset limits.

No, your long-time, live-in partner *who is not your legal spouse* will not get this exemption. Get married if you are worried about a nursing home stay forcing you to sell the home.

Long-term care insurance (LTC) helps pay for nursing home or in-home care. If you have insurance to pay for your nursing home stay, you won't have to worry about losing your home to Medicaid.

So why doesn't everyone buy this type of insurance? It is expensive! Many people wait too long to look into this type of insurance until they are too sick to medically qualify. You need to buy this type of insurance when you are young (in your 50s) and healthy.

Depending on how much insurance you purchased, and how long you are in a nursing home, there is a risk that you could *still run out of insurance and still end up on Medicaid.*

A basic LTC policy for a 65-year-old female in the Midwest with a $150 to $200 daily benefit for 3 to 5 years of coverage will cost you $3,000 to $4,000 per year. That is if you are healthy. It will cost more if you are not healthy. You may not be able to get it at all if you are very sick.

I'm no longer a fan of this type of insurance after seeing how high these companies jack up the rates as people age.

Too many people pay on their LTC insurance for years only to finally cancel it when the price reaches $500 per month. Instead of LTC, I recommend short-term care insurance plans and file it under "something is better than nothing." At least if you never use this type of insurance, it didn't cost you an arm and a leg.

As I mentioned in the introduction, I purchased a life insurance policy with Living Benefits to plan for my own nursing home costs. Ask a life insurance agent near you for information on this type of life insurance.

A Lady Bird Deed lets you keep living in your house, but after you die, it automatically goes to someone else, like your kids. It helps you avoid having to give up your house for nursing home costs and helps avoid probate. Lady Bird Deeds are only available in Florida, Michigan, Texas, West Virginia, and Vermont. This type of deed is cheap to set up!

If you don't live in a state that allows a Lady Bird Deed, don't worry. Your state has something that is similar called a Life Estate. It lets you live in your house until you pass away, then the house goes to your beneficiary. A Life Estate is used mainly for property. You give yourself the right to live in and control your property while you are alive and when you die, the ownership automatically transfers to the person you named on your deed called a remainderman.

Once you set this up, you are usually not able to change it! The person you chose to take over after your death now has some legal rights so don't go into this type of arrangement lightly. Setting up a Life Estate is also inexpensive.

Here are the brief differences between a Lady Bird deed and a traditional Life Estate:

1. Control

- With a **Lady Bird Deed**, you retain full control during your lifetime, including the ability to sell, mortgage, or revoke the deed without the remainderman's consent.

- With a **Life Estate,** you share ownership with the remainderman and cannot sell or modify the property without their consent.

2. Medicaid Estate Recovery

- A **Lady Bird Deed** avoids probate, so the property is protected from Medicaid Estate Recovery.

- A **Life Estate** also avoids probate, but Medicaid may still count the life estate's value as an asset during your lifetime. You could still end up with a lien on your house!

Lady Bird deeds are often preferred for their flexibility and Medicaid planning advantages — but again, they are only available in 5 states.

MORE ADVANCED ESTATE PLANNING OPTIONS

An **Irrevocable Trust** is a more complex and comprehensive way to protect your house and money. This is not cheap to set up! You put your stuff in the trust, and then it belongs to the trust, not you. Since you don't own anything, your nursing home costs will be covered by Medicaid. This type of trust is not to be confused with a **Living Trust**. You or your parents may have a Living Trust which is a Revocable Trust. A Living Trust allows you to change it at any time while you are living.

A Living Trust avoids probate but not Medicaid Estate Recovery!

With an irrevocable trust, you can't change your mind and take your stuff back. Of course, this is a massive oversimplification of a complex topic, but this is the gist of it.

A **Medicaid Asset Protection Trust (MAPT)** is a special kind of trust that helps you get Medicaid to pay for a nursing home, but still keeps your house safe. It's similar but different from an irrevocable trust because this trust is set up specifically to avoid Medicaid.

You have to plan ahead to set this type of trust up at least 5 years before you need Medicaid. With a MAPT you can still receive income from the trust assets, but you can't access the principal.

If your adult daughter has been living with you and providing your care for at least 2 years before you enter a nursing home, you might be able to transfer your home to her without penalty using the Caregiver Child Exemption. This varies by state. Check with your state's Medicaid program for details in your area.

FREQUENTLY ASKED QUESTIONS

"I'm on Medicaid but not in a nursing home. Is my house still subject to a lien to pay back Medicaid for my healthcare?"

No, not yet. For now, the Medicaid Estate Recovery Program is for debts to a nursing home, not regular healthcare costs (such as doctor visits, hospital stays, or prescription drugs). *But this can change in the future.*

"Can Medicaid take my spouse's income while I'm in a nursing home?"

No, Medicaid won't take your spouse's income while you're in a nursing home. Under spousal impoverishment rules, your spouse (called the Community Spouse) is allowed to keep a portion of your income or all of it, depending on her needs. Medicaid only considers your income when determining your eligibility for nursing home coverage.

"What happens if I rent and don't own a house?"

You'll pay for your nursing home care out of your own money. If you don't have enough to do that, you'll qualify for Medicaid. The state can't go after your kids for your unpaid Medicaid bills after you die. Medicaid Estate Recovery is focused on your assets. If you don't have any other major assets, there is nothing for Medicaid to recover.

POINTS TO REMEMBER

- Your state government can put a lien on your home and assets through Medicaid Estate Recovery.

- You can protect your home and assets. For specific help, contact an attorney! You have many options.

- The 5-year look-back period matters! You need to plan in advance to protect your assets. If you need to go into a nursing home immediately, you usually can't do anything to protect your assets. It is too late.

- If your spouse qualifies for Medicaid to cover his nursing home stay, you are not forced to sell a house that you jointly own to pay for his care while you are alive or while a disabled child is living in it.

- If you are living with your partner, but are not legally married, the house is not protected from Medicaid Estate Recovery.

- What type of estate planning options you have available to you are dependent on the state you live in.

- Lady Bird Deeds are a very popular, flexible and inexpensive way to protect your house from Medicaid Estate Recovery, but this type of planning tool is only available in 5 states.

- In states without a Lady Bird Deed option, you can use a Life Estate for protection.

CHAPTER 23

WORKING WITH AN INSURANCE AGENT

You may be leery of working with insurance agents. Many people think we get paid more to push X over Y, and *sometimes that is true.*

Our company doesn't work that way.

Our agents get paid the same regardless if you choose X, Y, or Z. Some companies pay us more or less than others, but our agents are not paid more or less when a company pays our agency less. We want our agents to help you come to the decision of what plan best suits your needs regardless of their commission.

> Our company does not represent all the insurance companies in the nation. We pick and choose.

We add and subtract companies based on their performance. We represent the largest, national Medicare insurance companies that are household names. We also represent many small, regional companies you may never have heard of.

The great thing about being an independent, family company is that we can represent the companies *we feel bring value to our clients.*

It is hard to master the ins and outs of so many companies. And if it is in your best interest, there will be times when we will refer you to a company that we do not represent.

We've done this for over 45 years and taking care of our clients is our priority, even if they don't buy with us.

Do you still have a lot of questions about Medicare?

Simply schedule your free consultation with our team. We are licensed in all 50 states, and you can call us as many times as you need to until you feel comfortable proceeding.

There is a yellow box on **THEMEDICAREFAMILY.COM** website where you can book an appointment to enroll or just to have a consultation to answer your questions about Medicare insurance. You can also just call in to book your appointment at 1-800-970-1964.

Obviously, I urge you to choose our family to work with. Not only are our services free to you, *but we love what we do, and it shows.* You don't pay for our advice or help enrolling because we are paid as independent contractors by the insurance companies.

Now that I have plugged my family company, let's talk about insurance agents in general.

PICKING THE RIGHT AGENT

There are over 40,000 Medicare agents in the U.S. Feel free to interview several before you pick one.

Not all agents have the same breadth of experience — everyone has to start somewhere — but a more experienced agent has learned a lot that can benefit you. Some have an obvious bias and seem to push a particular company. If your agent is pushing one particular company remember that it is rare for one company to be vastly superior to all others. You know when you trust someone, go with your gut.

💡 *Some agents are not able nor willing to take all the annual testing (and it takes many, many hours) to be able to sell all the various Medicare Advantage and Part D drug plans in your area. These agents just offer you a few choices because these are the options they know.*

Some agents refuse to sell either Medicare Supplements because they pay a lower commission, or Medicare Advantage because there is too much testing.

A great agent is able and willing to present you with dozens of options, without a clear bias in favor of any one insurance company.

A good agent:

- **Represents multiple companies** to offer you a variety of plans, not just one company.

- **Listens to your needs.** Look for someone who takes the time to understand your specific needs and concerns. A good agent won't rush you into decisions.

- **Is transparent.** Is your agent getting paid a bonus for selling you this plan? Ask.

- **Is knowledgeable and experienced.** Your agent should be able to explain Medicare Supplement *and* Medicare Advantage plans. Not just one or the other.

- **Offers support** after you enroll. When you need help, you don't want to be on hold with the insurance company; you want a real person to talk to or email.

- **Has a good record.** You could go the extra step to check your state's insurance disciplinary board and see if your agent has a history of complaints. Checking online reviews is also helpful.

- **Provides Annual Plan Reviews.** If your agent doesn't provide this, move on, because each year you'll need to review your plan and decide if you want to stay or move.

CAPTIVE AGENT VS. INDEPENDENT AGENT

When you work with an agent employed by a specific insurance company (an employed agent or captive agent), he must sell their plans to pay his bills. It's rare — if not unheard of — for an employed agent to tell you his products are not competitively priced and refer you to a competitor.

I've spent nearly 30 years as an independent agent. Even if you don't choose to work with our family, I recommend that you find another independent agency to work with. Independent agents work for themselves. They are not beholden to one insurance company. They can't be pushed to hit a sales quota.

If your agent has a company logo on his shirt, chances are he's only able to represent that one insurance company. It may offer the best rates and benefits this year, but in the future, when it almost assuredly won't be the most competitive plan, a captive agent won't alert you to another plan from another company. Independent agents do this every day.

A good independent agent represents dozens and dozens of companies to give as many options as possible in one stop. If you want to compare 10 plans working directly with the insurance companies, you'd have to call up 10 separate captive agents. Or you can call a well-educated independent agent.

If you decide to call 10 different insurance companies and do your own research, keep in mind they can't compare and contrast competitors' plans for you. They can only speak to their plans. This leaves you with a lot of work on your own.

After the sale, you are just an 11-digit number to your insurance company. Many of them force you into long phone lines to get a simple question answered. That is if you don't hear the dreaded, "Due to high call volume, please call back later."

> A lot of what we do is help fix the Medicare mistakes people make. Sometimes we can, sometimes we can't, but we are always willing to try!

Another hallmark of a good independent agent is the type of service they offer *after the sale*. An insurance agent is a middleman. It's nice to have someone in the middle to help you with the insurance company!

We have a large **Client Care Team** to help with all your needs after you enroll. Some agents just tell you to call your insurance company and tough it out alone when you have questions.

AGENT COMMISSIONS

If you have a cynical bone, like many of us do, you might assume that I prefer a Medicare Supplement plan because, as an insurance agent, I earn a higher commission.

That's a fair assumption. Agents are paid a higher commission when you enroll into a Medicare Advantage plan!

We get paid about the same by each Medicare Supplement company, but one company pays us *considerably less*. I'm quick to point that out when I sell one of the most popular Medicare Supplement plans, because I found that since they are a well-known company, people *assume we are paid more.*

If I only had my wallet in mind, I'd never sell for that company, nor would I sell Medicare Supplements at all. You can easily find agencies that say Medicare Supplements are inferior to Medicare Advantage. Some refuse to sell Medicare Supplements at all *and now you know why!*

Insurance companies almost always sell both Medicare Supplement and Medicare Advantage plans. They make much, much more money when you enroll into a Medicare Advantage plan. This is why you rarely ever see TV ads about Medicare Supplements.

My parents founded our company to do what is best for the client. When you call into The Medicare Family, you can rest assured that the agent who works with you will not be paid more to push one plan over another. We shield our team from bonuses companies offer precisely because we don't want them to be swayed financially.

THE CHOICE SHOULD BE YOURS

If you feel pushed to purchase a certain product, then there is probably a reason — $.

But it's your future. Your bank account. Your health. You should be in the driver seat.

So, what do most people choose?

Last year 70% of the people we helped enroll in Medicare chose a Medicare Supplement plan. Medicare Supplements are expensive when compared with a Medicare Advantage plan with a $0 monthly premium. But when properly educated about the risks and rewards of both types of plans, our clients overwhelmingly chose Medicare Supplements.

Remember, we get paid LESS when you choose a Medicare Supplement!

Our interest is in each client choosing the plan that best fits their individual needs. We research and then educate you about plan options *in your area*. You make the final decision. A good Medicare insurance agent should guide, not push you!

Up front, we want you to know it's going to be rocky. Change is constant and scary. We've weathered some massive changes to Medicare over the past 40 years. *Changes to Medicare will continue to come and they will hurt.*

Don't go it alone. A good insurance agent is worth her weight in gold.

POINTS TO REMEMBER

- Not all insurance agents are willing nor able (certified) to sell a variety of Medicare plans. Ask how many companies they represent.

- Some insurance agents express obvious bias toward a certain type of plan, often because it pays them more commissions.

- No agent is allowed to use high-pressure sales tactics, but some try.

- Captive sales agents only work for one insurance company.

- Independent agents can represent as many companies as they wish. A good agent offers you a lot of choices.

- Find an agency that offers help after the sale and doesn't force you to solve your issues with the insurance company alone.

- You have a lot of choices, so choose an agency that will still be around later when you have inevitable problems.

- Read reviews. See what other people are saying before you choose an agency to work with.

CHAPTER 24

SOCIAL SECURITY

You've worked hard your whole life and now it's time to enjoy retirement. That's where Social Security comes in.

Everyone will get a different amount based on how much each person paid in. Some will get very little and others will get close to $5,000 per month. You can see how much you've paid in and what your estimated benefits will be at different ages by setting up your account at **SSA.GOV**.

If you plan to draw Social Security as a Spouse, Ex-Spouse or Widow, you won't have access to that data in your SSA account. Ask your spouse to set up his account if you want to estimate Spousal Social Security benefits. For Ex-Spouse benefit amounts, you'll have to take your marriage license and divorce decree into the SSA office near you.

When should you start drawing benefits?
This is the million-dollar question!

If you think you'll live to 90, draw at 70 so you can get the largest check possible. If you think that you'll live to age 90, but you really need the money to survive now, take it! Even though you are locking in a lower benefit, it may be your lifeline to paying your bills today.

Just like with health benefits, there is no right answer for everyone. This is my attempt to oversimplify the government's crazy rules.

I can't cover it all, so when a topic leaves you with more questions, head over to the government's website **SSA.GOV.**

Let's start at the beginning of the program.

Social Security started in the 1930s. It was meant to be a safety net for *the few people who lived past normal life expectancy.* It was never intended to provide a retirement benefit for every American! Yet today, everyone expects to live long enough to collect a benefit. This leads to the funding problems we now have. The history is actually pretty interesting, but I'll let you do that research on your own.

WHO QUALIFIES?

If you've worked and paid Social Security payroll taxes, you were earning credits toward qualifying for a benefit. You need 40 credits and you can earn 4 credits a year. So, it takes about 10 years to earn enough credits to qualify for Social Security benefits. The more you work and the more you pay into the system, the higher your check will be later. But it's not just your work history that matters. How old you are when you start drawing benefits is important too.

If you draw retirement benefits at your earliest opportunity, age 62, you'll lock in a 30% reduction in your benefits. If you wait to start drawing at your Full Retirement Age (FRA) you'd take home 100% of the amount you are eligible to receive.

You also have the option to wait **past** your FRA and draw at your latest opportunity, age 70, to get the highest benefit.

Don't panic if you were a stay-at-home mom and didn't pay into Social Security. I'll explain below how you can draw based on your spouse or ex-spouse's work record.

AGE IS EVERYTHING

Twenty years ago, President Reagan changed the age to receive your full benefits from age 65, slowly phasing in until everyone will reach FRA at age 67. That phase-in is not yet complete. You may reach your FRA at 66 and 8 months. Your Full Retirement Age depends on the year you were born. Refer to the chart below to determine your FRA:

Full Retirement Age for Social Security Based on Year of Birth

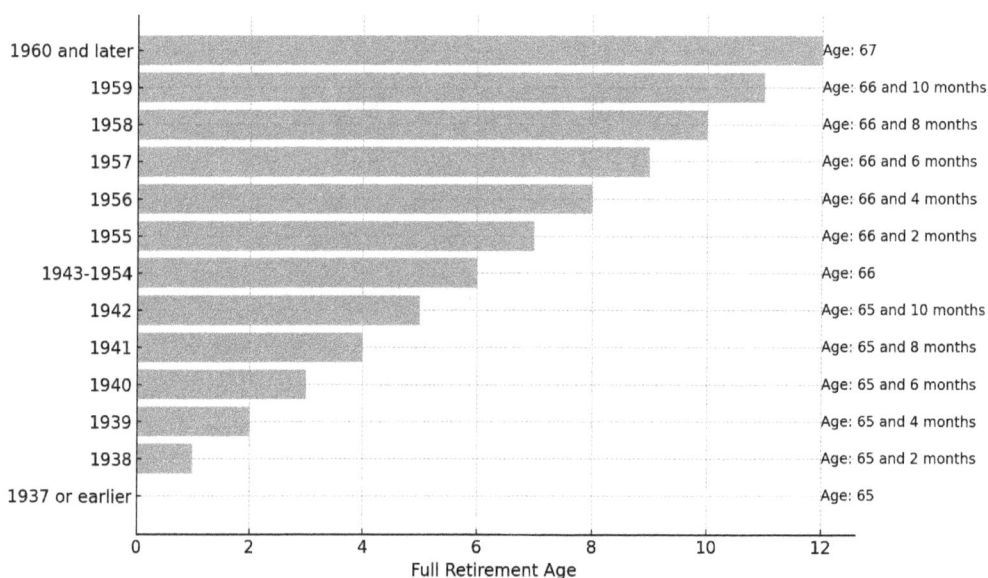

Year of Birth	Full Retirement Age
1960 and later	Age: 67
1959	Age: 66 and 10 months
1958	Age: 66 and 8 months
1957	Age: 66 and 6 months
1956	Age: 66 and 4 months
1955	Age: 66 and 2 months
1943-1954	Age: 66
1942	Age: 65 and 10 months
1941	Age: 65 and 8 months
1940	Age: 65 and 6 months
1939	Age: 65 and 4 months
1938	Age: 65 and 2 months
1937 or earlier	Age: 65

Full Retirement Age

💡 If you were born in 1960 or later, the age of full benefits levels out at age 67.

FREQUENTLY ASKED QUESTIONS

"How much will I get from Social Security?"

I can tell you the AVERAGE person will get about $1,976 per month in 2025. The maximum benefit is $4,018 per month at Full Retirement Age. Those who delay claiming benefits until age 70 can receive up to $5,108 per month, due to delayed retirement credits. The smallest check will be about $50 per month with 11 years paying into FICA and about $1,000 per month with 30 years paying into Social Security.

"My ex was in the NFL and made millions. Why is my spousal benefit so low?"

Because Social Security doesn't tax every dollar (Medicare does). In 2025, only the first $176,100 is subject to Social Security FICA taxes.

"Why is there a limit? It's my money, just let me have it."

According to the government, it's their money. *Ahem*. You must follow their rules, and they say you are NOT retired if you are still working full time. If you draw your social security earlier than your Full Retirement Age, you have an earned income limit. If you exceed that, they take some or even all your Social Security away (you may live long enough to get it back later).

APPLYING FOR SOCIAL SECURITY

There are three primary ways to apply: over the phone, online, and in person. While it is possible to apply over the phone, the wait times are very, very long. The best way to apply or at least ATTEMPT to apply is online. Typically, there is NO need to apply in person.

If your application is considered simple, please apply online! (Simple means you are applying for regular retirement benefits on your own work record.) It should be fast and easy to apply at **SSA.GOV**.

If you must provide them with proof of a change of name, citizenship papers, or proof of marriage or divorce, *it's just easier to apply in person.*

I know that most people don't want to go in person, but you may get the run-around if you don't. And some people are simply not allowed to apply online, such as those applying for widow benefits.

Spouses can technically apply over the phone and mail in proof of

HOW MUCH OF YOUR FULL RETIREMENT AGE BENEFIT WILL YOU GET?

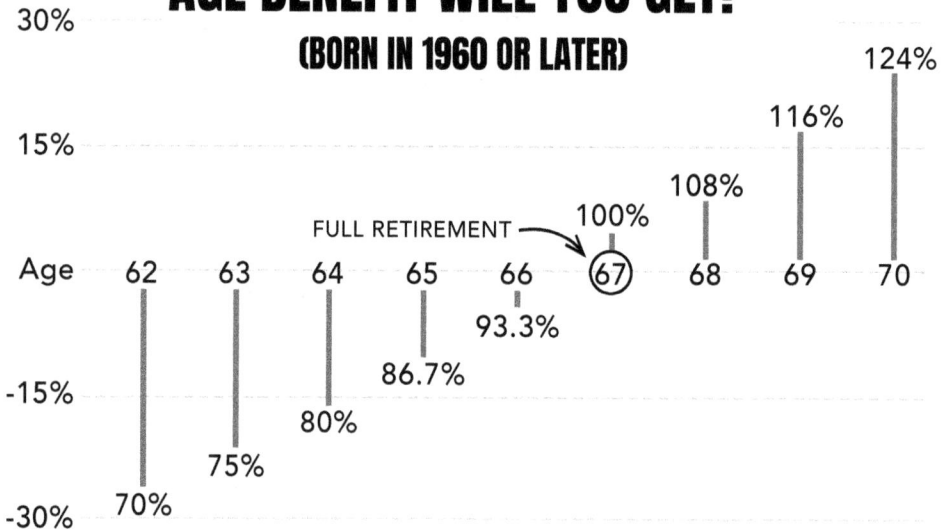

(BORN IN 1960 OR LATER)

30%

15%

FULL RETIREMENT → 100%

124%

116%

108%

Age   62   63   64   65   66   (67)   68   69   70

93.3%

86.7%

-15%

80%

75%

-30%   70%

marriage. As already stated several times, do not mail things into the SSA unless you have no other option.

1. The SSA is likely to "lose" your documents. Then you have to go back a second time.

2. They only accept original documents or certified copies which may cause you to have to go back and get new documents if they lose them!

Sure, there are great, experienced, and friendly people working for the government, but you hear the complaints just like I do.

When I call the SSA, my wait time is so long (more than 30 minutes) that I usually have to hang up because my next appointment is ready. If you have to call the SSA, only do it first thing in the morning and clear your schedule so you can wait and wait. Then be nice and patient, even if they have clearly messed up on their end or lost your paperwork again.

If you get an answer that sounds incorrect, ask him to cite the Program Operations Manual System (POMS). This is kind of rude. You are asking him to prove he is correct, and if you are non-confrontational, it may not be your style but do it anyway. If he is correct, fantastic, no harm done. If the employee gave you incorrect information, this is his chance to read the regulations and get educated.

GETTING PAID

The exact timing of your first payment depends on when your birthday falls within the month. You'll be paid by direct deposit or a Direct Express card (like a debit card). Please opt for direct deposit (if you have a bank account) to avoid fraud and delays!

- Social Security benefits are *paid in arrears*, meaning you receive the payment for the current month in the following month.
- The exact date of your payment depends on your birth date:
  - ⇨ If your birthday is on the 1st to the 10th of the month, you'll get your payment on the second Wednesday of the following month.
  - ⇨ If your birthday is on the 11th to the 20th, your payment will be on the third Wednesday.
  - ⇨ If your birthday is on the 21st to the 31st, your payment will arrive on the fourth Wednesday.

So, depending on the exact timing, your first check could arrive in about 4 to 6 weeks. If your payment is scheduled on a holiday, they pay you a day early, not late.

If you don't have a bank account, the Direct Express card is perfect! It's like a prepaid debit card that lets you spend your benefits, pay bills, or get cash from an ATM, all without needing a bank. It's easy, safe, and you'll still get your payments on time. So, whether you choose direct deposit or the debit card, you'll be all set!

There are some risks with the debit card that you will hear about, such as:

ATM Fees: While you can withdraw money for free at certain ATMs, using out-of-network ATMs can result in fees. It's important to check the ATM network to avoid extra charges.

Limited Access to Cash: You can only withdraw a certain amount of cash per day from an ATM, which can be a problem if you need a large sum at once.

Lost or Stolen Cards: If your debit card is lost or stolen, you'll need to report it and wait for a replacement. While Direct Express has protections in place, this could delay access to your money temporarily.

Customer Service Delays: Some people report difficulties with reaching customer service or experience delays in resolving issues like lost cards or unauthorized charges.

No Interest on Balances: Unlike a bank account, any money left on the card doesn't earn interest, so you're not getting any extra benefit from keeping funds on the debit card.

DEATH AND REPAYMENT

Since you are paid a month in arrears, if you die on the last day of that month, your family will have to return the whole check. If your direct deposit hits your bank account after your death, the bank is required to return it to the SSA.

APPLYING PAST AGE 70

Every year I hear from people that tell me their dad (let's call him Jim) is still working and hasn't filed for Social Security yet and he's 80 years old. What happens in Jim's situation?

Social Security stops growing at age 70. There is no benefit in delaying your benefits past age 70. But Jim is now 80 years old. He will get the amount *he was eligible for at age 70*. Since he doesn't file until age 80, he will get his benefit adjusted for inflation through the annual COLA increases, but essentially, he will get the amount he was eligible for at age 70. Why did Jim not draw at age 70? Typically, this is because he was still working full-time and was under the incorrect impression that he could NOT draw his Social Security while he was still working. A costly mistake!

💡 *Jim can get 6 months of retroactive payments, but not the full 10 years of payments that he is due.*

WHEN TO DRAW

Now you know how to apply, but when you apply depends on when you need the money and when you just plain want it. There is no right or wrong answer. Sure, you'll get less if you draw it sooner, but by getting your money sooner it's worth more. A dollar today is more valuable than a dollar in 5 to 7 years. Many people draw a benefit not to live on, but to invest.

It's your choice whether to draw as soon as possible (age 62) or wait till age 70, or any age in between.

If you haven't already, set up your free account at **SSA.GOV**. Do it now. See how much you've paid in and see the estimate of how much you could draw at every age.

You can't access your spouse or your former spouse's information online. You'll have to take a copy of your marriage certificate and divorce decree into the SSA to get that information.

What you will see online is only an **estimate.** That estimate is based on you continuing to work at your current job until the age you draw.

Factors that can lower the estimate you see on SSA.GOV:

1. **Not Working 35 Years** – Social Security is based on your highest 35 years of earnings. If you worked fewer than 35 years, those missing years are filled in with zeroes, which lowers your average earnings and, in turn, your benefit. If you keep working and replace those years with zeroes, your benefit will go up.

2. **Lower Future Earnings** – The estimate assumes you'll continue earning *at the same income level until you retire.* If you earn less than expected in the coming years or stop working, your benefit will be lower than the estimate.

3. **Inflation Estimates** – The SSA uses assumptions about future inflation and wage growth. If inflation or wage growth turns out to be lower than expected, your actual benefit may not match the estimate.

These factors can all affect what you'll eventually receive, so it's good to keep them in mind when you look at those online estimates!

There is a lot of wiggle room in the estimate you see online. That is without factoring in a reduction in benefits which is likely due to the Social Security funding problem.

Common questions:

- "If I want to quit working at age 60, and wait till age 62 to draw, will my amount be a lower amount than what I see on **SSA.GOV**." Yes.
- "If I stop working at age 55, will it lower my estimated benefit?" Yes.
- "If I get a higher paying job for the next few years prior to retirement, will it *increase* my benefit?" Possibly, if a new year of earnings is higher than one of the years used to calculate your benefit.

BENEFIT CALCULATOR

Your Social Security payments are calculated based on your highest 35 years of earnings. Not your highest 5 or your last 10 years, those are common myths.

Let me walk you through a simplified example to show how the SSA determines your benefit.

Step 1 – Your Record of Earnings

First, the SSA takes your highest 35 years of earnings. If you didn't work for 35 years, they fill in zeros for the missing years. The more zeroes, the lower your benefit will be. Let's assume you have 35 years of earnings and no zeros.

Step 2 – Adjust for Inflation (They call this Indexing)

The SSA adjusts your past earnings to account for inflation, so earnings from earlier years are increased to reflect today's value.

Step 3 – Calculate the Average Indexed Monthly Earnings (AIME)

Once your earnings are adjusted for inflation, the SSA adds up your highest 35 years of indexed earnings and divides the total by 420 (the number of months in 35 years). This gives you your Average Indexed Monthly Earnings (AIME).

If your 35 years of earnings is $2,940,000, divide that by 420 for a total of $7,000

So, your AIME is $7,000.

Step 4 – Apply the Social Security Formula to Calculate Your Primary Insurance Amount (PIA)

Using the formula for 2024:

- 90% of the first $1,280 of AIME.

- 32% of the AIME between $1,281 and $6,493.

- 15% of the AIME over $6,493.

Here's the breakdown:

- **90% of the first $1,280**:
  $1,280 × 0.90 = $1,152

- **32% of the amount between $1,281 and $6,493**:
  ($6,493 − $1,280) × 0.32 = $1,666.56

- **15% of the amount over $6,493**:
  ($7,000 − $6,493) × 0.15 = $75.45

Now, add them together to get your **PIA:**

PIA = $1,152 + $1,666.56 + $75.45 = $2,894.01

So, your Primary Insurance Amount (PIA) is $2,894 per month if you claim benefits at your FRA.

Step 5 – Adjust for Early or Delayed Retirement

If you claim before or after your FRA, your benefits will be adjusted. Here's how it works for claiming at 62 or 70:

1. Claiming at age 62:

   ⇨ You will receive 70% of your PIA, because you're claiming early.

   ⇨ This reduction is permanent. Your amount won't increase when you reach your FRA later.

   ⇨ So, if you claim at age 62, your monthly benefit will be $2,026.

2. Claiming at age 70:

   ⇨ You will receive 124% of your PIA, thanks to Delayed Retirement Credits.

   ⇨ If you wait until age 70, your monthly benefit will be $3,588.

Summary:

- If you claim at age 62, your benefit will be $2,026 per month.
- If you claim at your FRA (around 66 or 67), you will get your full benefit of $2,894 per month.
- If you wait until age 70, your benefit will increase to $3,588 per month.

This shows how waiting until later can significantly boost your monthly Social Security payment if you think you are healthy enough to live to the break-even point.

DELAYING UNTIL AGE 70

To calculate the break-even point, we need to figure out how long it will take if you wait until age 70 compared to claiming Social Security at age 62. This break-even point is when the total benefits received from claiming at age 70 surpass the total benefits you would have received by starting at age 62.

Step 1 – Sample Monthly Benefits[1]

- Benefit at age 62 is $2,026 per month.
- Benefit at age 70 is $3,588 per month.

Step 2 – Calculate Total Benefits from Age 62 to 70

If you claim at age 62, you will receive $2,026 per month for 8 years (from age 62 to 70).

$2,026 × 12 × 8 = $194,496

By the time you turn 70, you would have received a total of $194,496 if you claimed at 62.

Step 3 – Calculate Monthly Difference

If you wait until age 70, you'll get $3,588 per month, which is $1,562 more per month than if you claimed at 62.

$3,588 − $2,026 = $1,562

Step 4 – Calculate Your Break-Even Point

Now, we divide the total amount you would have received by age 70 vs. claiming at age 62, by the difference in monthly benefits:

$194,496 / 1,562 = 124.5 months

---

1   All figures courtesy of ChatGPT. This girl can't do that math on her own!

Step 5 – Determine Your Break-Even Age

If you start collecting at age 70, the break-even point is 10 years and 5 months later, which means you'll need to live until about age 80 and 5 months if you wait until 70 to collect SSA instead of claiming at 62.

Be Realistic About Your Longevity

Look at your family history and your own health realistically. How long do you expect to live? Who cares if you get 24% per month MORE if you wait till age 70 *if everyone in your family dies in their mid 70s*?

Deciding when to draw Social Security is a very personal choice, and there's no one-size-fits-all answer. It depends on your health, finances, and how long you think you'll live. Some people need the money as soon as they're eligible, while others can afford to wait and maximize their benefit. It's all about what works best for *you* and your situation. Just like choosing the best health insurance option, *it's all a gamble!*

Now, let's see WHO qualifies for Social Security.

You may think that every American qualifies for about $1,500 per month at age 65. I've heard that myth thousands of times. In reality, not everyone qualifies for Social Security benefits.

If you or your spouse have worked and paid into Social Security FICA payroll taxes for at least 10 years, you qualify for a Social Security retirement benefit for life.

💡 *While our office can give you advice and help enrolling into Medicare, we can't give advice on Social Security. When you have specific questions, you'll have to go into your local SSA office or call the national office at 1-800-772-1213.*

There are almost 3,000 rules for the 1,200 SSA employees to master. They have an operations manual that is 20,000 pages. This is a lot of information to digest! You need to know they face these hurdles because *you can't rely on them to give you correct information.*

Sadly, you may have to go into the SSA armed with proof and argue with them until they look up the rule and see you are correct. Too many people are turned away, only to go home and find out via Google that they were eligible for benefits. Then they have to go back to the SSA again. It's a cycle of frustration!

FILE AND SUSPEND

Contrary to popular belief, the program known as **File and Suspend** no longer exists. Here's a quick explanation before we get back to the nitty gritty of SSA benefits.

Social Security ended the File and Suspend loophole back in 2016. Before 2016, the File and Suspend strategy allowed a person (usually the higher earner in a couple) to file for benefits and then immediately suspend them. This did two key things:

1. **It allowed the spouse to claim spousal benefits** based on the higher earner's record, even though the higher earner wasn't actually collecting their own benefits.

2. **It let the higher earner's own benefits continue to grow** by earning delayed retirement credits (about 8% per year) until age 70.

This strategy was a popular way for couples to maximize their Social Security benefits by allowing the higher earner to boost their benefit while the lower-earning spouse could still receive spousal benefits during that time.

The Bipartisan Budget Act of 2015 was aimed at closing certain loopholes. The File and Suspend strategy was seen as a loophole that allowed some individuals to game the system.

Essentially, Congress felt the strategy was allowing wealthier individuals to increase their lifetime benefits in a way that strained the Social Security trust fund.

Now, if you suspend your benefits after filing, your spouse (or any other dependents) can't collect benefits on your record while your benefits are suspended. If you suspend your benefits, all benefits based on your record will also stop.

What does this mean for you now?

- If you **file** for Social Security and later **suspend** your benefits, your spouse or dependents **can't collect** spousal or dependent benefits during the suspension.

- However, if you **suspend your benefits after reaching Full Retirement Age,** your own benefit will still continue to grow by **8% per year** up until age 70, but you can't use File and Suspend to let others collect during that time.

Now, when you suspend your benefits, no one can collect on your record until you start your benefits up again.

GO TO THE SSA PREPARED

Save yourself time and a lot of frustration, avoiding several trips to your local SSA, by learning on your own as much as you can about your unique situation.

The government employees cannot give you advice. They can explain your rights, *but not recommend what you should do.*

There are Registered Social Security Analysts (RSSA) that you can hire. Some Certified Professional Advisors (CFP) often understand Social Security. Many don't. When you are choosing which professional to hire for retirement advice, *ask how long they've advised on this topic and how much experience they have.*

Unfortunately, most of the "free dinner seminars" to teach you "how to optimize your Social Security" are just a guise to sell you an investment. They know that retirees have money in their 401(k), IRA, or bank accounts, and they want to help you invest it. There is no magic to optimizing your Social Security. What they will tell you is the longer you wait to draw, the higher your benefit will be.

Learn as much as you can, but never feel pressured to sign up for anything, especially if they put a time limit on it. Run if "This deal only lasts for 15 more minutes!"

If you call the SSA and don't get the information you need, or the information sounds incorrect (because you've done your homework), hang up and call back again.

One of my clients recently told me she called the SSA and they told her she was ineligible to draw spousal benefits. She had watched my videos and knew to hang up and call back to talk to another person. Sure enough, the next employee knew the rules and was able to help her. Sadly, many people would have stopped with the first answer and lost thousands of dollars in retirement!

> This may be the most valuable piece of advice in the entire book. This goes for information you get not just from Social Security but from Medicare and the IRS as well: Call a few times, see if you get the SAME information before you accept their information as reliable.

COMMON REASONS FOR MISTAKES

1. You got married or divorced and changed your name and didn't tell the SSA.

2. Your employer used your wrong Social Security number.

3. Your employer never paid the money to the government (and your employer is now long gone).

With all things government, it takes time to get results. Take *proof* of marriage or divorce, earnings such as a W-2 form, a copy of your old tax returns, any other documents that showed their mistake. It's best to go in person because they need to see your documents.

PRIMARY INSURANCE AMOUNT

Your Primary Insurance Amount (PIA) is how the SSA determines what to pay you. Earlier in this chapter, you learned that you can earn 100% of your benefit at your Full Retirement Age. But you'll also see that you can earn 124% of your benefit at age 70.

Note that I don't use the term PIA in any of my educational videos. I use the term FRA, for Full Retirement Age, which isn't as accurate *but remember I'm trying to simplify.*

You reach your PIA at your Full Retirement Age. They take your highest 35 years of earnings (you may have some years with $0s) and index that for inflation. They round up and down and have some other calculations they do to help raise the benefits of the lowest earners, and voila, they arrive at your PIA.

> If you qualify for Social Security disability, you will get a monthly check equal to your PIA, even though you are not yet at your Full Retirement Age.

The government automatically raises your PIA to when there is an increase in benefits due to a COLA.

DELAYED RETIREMENT CREDITS

For every year that you wait to draw your Social Security past your Full Retirement Age, you'll earn a guaranteed 8% return up to age 70. This is basically the government bribing you to draw later. These are called **Delayed Retirement Credits** (DRC). *These extra credits will not benefit* *your spouse if she draws on your record. But they will benefit your widow. I'll get into this more later.*

DIVORCE AND REMARRIAGE

Many people are eligible for several benefits. I will use my own case as an example.

- Even though I was a stay-at-home mom for five years, I had a good job later (I trained Medicare insurance agents for a living) and qualified to draw off my **own work record**.

- I divorced my first husband (a great guy, by the way) after a 24-year marriage. I could have drawn off my **former spouse's work record**, but I remarried Dave (also a great guy).

- Since Dave and I have been married for at least one year, I now qualify to draw as a **spousal** off his work record.

- But wait, I'm the higher earner, so both men could potentially draw off MY work record. I will never draw off either of their Social Security work records.

- My ex is remarried. But if his current wife and I both die, he becomes a **widower**. He would then be eligible again to draw off my work record or hers, whichever was higher.

- If I die, both my ex and my current spouse could draw widower benefits off my work record.

> You may be eligible for several Social Security benefits, but you can only draw one benefit at a time.

You may be able to draw a benefit:

1. Off your **own work record** because you paid into Social Security FICA payroll taxes at least ten years (they don't need to be consecutive) and you are age 62 or qualify for disability.

2. Off the **work record of your spouse** if your spouse qualifies and you've been married at least one year, you are at least age 62, and your spouse is drawing his own Social Security benefits.

3. Off the work record of a **qualified former spouse** if your marriage lasted at least 10 consecutive years and you are currently single (even if you had remarried and re-divorced).

4. Off a **parent's work record** if you are a minor and your parent is drawing their own Social Security or a Disability payment.

5. Off your **deceased spouse's work record** if you are a qualified survivor and the marriage lasted at least 9 months, or you had a minor child together.

6. Off your **deceased former spouse's work record**, if that marriage lasted at least 10 years and you are age 60, currently single, and only working part time.

In all these scenarios, drawing benefits off another person's work record will not in any way reduce the amount of social security benefits that worker receives!

It's unfortunate how many women have told me they are not taking a higher social security benefit off their former spouse because it would anger him, his new wife, or their kids.

Spread the word! Drawing Social Security benefits off another person's work record does not lower their benefit! No harm to your ex. There is no impact on his new wife.

Social Security is not negotiated in a divorce court.

Marital assets are divided in the divorce. If you were awarded alimony and he is behind, as soon as your former spouse draws his Social Security you can file to garnish it. You can also garnish for back child support (even if the kids are grown or deceased, this money goes to you).

GARNISHMENTS EXPLAINED

💡 *People who owe back state and federal income taxes are reluctant to file for Social Security benefits because they assume the government will hold their whole check. That's not true. The government can only garnish 15% of your check each month. You have a minimum of $750 per month in Social Security benefits that is protected from tax garnishment. This means if your monthly benefit is less than $750, it cannot be garnished for back taxes. There is no minimum protected amount for back child support and alimony.*

The amount of your Social Security that can be garnished depends on several factors, including whether you are supporting another family. Here's a breakdown of the limits:

1. If you are supporting another spouse or child, up to 50% of your Social Security benefits can be garnished for back child support and/or alimony payments.

2. If you are not supporting another spouse or child, up to 60% of your benefits can be garnished.

3. If payments are over 12 weeks late, these limits increase to 55% and 65%, respectively.

Supplemental Security Income (SSI), however, is not subject to garnishment for alimony or child support.

If you're concerned about garnishment, it's always a good idea to consult a legal professional to understand how state laws may impact your specific case.

COST OF LIVING ADJUSTMENTS

The government tells us we get a benefit that will keep pace with inflation and most years we get a Cost of Living Adjustment (COLA). 2023 was a year with high inflation and a record high COLA of 8.7%. But that was not the actual rate of inflation for retirees. The government thinks we don't notice, but we do. A typical COLA increase is 1% to 3%.

COLA helps *but doesn't make your benefits keep pace with actual inflation* because it's not based on things retirees actually spend money on, such as medications.

Scam Alert: COLAs do happen most years and occur automatically in January. You don't have to apply for the raise. **Any emails that tell you to apply or call in are scams.**

SUPPLEMENTAL SECURITY INCOME

If you qualify for regular Social Security retirement, but your benefit is very low because you didn't work much and had a low paying job, you may qualify for SSI if your income stays under the annual limit. In 2025 that is **$9,204 per year ($767 per month)** for an individual and **$13,080 per year ($1,090 per month)** for a couple.

These limits refer to countable income, meaning some types of income (like a portion of earned wages, housing subsidies, or SNAP benefits) may not count fully or at all against the limit. Some states provide additional supplemental payments, which can affect these limits slightly.

To apply, you can start the process at **SSA.GOV** but then you'll need to go in for a follow-up appointment to show proof of your financial need.

People often confuse Supplemental Security Income (SSI) with the program for the disabled (SSDI). To make it more confusing, one person can be on both programs!

SSI is a program that helps people who don't have much money and need extra help to pay for their food and housing. To receive this benefit, you must be 65 or older or be any age if you are blind or have a disability. Unlike regular Social Security benefits, you don't have to have worked and paid into the system to qualify for SSI.

If you qualify for SSI, you may also qualify for Medicaid to help with medical bills and food stamps for groceries.

How to qualify for SSI

You can't have much income, money saved, or many assets. If you are single, you can't have more than $2,000 in assets and if you are married it's $3,000. They won't count your house or the car you drive. Things you own that could disqualify you from SSI include cash, investments, land of a house you don't live in, cash value of life insurance with a value over $1,500.

How people commonly lose SSI benefits

This seems cruel, but COLA adjustments in your Social Security checks could cause you to make too much money to keep your SSI. You can't decline COLA and it may end up hurting more than it helps you.

Many people may lose SSI and other forms of assistance when they receive an inheritance. This is something to immediately contact an estate planning attorney for help with because you can buy a new car, remodel your bathroom, or use the money for other things *so you can again qualify for assistance.*

Marriage affects your eligibility for SSI because your spouse's income is now included. But don't think just living together is a work-around because the government considers that free housing as in-kind support and maintenance. It is important to report your living situation to the SSA so they can adjust your payments so you don't get yourself into an overpayment situation.

SOCIAL SECURITY IS GENDER NEUTRAL

If you out-earned your spouse, you will draw your own higher benefit, and your lower-earning spouse may be able to draw off your work record.

People think the female always draws off the male, and that's generally been true for the 80 years of the Social Security program because men typically out-earned women. But it can be the other way around too.

As my generation (born in the 1960s) reaches retirement age, more couples will draw their own benefits. Spousal benefits only come into play when ½ of your spouse's Social Security is more than all your own benefits. If your spouse just slightly out-earned you, you'll only draw your own Social Security.

THE FRUSTRATING REALITY

When the government forces us to contribute to Social Security, many are under the misconception there is a pot of money sitting in Washington, DC with our name on it.

Yes, you are forced to pay into the system. But the system is based on the premise that not everyone will live to draw their money. It's all a gamble, remember? It's baked into the system that many will pay in much more than they ever draw out. It's not a flaw of the system, it's the foundation. Benefits are weighted to pay the lower earners more.

NOT YOUR SOLE SOURCE OF INCOME

Social Security was never meant to be your sole source of retirement. Never!

Day #1, back in the 1930s, when FDR signed Social Security into law, it was projected to *only be drawn by a few people*. Life expectancy back then was age 57. Few lived to draw Social Security.

Social Security was only meant to provide ⅓ of your retirement. Back in the 1930s people commonly had company pensions to provide ⅓ of their retirement. The government expected retirees to save another ⅓ on their own, so they could maintain their standard of living in the very few years they would be retired.

Now, 80-some years since FDR signed Social Security into law, a lot has changed in our society:

1. People are having fewer and fewer kids.

2. People are living longer.

As discussed earlier in this book, everyone expects to live long enough to draw Social Security, but getting a company pension is rare. Sure, some have 401(k) accounts at work, but they are not as rich as prior pension plans, and not all people have access to a 401(k).

The rest of us can set up an IRA, but many are paying for college, helping their adult kids or parents, and don't have any money left to save for retirement. You are not alone!

Many Americans live off their monthly Social Security check ONLY.

How can they afford to do that? Many people:

- Trim their budgets to survive.

- Move into smaller homes, or sell and become renters.

- Take a Reverse Mortgage (a last resort when you don't want to move but are house rich and cash poor).

- Rely on family members to get by financially.

- Move to Mexico, Costa Rica, or Thailand — areas with large expatriate communities to stretch the American dollar.

That is why it is critical you are learning this information. It is likely to help you or someone you know increase their benefits. *Please share this book*. Nothing has been more gratifying than people writing to tell me they got a raise in retirement because one of my videos alerted them to a higher benefit via divorce or death that they didn't know they qualified for.

POINTS TO REMEMBER

- You or your spouse must work 10 years and pay into Social Security to receive a benefit.

- If you can, apply online, but if you need to mail in documents, it might be faster to just go in person to apply.

- Check your earnings record for errors.

- Your Full Retirement Age (FRA) varies depending on when you were born.

- If you draw earlier than FRA, you lock in a permanently lower amount.

- If you draw past your FRA, you get a guaranteed additional 8% each year till age 70.

- There is no right time to retire. You have to make a personal decision based on your health and budget.

- If you owe back taxes, child support, or alimony, your benefits can be garnished (but regular creditors can't garnish your Social Security benefits).

- If we have inflation, your check will go up with a COLA increase.

- How much you draw off *your own work record* is based on the highest 35 years of earnings, not the top 5 or the last 10 years; both are modern myths.

- Apply 4 months before you want your benefits to start.

- SSI is a form of financial assistance. Even if you receive Social Security, you may also qualify for SSI to help you survive.

- If your income or assets increase, you can lose SSI. Be truthful with the SSA so you don't get into an overpayment situation.

- Social Security benefits stop growing at age 70. You should file by then to avoid losing out on payments.

- If you delay filing past 70, you can receive up to six months of retroactive payments — but not the full amount you missed since turning 70.

CHAPTER 25

SPOUSAL SOCIAL SECURITY BENEFITS

When it comes to Social Security, it's not just about what you've earned yourself; your spouse's work record can open up a whole new set of benefits for you. Whether you're the higher or lower earner in the relationship, understanding spousal benefits can help you and your partner maximize what you've got coming in retirement.

If you spent years raising a family or running the household and didn't work enough to qualify for your own Social Security benefits, don't worry, spousal benefits have you covered!

Even if you didn't pay into Social Security, you can still get up to 50% of your spouse's benefit. This is great news for stay-at-home parents who worked hard in their own way. Social Security recognizes how important your role was, so you won't miss out when it's time for retirement. You'll still get the support you deserve, based on your spouse's work history.

> The great thing is that spousal benefits
> don't reduce what your spouse receives.

Whether you've worked a little, a lot, or not at all, you can still tap into your spouse's Social Security benefit to help ensure your financial security in retirement. However, the timing of when both of you start drawing benefits can impact how much you'll receive, so it's important to understand the rules and make a strategy that works best for your situation.

Let's break it all down.

- **How do you qualify?** You must be married for at least one year.

- **What percentage of your spouse's benefit can you claim?** Up to 50% of the amount that your spouse is entitled to at his Full Retirement Age.

- **How to apply?** Online, over the phone, or in person. The SSA needs proof of marriage and divorce, which might mean going in person is faster.

- **How much will it reduce my spouse's own retirement if I file for spousal benefits?** None at all.

First, let's talk about how spousal benefits work. To be eligible, your spouse needs to have started collecting his own Social Security retirement benefits.

> If he wants to wait until 70, you can't claim as a spouse until then. You two need to calculate how much money you are giving up by not drawing all those years and it may change your plans.

I'm often told, "I understand I'll take a reduction for drawing at age 62, but that's OK because when my spouse later draws his own Social Security, I'll be able to get 50% of his benefits since I'll then be at my own FRA." This is incorrect.

You can start getting spousal benefits as early as age 62, but keep in mind that starting early means your monthly checks will be smaller. If you wait until your Full Retirement Age (around 66 or 67), you'll get 50% of your spouse's full benefit amount. But if you decide to start at 62, the amount you'll be eligible to draw as a spouse goes down to around 30%.

So, when it comes to Social Security, timing really does matter!

This doesn't mean I don't support you drawing early, I just want you to understand the amount you draw is permanently reduced. Your check will not increase when you reach your FRA. So, make sure you are happy with that reduced benefit for as long as your spouse lives. If you outlive him, you can move to a higher benefit as a widow.

THE SPOUSAL TOP-OFF PROGRAM

If your spousal benefit is higher than what you'd get from your own work history, Social Security will still pay out. You draw your lower benefit and some from your spouse's higher benefit. This is called the spousal top-off. (My explanation here is accurate, but the term "top-off" is unofficial and not used by the government.)

Let's walk through Vani and Mark's situation:

- Vani was a homemaker and worked part-time jobs.
- Vani's retirement benefit is based on her own work record because she earned 40 credits.
- She'll receive **$800 per month** at her FRA.
- Her spouse Mark's benefit at his FRA is **$3,500 per month**.
- Vani is eligible for ½ of Mark's benefit, which is **$1,750**.
- The SSA pays Vani her own $800 and the top-off is the extra money she needs to get to **$1,750**.
- Vani's spousal top-off is **$950**.
- I never explain spousal benefits this way in my videos. I just say "Vani is eligible for ½ of Mark's amount if she waits to draw until her FRA." What Vani wants to know is how much money she can get. *She doesn't care how the government bookkeeps it!*

> Social Security does the math for you, so you
> don't have to choose which benefit to draw —
> you'll automatically get whichever benefit is larger.

One of the key things to understand is **your spouse's benefit doesn't get reduced** when you start drawing spousal benefits. In other words, if your spouse is getting $2,000 per month, you can collect up to 50% of that amount as a spousal benefit without affecting the $2,000 he is getting.

Social Security recognizes the value of the work you did at home, and spousal benefits ensure that even if you weren't paying into the system, you still have access to retirement income. This is a big relief for many families, especially those where one spouse earned significantly more than the other, or where one spouse didn't work outside the home for many years.

QUALIFYING FOR SPOUSAL BENEFITS

To qualify for spousal Social Security benefits, you must typically be legally married to your spouse. However, there are exceptions where you may still qualify for benefits even if you're no longer married or were in certain other types of relationships. You might have benefits waiting for you!

DIVORCED SPOUSES

You can still qualify for spousal benefits based on your ex-spouse's record if:

- You were married for at least 10 years.
- You are currently unmarried.
- Your ex-spouse is eligible for Social Security benefits, meaning he is age 62 whether he's claimed his Social Security or not.
- You are also at least 62 years old.

- The spousal benefit you are eligible for is higher than the benefit based on your own work record.

- You will need your *original* marriage license or a *certified copy* to file for benefits, along with your divorce decree. Get a copy at the courthouse in the county where you married. It's a small fee and takes a few weeks, so start early.

- You have been divorced for at least 2 years.

THE 2-YEAR RULE EXPLAINED

If you're divorced and looking to collect Social Security benefits based on your ex-spouse's work record, there's a little catch: you usually need to have been divorced for at least two years before you can claim those benefits — **but only if your ex hasn't started collecting yet.** If your ex is already receiving Social Security, you can apply right away. It's like the Social Security folks want to make sure the dust has fully settled before you start drawing on your ex's work history.

"My divorce decree says I can't draw Social Security off my ex." This is unenforceable.

There is nothing you could sign in your divorce decree that allows you to give up your rights to draw Social Security benefits. Meaning, that clause your ex's attorney inserted into your paperwork *is not binding*.

Why do attorneys put unenforceable language in divorce paperwork?

1. Misunderstanding

Sometimes, attorneys may not realize certain provisions aren't enforceable. Not all attorneys are well versed in Social Security law.

2. Some attorneys are jerks.

There, I said it. (I'm an attorney so I can say it.)

3. Client Demands

Your ex-spouse might have insisted on his attorney including certain terms in the paperwork, even if the attorney knows they may not be enforceable. That makes them both jerks.

4. Ambiguity on Your Part

I think some women see, "I give up all rights to his retirement" in their divorce paperwork and assume that means not only his pension at work, but also his Social Security benefits. This isn't the fault of your ex's attorney, but your own attorney for not explaining to you this language *doesn't include Social Security benefits.*

> Spousal benefits are based on the 35 highest years of earnings, not the income during the marriage.

The amount you receive as a spouse is based on your ex's 35 highest earning years — even if those years occurred before, during, or after your marriage. You are not limited to the years you were married to him.

Chris and Karen married young:

They were married from age 18 to 28. Chris was a drinker. He didn't work much. Karen supported them financially.

They divorced because he refused to work (sound familiar?).

But then Chris got into a groove in his 30s and got rich!

Chris far out-earned Karen over their careers. She is eligible to draw as a former spouse on the amount of money he is eligible to receive at his Full Retirement Age. *Even though he was broke during their marriage.*

> You don't earn more or less based on what number wife you were.

The first wife who was married to Ed for 30 years is eligible to earn the same spousal benefit as his new wife of only 1 year. Neither has priority; they can each draw up to 50% as a spouse off Ed's work record (as long as they meet the other qualifications). Ed could have a current wife and three prior marriages that all lasted 10 years.

All four women are eligible to draw the same percentage from his work record — **no one gets priority over the others**. But the actual dollar amount each one receives can be very different. Why? Because they all chose to start drawing at different ages. The earlier they filed, the bigger the reduction in their monthly check. Social Security doesn't care which wife or ex-wife was first, last, or in the middle — everyone who qualifies gets their fair share, based on their own filing decisions.

COMMON-LAW MARRIAGE

A lot of couples think they're in a common-law marriage just because they've lived together for years. But that's not how the government sees it. While some states recognize common-law marriage, most do not. If you live in one of the few states that do, you might qualify for spousal Social Security benefits — but only if you meet all the specific requirements. To be eligible, you must:

- Have been living together in a state that recognizes common-law marriages at the time the marriage began.

- Provide documentation (affidavits or other legal proof) that shows you were in a common-law marriage.

The Social Security Administration will evaluate your case based on the laws of the state where you live or where the common-law marriage was established. Most states have outlawed common-law marriage, but it is possible (I didn't say easy) to prove common-law marriage.

These are the states that currently recognize common law marriage:

- Colorado
- Kansas
- Texas
- DC
- Montana
- Utah
- Iowa
- New Hampshire

Check out these forms if you need to verify your marriage: **SS-754 and SS-753.** These forms will give you an idea of what proof you need to win your case.

Grandfathered Common-Law States

These states no longer recognize common-law marriage but they will grandfather in your marriage if you met the requirements *before they changed their laws.* Here are the dates they stopped recognizing common-law marriages. If you met the requirements before these dates, you have a good chance of getting it approved:

- **Alabama** – January 1, 2017
- **Ohio** – October 10, 1991
- **Georgia** – January 1, 1997
- **Idaho** – January 1, 1996
- **Pennsylvania** – January 1, 2005
- **Florida** – January 1, 1968
- **South Carolina** – July 1, 2019

Proving you meet the requirements will vary depending on your state. If you think you may qualify, it's worth looking into.

SAME-SEX MARRIAGE

Any legally married couples are eligible for spousal benefits. Gender is irrelevant. The Supreme Court rulings that legalized same-sex marriage across the U.S. mean all legally married couples have the same rights to spousal Social Security benefits.

You can't get Social Security if you only have a civil union or domestic partnership. In most cases, if you want spousal Social Security benefits, you have to be legally married.

PUTATIVE SPOUSE

A Putative Spouse is someone who **believes in good faith** that she was legally married, but due to some legal defect (like an undisclosed prior marriage or an invalid marriage license), the marriage is not legally valid. In this situation, a putative spouse may be entitled to many of the same rights as a legal spouse, depending on the state where she lives.

If the state where you live or where the marriage took place recognizes your rights as a putative spouse, then you may be able to claim spousal Social Security benefits based on your putative spouse's work record.

Conditions for drawing as a putative spouse:

1. **Good Faith Belief** – You must have believed in good faith that you were legally married.

2. **State Law** – The state you live in or where the marriage occurred must recognize putative spouses.

3. **Other Requirements** – You'll still need to meet the general requirements for spousal Social Security benefits, such as being married for at least 1 year for regular spousal benefits, or at least 10 years for divorced spousal benefits.

Let's look at Pearl and Paul's case as an example:

Pearl was married to Paul. She had every reason to believe it was a valid marriage, but 30 years later discovered that Paul was still legally married to someone else. The state might recognize Pearl as a **putative spouse**. If so, and if all other conditions are met, she could still be eligible to draw Social Security spousal benefits. It will depend on her specific state law and whether the SSA recognizes her rights as a putative spouse. If you're in this situation, it's a good idea to consult with an attorney to determine your eligibility.

While being legally married is the typical requirement, there are exceptions. Always be sure to check your specific situation to see if you qualify under these exceptions.

MARRIAGE AND DIVORCE RULES ARE DIFFERENT

To claim benefits when you are married, you only have to be legally married for **one year**. You don't have to live together. You don't have to change your surname. You might even be legally separated for the past 20 years or more!

A lot of retirees don't want to mess with the legalities of divorce or remarriage. But marriage gives certain protections for Medicare, and especially Social Security, that often make a dramatic financial difference.

COHABITATION

Ted and Jane have lived together for 30 years. They raised three kids, shared all assets, and in all ways acted like a married couple. Jane was a stay-at-home mom most of her life. Ted vowed never to marry. He "doesn't need a paper to prove he loves her" bla bla bla.

Ted dies. Jane doesn't live in a state that recognizes common-law marriage. She can't claim Social Security widow benefits off Ted's work history. She didn't work much, so her monthly check is under $1000. If she's lucky, she may have inherited enough money to live on, or it may be a struggle.

If you are in a Ted and Jane situation right now, get married! After only one year of marriage, Jane qualifies for up to 50% of Ted's Social Security benefits. After only 9 months of marriage, if Ted dies, Jane is eligible for up to 100% of his Social Security check as a widow.

> If you are going to draw Spousal Social Security, there is no benefit to waiting past your Full Retirement Age.

Your amount will max out at your Full Retirement Age, *even if your spouse drew his own benefits early*. Your benefits are based on what he was eligible to draw at his Full Retirement Age, not the age he actually started Social Security. He may have taken a reduction, *but that won't impact your ability to draw 50% of what he was eligible to draw had he waited till his own Full Retirement Age.*

What if you marry and divorce the same spouse? Can you add up the years to qualify for spousal benefits?

Unfortunately, you can't add up the years from two separate marriages to the same spouse to qualify for spousal Social Security benefits.

Let's summarize marriage, divorce, and remarriage rules:

- To be eligible for spousal benefits, you must be married for only one year.

- To qualify for spousal benefits when you are divorced, your prior marriage must have lasted for *at least 10 continuous years.*

If you divorce and remarry the same person, you can't add the years together to qualify. If the first marriage lasted 10+ years, you qualify under divorce rules. If the first marriage only lasted 5 years and then you remarry, you'll qualify as a spouse after 1 year of the new marriage.

TWO DIFFERENT WAITING PERIODS

If you are drawing spousal benefits off a former spouse and you remarry, *those benefits stop.* You then have to wait one year to be eligible to draw off your new spouse (assuming ½ of his Social Security benefit is more than all of your own). So, what do you do for the one year? If you can draw off your own work history, you'll draw your own benefits. Then when the year is up, you can move up to the spousal benefit on your new spouse's work record.

Let's look at Ida's situation:

Ida was married to Norm for 10 years. She divorced him. She had to wait two years after her divorce was final to be able to draw spousal benefits off Norm's work record. Instead, she immediately married John. As soon as she married John, she lost her ability to draw on Norm's work record. She had to wait a year after marrying John before she could draw off his work record. If she later divorced John, she is again single and eligible to again draw off Norm's work record!

ABUSE AND HARASSMENT

Women in abusive relationships don't want to poke the bear. The thought of drawing Social Security off their ex's work record can feel risky — like it might set him off and lead to more problems.

Women always ask me these questions:

- Does the SSA notify my ex when I apply to draw Social Security off his work record? No.
- If he calls the SSA and asks, will they tell him she is drawing off his work record? Yes, but he'll have to wait on the phone for 30 minutes to 2 hours, like the rest of us to get that info.
- Will it reduce his own benefits? Not at all.
- Why would he care then? Some people still do!

OFF-THE-BOOKS INCOME

What to do about spousal Social Security when your spouse was paid under the table and didn't contribute to FICA?

If your spouse was paid in cash or off the books and didn't report his income, claiming spousal Social Security benefits can be tough.

Social Security is based on reported earnings — no taxes paid means no record, which can reduce or even eliminate your benefits.

Here's what you can do if your spouse was paid under the table:

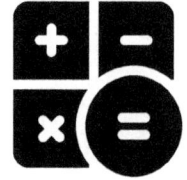

1. Verify Any Reported Earnings

You are not allowed to check your spouse's Social Security earnings record at **SSA.GOV**. Let's say he left it open and you walked by and saw it. Even if your spouse was paid under the table, he may have reported some income or worked other jobs where they paid into Social Security. It's crucial to know what's been officially recorded.

If you can ask him, ask him.

If you are divorced, the only way to find this information is to take a copy of your marriage license and divorce decree into your local SSA office.

2. Encourage Reporting Future Earnings

If your spouse is still working, encourage him to start reporting all future income and paying Social Security taxes. This will help build up his earnings record, which will not only benefit him in retirement but will also impact your eligibility for spousal benefits.

3. Review Other Sources of Income

If your spouse has minimal or no reported Social Security earnings, you may want to focus on other retirement resources like:

- **Pension plans** – Some employers offer pensions that don't require Social Security taxes, so check whether your spouse is eligible for any other retirement benefits.

- **Personal savings or investments** – Consider how savings, IRAs, or other investments can fill the gap left by missing Social Security benefits.

4. Claim Your Own Social Security (If Eligible)

If your spouse's under-the-table work means his earnings record is limited, you may still be eligible for Social Security benefits *based on your own work history.* You can compare your own benefits to the potential spousal benefit and see which provides a higher payout. Social Security automatically gives you the higher of the two when you file.

5. Consult with a Social Security Expert or Tax Professional

In complex situations where under-the-table work is involved, it's a good idea to speak with a **Social Security expert** or **tax professional** to assess your options. They can help you understand what your spouse's limited earnings record means for your spousal benefit and if there's any way to correct or improve the situation.

6. Legal Effects

Be aware that unreported income can carry **legal consequences**. If the IRS or SSA discovers unreported earnings, there could be fines, penalties, and back taxes owed. This might not directly impact your Social Security spousal benefits, but it's something to keep in mind when addressing the situation.

FOREIGN-BORN SPOUSE

Your foreign-born spouse can qualify for Social Security spousal benefits, but the process depends on several factors, including your spouse's legal status in the U.S., where she lives, and whether she meets the general eligibility requirements.

Here's how it works.

For your foreign-born spouse to qualify for Social Security spousal benefits, the same basic requirements apply as they do for any spouse:

- You must be **legally married**.

- You must have worked and paid into Social Security for at least **10 years**.

- Your spouse must be at least **62 years old** to begin receiving spousal benefits.

- You must have already filed for your own Social Security benefits for your spouse to claim spousal benefits.

- Your foreign-born spouse needs to have a valid *legal residency status* to collect Social Security spousal benefits. The key residency statuses are:

  ⇨ **U.S. Citizen** – If your spouse is a naturalized U.S. citizen, she will qualify for spousal benefits just like any other American citizen.

  ⇨ **Permanent Resident (Green Card Holder)** – If your spouse is a lawful permanent resident, she can also qualify for spousal benefits.

Spouse Living in the U.S. vs. Abroad

- **Living in the U.S.** – If your foreign-born spouse lives in the U.S., they can receive spousal benefits as long as they meet the general requirements.

- **Living Abroad** – If your spouse lives abroad, there are additional rules. The U.S. has **totalization agreements** with several countries that allow individuals to receive Social Security benefits while living outside the U.S. These agreements also help foreign-born individuals combine work credits from both countries to qualify for benefits.

If your spouse lives in a country *without a totalization agreement*, she may face restrictions on receiving Social Security benefits while living outside the U.S. For example, your spouse might be unable to collect benefits if they live in certain countries like North Korea or Cuba.

The U.S. has *totalization agreements with over 25 countries* that coordinate Social Security benefits for people who have worked in both countries.

If your spouse worked in one of these countries, she might be able to combine her work credits from her foreign country with her U.S. credits to qualify for Social Security benefits.

Some countries with totalization agreements include:

- Canada
- Germany
- Japan
- United Kingdom
- Australia
- South Korea

These agreements also allow Social Security benefits to be paid to individuals living abroad in participating countries. For example, you worked 5 years in the U.S. and 15 years in Canada. You can add the total years together to get a retirement benefit. You'll get proportional benefits from each country. You'll get two checks and your Canadian check will be much higher!

Additional Documentation

Your foreign-born spouse will need to provide additional documentation when applying for spousal benefits, including:

- **Proof of legal marriage** – You'll need to provide your marriage certificate.
- **Proof of age and identity** – A valid passport or birth certificate.
- **Immigration status** – Proof of permanent residency (green card) or U.S. citizenship.

Taxes for Foreign Spouses

If your spouse is a **non-U.S. citizen** and lives abroad, they may be subject to **taxes on their Social Security benefits**. In many cases, the U.S. will withhold **30%** of the Social Security benefit if they live in a country that does not have a tax treaty with the U.S. However, countries with tax treaties may have lower withholding rates or exemptions.

ANNULMENT

If you had your marriage annulled you can't get Spousal Social Security off your prior marriage, even if it lasted 10 years. If you annul the marriage, you are agreeing it never happened. Yes, you are usually doing this for religious reasons, but you lose Social Security too.

FREQUENTLY ASKED QUESTIONS

What happens to my spousal benefits if my spouse delays their Social Security past Full Retirement Age (FRA)?

If your spouse decides to wait past their Full Retirement Age (usually around 66 or 67) to collect Social Security, they'll get a bigger monthly check because of "delayed retirement credits." But here's the thing, your spousal benefits don't increase because of that. You can still get up to 50% of what your spouse was supposed to get at their FRA, even if they wait to claim their benefits until age 70. So, while their check might grow, your spousal benefits stay based on their FRA amount.

Can I collect spousal benefits if I keep working after I file for them?

Yes, you can! But if you're younger than your Full Retirement Age (FRA), how much you earn could reduce your spousal benefits. If you make more than the earnings limit set by Social Security that year, the SSA will hold back some of your benefits until you reach your FRA. After you hit FRA, though, you can work as much as you want, and your benefits won't be reduced.

How does it work if I can get both spousal benefits and survivor benefits?

If your spouse has passed away, survivor benefits can sometimes be higher than spousal benefits. Social Security will give you a higher amount, so don't worry about choosing! You can also get creative — claim one benefit first and let the other grow. For example, you could take spousal benefits early and let your own Social Security grow until you're 70, then switch over to that. It's all about getting the most out of what's available!

What happens to my spousal benefits if my spouse passes away?

When your spouse dies, you can start receiving survivor benefits, which can be up to 100% of what your spouse was getting. The exact amount depends on your age when you apply for survivor benefits. If you claim before your Full Retirement Age, you'll get a smaller amount each month, but if you wait until FRA or beyond, you'll get the full survivor benefit. So, waiting can mean a bigger check!

How do spousal benefits work if I've been married more than once?

If you've been married multiple times, you might be eligible for spousal benefits from an ex-spouse, as long as you were married to them for at least 10 years and you're currently single. Social Security will figure out which ex-spouse's record gives you the highest benefit, and that's what you'll receive. But you can't combine benefits from more than one ex, you'll just get the one that's most beneficial for you!

How does getting remarried affect survivor benefits?

If you're receiving survivor benefits because your spouse passed away, remarriage can change things. If you remarry before age 60 (or age 50 if you're disabled), you'll stop receiving those benefits. But if you remarry after 60, you can keep your survivor benefits even with your new marriage! So, timing really matters here.

Can my spouse file for their Social Security and then suspend it so I can get spousal benefits?

Unfortunately, that "file and suspend" option isn't available anymore — it was phased out in 2016. Now, your spouse has to actually start receiving their Social Security benefits before you can claim spousal benefits.

What happens to my spousal benefits if I get divorced and then remarry?

If you remarry, your spousal benefits from your previous marriage will stop. But don't worry, you can start collecting spousal benefits from your new spouse after you've been married for one year. Just remember, if your new spouse's benefits are lower than what you were getting from your ex-spouse, it might be worth thinking about how that change will affect your retirement income before you decide to remarry.

POINTS TO REMEMBER

- Spousal Social Security must be higher than your own benefits.

- You can draw as a spouse, even if you never worked and earned any Social Security credits on your own.

- If you did earn some benefits, you'll draw your own and then be "topped off" with your spousal amount.

- Drawing off your spouse's work record, will not reduce your spouse's own benefits.

- You may be eligible to draw off several people, but you can only draw on one person at a time.

- You can't give up your right to Social Security benefits in a divorce.

- If you remarry, you lose spousal benefits.

- If you again are single, you again qualify for spousal benefits.

- Neither the current spouse or any former spouse has priority. Several may be able to draw off the same worker's record.

- If you were never legally married, in most states, you are not eligible for spousal Social Security benefits.

- A few states still recognize Common-Law Spouses, but each state has different rules. If your state recognizes your marriage, the SSA will too.

- If you were never legally married for no fault of your own, you may be able to hire an attorney to plead as a Putative Spouse.

- If your marriage is annulled, you won't be able to draw benefits off your former spouse.

CHAPTER 26

WIDOW AND SURVIVOR BENEFITS

Before the 1970s, only women were allowed to claim a widow benefit; now men can get widower benefit. The SSA calls it a **survivor benefit**, but it's all the same thing.

If your spouse worked and paid into Social Security, the government can give you some of their benefits to help you after they're gone.

You can start getting these benefits as early as age 60 — or earlier if you're taking care of a child who is under 16 or disabled.

WHO QUALIFIES?

If you were married to someone who paid into Social Security long enough to qualify for benefits, you might be eligible for survivor benefits. You can get these benefits as early as age 60 (or 50 if you're disabled), but there are a few things to consider.

If you're already getting your own Social Security benefits, you may be able to switch to widow's benefits *if that amount is higher than what you're receiving.* On the other hand, if your widow's benefits are less, you can stick with your own. Many men qualify for this benefit, but it is often much less than their own, so they never draw off their deceased spouse.

You can also qualify for survivor benefits if:

- You were married to your spouse for at least 9 months before they passed away (with some exceptions).

- You're unmarried (or you've remarried after age 60 — or 50 if disabled — then you still might be eligible).

- Your spouse worked long enough under Social Security to qualify for benefits.

HOW TO APPLY

You can't apply for survivor's benefits online, so you'll need to either call the SSA (which I do not recommend) or visit your local office to apply. Make sure you have all the necessary documents, like your marriage certificate, divorce decree, and your Social Security number handy to make the process smoother. You can apply 4 months before you are eligible. So, if you want the benefit to start when you turn 60, make your appointment with the SSA 4 months earlier.

💡 *You won't need a copy of the death certificate as that information is forwarded to the SSA by the funeral home.*

THE NUMBERS

Now let's talk about numbers. The amount of money you receive depends on several factors:

- **Your age when you apply**. If you take the benefit at age 60, you'll get a reduced amount. The full survivor benefit is available when you reach Full Retirement Age, which is usually between 66 and 67 depending on your birth year. Waiting until your FRA means you'll receive 100% of your late spouse's benefit. If you claim early, at age 60, you'll get about 71.5% of what your spouse would have gotten. When you claim, you lock in that benefit amount for life.

- **What was your spouse's actual benefit?** The actual amount you'll receive is based on what your spouse was getting or was entitled to get at the time of their death. If your spouse claimed benefits early, your survivor's benefits will also be reduced.

Here's the good news. If your spouse delayed their benefits past their FRA, your widow's benefits might be higher because of the delayed retirement credits they earned. Those credits can increase the overall amount for widows.

MAXIMIZING BENEFITS

Timing matters. You'll have to factor in your health and financial need to plot a strategy for yourself.

You could:

- Take the survivor's benefits at age 60 and switch to your own retirement benefits later if your personal benefits will be higher at your FRA or age 70.

- Or, if your own retirement benefit is higher, you could take your benefit early and switch to the survivor's benefit later.

Many men believe they will die before their wife and try to work as long as possible to get their wife the highest survivor benefit possible.

Let's look at Tom and Mary as an example:

Mary worked part-time jobs so she could take care of the kids and later her parents. She won't draw much on her own work record, but she does qualify to get her own small benefit. She wants to draw it at age 62. She gets less than $1,000 per month.

Her husband Tom wants to wait to draw his benefits until the latest time possible, age 70. His goal is to beef up his own Social Security amount, not because everyone in his family lived till their 90s, but because of the opposite situation. All the men in his family died in their early 70s.

Tom is blocking Mary from drawing her spousal benefits. She cannot draw off his work record until he draws his own benefits. He is delaying to help her out later. Tom's goal is to increase how much Mary can draw later as a widow. He knows that he is likely to die before her.

Many men feel the same way and they worry about their wives surviving as a widow. Most women do not remarry (men do) so many women are very reliant on their Social Security benefits.

Delayed Retirement Credits (DRC) boost survivor benefits, not spousal benefits.

If Mary files for spousal Social Security while Tom is alive, the amount that she can get is based on what he was eligible for at **his Full Retirement Age.** None of the delayed credits up till age 70 will increase her benefit **while he is alive**.

But as a widow, Mary can benefit from the extra money Tom earned in those delayed retirement credits! As a widow, she can draw up to 100% of the amount Tom was **eligible for at his death**, including any delayed credits he earned.

It all depends on your situation, so be sure to run the numbers or talk to someone who can help you figure out what works best.

THE BOTTOM LINE

A widow who is already receiving Social Security benefits can receive either her own Social Security benefit or her spouse's, whichever amount is higher, *but not both*. When you and your spouse have been living off two checks and now you have to live off only one, it can be hard.

Widow's benefits can be a lifeline, especially when you're adjusting to life after losing a spouse. Understanding your options and timing is key to making sure you get the most out of what's available.

Remember, you don't have to make these decisions alone — whether you consult with a Social Security expert or work with a financial advisor, having a clear plan will make all the difference.

If you're unsure, don't rush. Sometimes waiting a little longer for benefits can result in a bigger monthly check for the rest of your life. Take your time and think about what works best for your situation. Only you know if you really need the money now, even if it is reduced, or if you can live off other sources of income and let your benefit grow.

Let's look at Betty's scenario.

- Betty is 60 years old.
- If she claims her own Social Security at 62, she'll receive $1,200 per month.
- Betty's Full Retirement Age is 66 years old.
- Betty's spouse recently died.
- If Betty's husband had lived, he would have received $2,500 per month at his FRA.

Betty can choose to claim her own retirement benefits at age 62, which would give her $1,200 per month. This would allow her to receive some income right away, while letting her widow's benefits grow until she reaches her FRA of 66. At that point, she can switch to her widow's benefit, which will have maxed out.

1. **Betty claims her own Social Security at age 62:**

    ⇨ From ages 62 to 66, she collects $1,200 per month for 48 months (4 years).

    ⇨ Total collected from age 62 to 66:
    $1,200 x 48 months = $57,600.

2. **Betty lets her widow benefits grow:**

    ⇨ Betty is eligible for widow's benefits starting at age 60, but if she claims early, her benefit will be reduced.

⇨ By waiting until her Full Retirement Age (66), she will receive 100% of her late husband's benefit. This means her benefit at age 66 will be $2,500 per month.

⇨ If Betty had taken the benefit at age 60, she would have only received about 71.5% of her husband's benefit, or $1,787 per month.

3. **At age 66, Betty switches to her widow's benefits:**

⇨ Once Betty reaches her Full Retirement Age of 66, she can then switch from her own Social Security benefit to the *full widow's benefit*, which is $2,500 per month.

This strategy allows Betty to collect a steady income starting at age 62 while giving her widow's benefit time to grow to its maximum amount. By age 66, she's set to receive significantly more each month for the rest of her life.

SWITCHING BENEFITS

What happens when you go from spousal benefits to widow benefits? Sometimes you are automatically switched up to a widow benefit, and other times you must choose when to switch. If you are drawing a spousal or ex-spousal Social Security benefit and your spouse or ex-spouse dies, what happens is based on YOUR age.

1. If you are **younger** than your Full Retirement Age, nothing happens.

2. You have the choice to switch over to a widow benefit or **wait to let it grow** and switch at your Full Retirement Age.

3. If you are age 50 and disabled, you may be able to draw as a disabled widow now.

4. If you are at, or older than your Full Retirement Age, your spousal benefit will **automatically convert** to the higher widow benefit.

EMPLOYMENT AND BENEFITS

If you're under your FRA and working while receiving widow benefits, you are subject to the annual earnings limit. If you earn more than the limit, part of your benefits will be withheld. The earnings limit changes each year. For 2025, it is $23,400. If you earn more than that, $1 in benefits will be withheld for every $2 you earn over the limit.

Once you hit your FRA, you can work and earn as much as you want without affecting your widow benefits. At that point, there's no penalty.

REMARRIAGE

If you remarry at ANY age, your spousal benefits stop. However, if you remarry after 60 (or 50 for the disabled), you're still eligible for widow benefits.

Let's say you marry for 10 years and divorce. You remarry. Your new spouse dies. Then your former spouse dies too. What are your options?

If both die, *you can switch to the higher of the two widow benefits*. You don't have to stick with the benefit from the spouse you were currently married to.

What if you are a widow over age 60 and you marry a higher earner. You want to draw spousal benefits off your new spouse's work record but what happens to your widow benefits?

First, you'll continue to receive your widow benefits since you remarried after age 60. You must be married at least one year to be eligible to draw a spousal benefit off your new spouse's work record. Your new spouse must be drawing his own Social Security for you to be able to draw as a spouse. You must be 62 or older to draw as a spouse.

So, if the survivor benefit is higher, you'll keep that. But if the spousal benefit is higher, you can switch over. You can't draw both benefits at the same time. If your new spouse dies before you, you then can choose when to move up to a survivor benefit again.

Many couples don't remarry because they want to keep their estates separate, but there are advantages to remarriage when it comes to Social Security!

💡 *Many people confuse this rule and think they can draw on a living ex-spouse AND remarry after age 60. You can never draw spousal benefits off a former living spouse after you remarry, at any age.*

A lot of people wonder if remarriage is even a good idea once they are at or near retirement age. Many people do not want to remarry and mingle their assets (their kids always have opinions). But for some people, usually women, remarriage opens up the chance for a higher Social Security benefit and a higher widow benefit.

In many cases, men will never draw any widower benefits when their spouse dies because men typically far out-earn their wives over the course of their working years.

People think you can get your own benefits and at least a little bit off their late spouse's work record, but that is not how Social Security works. For a widower to collect from his late wife, she had to have been the higher earner. The most many men get from Social Security when their wives die is the $255 death benefit.

THE DEATH BENEFIT

The SSA pays a one-time $255 lump-sum death benefit to surviving spouses or children. The benefit is paid automatically to eligible spouses and children who were already receiving family benefits on the deceased's record. If you were not receiving spousal Social Security, you must apply for this benefit *within two years of the date of death.*

If there is no eligible spouse or child, no one can claim this benefit (ex-spouses are not eligible).

How do you apply?

You can apply for the $255 death benefit over the phone by calling the SSA at 1-800-772-1213, but you will typically need to provide some documentation, including proof of death, if the SSA does not already have it on file.

I've heard of many people who received the death benefit payment automatically. That could happen if the SSA was notified quickly by the funeral home, but for most people, you will need to contact the SSA and file the claim yourself.

:💡: *The death benefit used to go up each year. Then the SSA capped the death benefit at $255 to prevent the benefit from increasing as monthly benefit payments rose. The cap was intended to be temporary, but the benefit has remained at $255 ever since, which saves the SSA money.*

CHILDREN AND OTHER SURVIVORS

If you have minor children under age 18 (or under 19 and still in high school), or a disabled child, they may be eligible for survivor benefits. Typically, children can receive up to 75% of your spouse's basic benefit.

Additionally, if you're caring for a child under 16 who is receiving survivor benefits, you might be eligible for benefits regardless of your age. These are called mother's or father's benefits, and they're available even if you haven't reached age 60.

POINTS TO REMEMBER

- Widow benefits are payments you can receive if your spouse passed away and had paid into Social Security.

- You can begin drawing a widow benefit as early as age 60 (age 50 if disabled) but claiming early reduces your benefits permanently.

- Men can receive benefits too. Since men typically have higher lifetime earnings, their social security benefits are higher than their spouse so they may not get any money as a widower.

- You can switch between your own Social Security benefits and widow benefits, depending on which is higher, but you can't collect both at the same time.

- Waiting till your FRA lets you get the maximum widow benefit.

- Widow benefits can't be applied for online.

- Remarriage after age 60 doesn't impact your widow benefits.

- Kids can qualify for a survivor benefit until they graduate high school.

- Any benefit taken before your FRA comes with an earned income limit!

CHAPTER 27

WORKING WHILE DRAWING BENEFITS

Let's say you are at your Full Retirement Age, drawing your Social Security, *and working full time*. Will your benefits increase since you are still working? Possibly.

Each year, the SSA talks to the IRS. They review the records of all Social Security beneficiaries who have wages reported for the previous year. If your latest year of earnings is *one of your highest 35 years*, the SSA recalculates your benefit and pays you any increase you are due! The increase is retroactive to January of the year after you earned the money.

That's good news. *I don't have a lot of good news so please savor this.*

Here is some bad news. If you continue to work, *but do not earn enough to drive up your benefits,* you will still continue to pay into FICA. This drives people nuts. As long as you are earning wages, you will pay those darn FICA payroll taxes. Why? The trust fund needs your taxes to pay others.

CORRECTING EARNINGS MISTAKES

Please look at your **SSA.GOV** account now. You may see some errors.

An easy error to spot is a $0 for earnings in a year you know that you worked. For example, I was a stay-at-home mom for five years. For the years 1993 to 1998, I had $0s. If you see $0 earnings for years that you know you worked, you must work to correct them!

Common reasons for mistakes on your account are marriage or divorce. You may have changed your last name and didn't tell the SSA. Or your employer used your wrong Social Security number.

Sometimes you had a corrupt employer who didn't send your payroll taxes to the government on purpose. He's now long gone, and you are left to try to fix the problem. Is it possible? Yes. But with all things involving the government it will take a lot of patience and evidence.

You'll need proof to get your earnings record updated. That can be tough if you don't have copies of your old tax records, or W-2s, or any other documents that showed you worked. It's best to go to the SSA in person and take all your documents to fix your earnings record.

WHEN SHOULD YOU RETIRE?

As with all things in this book, your situation will be unique to you. There is no one-size-fits-all answer. But let's take a crack at it.

You've looked at your **SSA.GOV** account, found no errors, and are curious about the estimated amounts. Most people hope to see a higher dollar amount than what they see online. This is when you might reconsider retiring at the age you'd chosen. Maybe you should work a few more years and lock in a higher monthly check.

Only you know how much you like your job. If it is too physically demanding or mentally stressful, I don't advocate staying in a job you hate for a few more years — you could die before you ever draw any of your Social Security.

If you want to draw a reduced amount at an early age and not look back, do it. There could be a possibility you could draw a larger benefit in the future as a widow.

Let's assume you want to delay retirement a few years. How much can a few more years of work help boost your benefits beyond the obvious?

- If you are at the height of your career, working a few more years will replace a few of your lower 35 years of earnings. Worth it!
- If you are at a low-paying job, and a higher earning year will be replaced with a lower year, maybe it's not worth it.
- If you are never going to draw your own Social Security and instead draw as a spouse, then working doesn't change your benefits.

If you're unsure, don't rush. Sometimes waiting a little longer for benefits can result in a bigger monthly check for the rest of your life. Take your time. Talk to a professional. Think about what works best for your situation. **Only you know if you really need the money now,** even if it is reduced, or if you can live off other sources of income and let your benefit grow.

EARNED INCOME LIMITS

Understanding how much you can earn without having your Social Security benefits reduced starts with learning the difference between active and passive income. If you want to draw Social Security at any time before your Full Retirement Age (FRA) and continue to work full time, you need to remember the earned income limit. In 2025, the limit is **$23,400**. If you earn more than that from active income (like wages or self-employment), your benefits will be reduced.

For every $2 you earn over the limit, $1 is withheld from your benefits. This rule really hits people hard who are under their FRA and continue to work full time!

Once you reach your FRA, there are **no earnings limits**, and you can work as much as you want without any penalty.

💡 *If you keep working after your FRA, you also continue to pay into Social Security payroll taxes!*

However, Passive Income (like rents, dividends, or withdrawals from your retirement accounts) won't count toward your earnings limit. This is why it's important to plan your income sources carefully if you want to retire early and avoid penalties on your Social Security benefits.

PASSIVE INCOME

Other sources of Passive Income:

1. **Interest** from savings accounts, bonds, or CDs.

2. **Dividends** from stocks and mutual funds.

3. **Capital gains** from selling investments like stocks, bonds, or real estate.

4. **Rental income** from properties you own.[1]

5. **Withdrawals from retirement accounts** like 401(k)s, IRAs, and Roth IRAs.

6. **Annuities** that provide regular payments.

7. **Royalties** from books, movies, or inventions.

8. **Alimony or child support** payments.

9. Other government benefits, like **Veterans benefits.**

10. **Inheritance or gifts** you receive.

11. **Profits from a business** where you are not actively involved in the day-to-day operations.

12. **Income from trusts or estates** where you are a beneficiary.

---

1   Rental income can sometimes be considered active income.

13. **Lottery or gambling winnings.**

14. **Court settlements** (like personal injury settlements as long as they are not tied to lost wages).

15. **Profits from selling personal property** like your car.

16. **Life insurance** proceeds where you are the beneficiary.

ACTIVE INCOME

Active income is money you earn by working or being actively involved in a business. You have to put in effort or time to make this type of income. Think of passive income you can make while asleep (interest) and active income you have to be doing something (like operating a forklift).

Attention Landlords:

If a realtor owns several rental properties and is *actively involved in the day-to-day operations* — such as finding tenants, handling repairs, collecting rent, or managing the property directly — this could be considered **active income**. In this case, the realtor is working regularly to maintain the rental business, so the IRS might classify this as active income rather than passive.

Let's look at Opal:

Opal owns 3 rental properties. She handles everything herself — marketing the properties, interviewing tenants, doing maintenance, and even collecting rent. *Since she's directly involved in the operation of her rental business on a regular basis,* the income she earns from these properties could be classified as **active income**. This means it might count against her Social Security earned income limit if she's drawing benefits before her Full Retirement Age.

If Opal hired a management company to oversee the day-to-day and she was simply collecting rent from her properties, that would be **passive income**, which wouldn't count against her Social Security benefits.

The key difference is how **involved** Opal is in the day-to-day operations of the rental property. So, if you own a few rentals you could fall into either camp, based on how active you are in the business.

Other examples of Active Income:

1. **Wages, salary, bonuses, commissions** from a job where you work for an employer.

2. **Self-employment income**, like from a freelance business or a small business you run.

3. **Bonuses and commissions** earned by doing extra work or selling something.

4. **Rental income** when you're actively managing properties, like Opal the realtor who does all the work herself.

5. **Income from a business** where you're actively involved in its day-to-day operations.

Key Points of the Special Wage Payment Rule:

This type of income (like vacation pay, severance, bonuses, etc.) received after retirement is NOT counted toward your Social Security's earnings limit.

The payment must be for work performed **before** you retired. Your employer may need to **report the vacation pay separately** on your W-2 under **"Noncovered Pension or Special Wage Payments"** so SSA knows not to count it against your benefits.

How This Works:

▪ Marvin retires at 63 on December 31, 2024.

- In January 2025, he receives a lump-sum payout of $15,000 for unused vacation time.

- Since the vacation pay was earned before he retired, it falls under the **Special Wage Payment Rule** and **will not** count toward the $23,400 earnings limit for 2025.

How does working in retirement affect benefits?

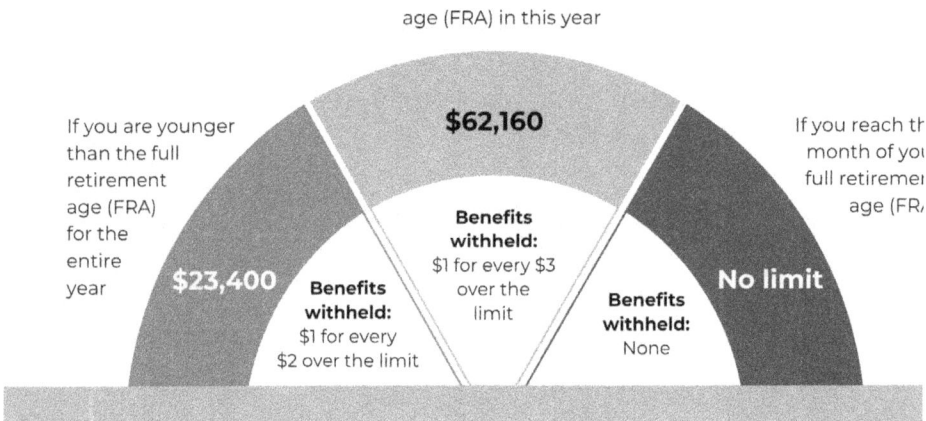

age (FRA) in this year

If you are younger than the full retirement age (FRA) for the entire year

$23,400

Benefits withheld: $1 for every $2 over the limit

$62,160

Benefits withheld: $1 for every $3 over the limit

Benefits withheld: None

No limit

If you reach th month of yo full retireme age (FR/

Now that I've explained what active income is, let's see how having too much of it impacts dollar amounts when you draw your Social Security benefits earlier than your Full Retirement Age. When your active income exceeds the earned income limit, some or all of your Social Security benefits will be reduced. **The earned income limit is higher and the formula for how they deduct money when you go over the limit is HIGHER in the year you reach your Full Retirement Age!**

Let's look at how Becky's Social Security benefits would be affected by working too much.

Becky is 62 and has decided to start drawing her benefits early. She's also working full time and expects to earn $20,000 over the annual earned income limit. For every $2 Becky earns over that limit, $1 will be withheld from her benefits.

Since she is $20,000 over the limit, half of that amount will be withheld from her Social Security check.

This means $10,000 will be withheld from Becky's Social Security benefits for that year if she notified the government that she was going to earn more than allowed. If Becky was supposed to receive $1,200 a month in benefits ($14,400 per year), she would now only receive $4,400 for the year.

Even though Becky still gets some Social Security, the penalty for working full time before reaching Full Retirement Age (FRA) significantly reduces her benefits.

Will Becky ever get that money back? Possibly.

Not in one lump sum, but once Becky reaches her FRA, the SSA will add a little bit more to each of her monthly checks until she dies. If she lives long enough, she will eventually get all that money back. Here is an estimate of how that would look:

If Becky's FRA is 67, and the average person lives until 85, that gives her about 19 more years to live. The SSA would spread out the $10,000 it owes her over those years.

Let's change the scenario: Becky doesn't tell the SSA she plans to earn over the limit. The government doesn't find out until she files her tax returns.

Becky was overpaid last year. Previously, the SSA only withheld **10% of your monthly benefit** to recover overpayments. A new rule in March of 2025 allows **Social Security to take 100% of your check** until the overpaid amount is fully recovered.

For example, if Becky owes **$2,000** and her monthly benefit is **$1,500,** SSA will **withhold her entire check for the first month** and then **take $500 from the second month's check,** allowing her to receive the remaining **$1,000**. Once the debt is fully repaid, her full benefit resumes.

If this creates a **financial hardship**, you **don't have to accept full withholding** — you can **request a lower repayment amount** or **apply for a waiver.** To do this, contact SSA immediately or **file Form SSA-632-BK** to request help. If you qualify for Supplemental Security Income (SSI), your withholding is still **limited to 10%** of your benefit.

IMPACT OF INCARCERATION

If you are incarcerated for 30 days or more, your Social Security benefits will stop. However, your spouse or children who are drawing benefits based on your record will continue to receive their payments. You can reapply for benefits upon your release, and payments can start the month following your release.

Medicare works differently. While you're incarcerated, you can retain Medicare Parts A and B, but you will need to cancel Part B if you don't want to keep paying the premiums while in prison. Upon release, you can re-enroll and avoid late penalties if you take advantage of the Special Enrollment Period.

POINTS TO REMEMBER

- Social Security benefits are calculated based on your 35 highest-earning years.

- Your Full Retirement Age (FRA) is based on your year of birth.

- You can start collecting Social Security as early as age 62, but doing so permanently reduces your monthly benefit compared to waiting until your FRA.

- Delaying benefits beyond your FRA can increase your monthly payout by 8% per year up to age 70. These are called Delayed Retirement Credits (DRC).

- Spouses don't benefit from DRCs. Survivors do!

- At your FRA, you can work and earn as much as you want.

- Prior to your FRA, you have a limit on your active income.

- Passive income is unlimited!

- Just because passive income doesn't matter for Social Security doesn't mean it isn't taxable income for tax purposes and Medicare IRMAA calculations.

- The year you reach FRA the earned income limits are more lenient.

- If your Social Security benefits are reduced because you earned too much, you may be able to get it all back later in monthly installments if you live long enough. This is not a lump sum payment!

- If that's too much, you can ask for a lower amount or a waiver.

CHAPTER 28

SUSPENDING BENEFITS

Sometimes people start their Social Security benefits and realize they want to make a change — and that's okay!

You may have started your Social Security at 65 when you started your Medicare. Many people do this. Then you realized that you are likely to live to 90, like your parents, and you regret having drawn benefits early. Or you didn't realize that you had to limit your income prior to your FRA.

You've got three options to stop your benefits: **Withdraw, Voluntary Suspension, or Voluntary Withholding.**

Knowing the difference helps you make the best choice for your situation and get the most out of your benefits.

WITHDRAWING YOUR BENEFITS

Withdrawing your benefits lets you stop and give back what you've already received, kind of like a do-over. I also call this "unretiring." If you realized you claimed too early or don't need the money, you can pay it all back. You can't make payments. You have to write the SSA a check for the full amount — but you won't owe interest.

You have to do this *before* you've been drawing for 365 days.

You can only do this once in your lifetime.

There is no waiting period if you change your mind again and decide you do want the money! Just reapply for Social Security when you are ready.

VOLUNTARY SUSPENSION

Voluntary Suspension is more like hitting the pause button to let your payments grow bigger.

This is especially helpful if your circumstances change, like landing a new job, getting a raise, or realizing you don't need the money right away. **Build your nest egg!**

Once you hit your FRA, you're allowed to suspend your benefits. This means that even though you're entitled to start collecting, you choose to pause those payments. The reason many people do this is to take advantage of **Delayed Retirement Credits (DRCs)**. By delaying your benefits, they increase by about 8% each year until you reach age 70. It's essentially like getting a raise each year you wait.

💡 Let's break that down. If your FRA is 66 and you decide to suspend your benefits right away, you can let them grow until you hit 70. In that time, your monthly benefit will increase by a total of 32% (that's 8% per year for four years). So, if your monthly benefit at FRA was going to be $2,000, delaying until 70 would bump that up to $2,640 per month. Not bad, right?

VOLUNTARY WITHHOLDING

If you've been drawing benefits for more than 1 year and you are not yet at your FRA, you can't use the withdrawal or suspension options. If you know that your income will put you into an overpayment situation, contact the SSA and ask for a **Voluntary Withholding of Benefits.** Your amount is still locked in since you drew early but you won't get into an overpayment situation.

IMPACT ON YOUR SPOUSE AND KIDS

One thing to keep in mind, if you withdraw or suspend your benefits, *any spousal benefits based on your record will also be paused.* So, if your spouse is receiving a check based on your work history, her payments would stop until you resume your own benefits.

If your spouse is counting on that extra money coming in each month, you'll need to have a good chat about how this will affect your household budget.

For some couples, this might be no big deal if you've got other savings or income to rely on. But for others, it could be a little tight. That's why it's important to weigh the pros and cons together, to see if boosting your future payments is worth the temporary pinch. Just like grandma always said, "a bird in the hand is worth two in the bush," so be sure the trade-off works for your situation!

RESUMING YOUR BENEFITS

It's actually easier to get your Social Security benefits the second time! When you're ready to resume your Social Security benefits, you don't need to go through the whole process like you did the first time. It's more like hitting the "play" button after you paused — it just starts back up again.

Simply call the SSA.

If you want to restart *before you turn 70,* you just have to let Social Security know, but it's much simpler than applying for the first time.

If you want to *wait until 70,* your benefits automatically start up again, no extra steps needed!

GREAT NEWS - LUMP SUM BENEFIT OPTION

If you wait until after your Full Retirement Age (FRA) to apply for Social Security, you can ask for a lump sum payment of up to 6 months of back benefits. For example, if you apply in January but could have started your benefits the previous July, Social Security will send you a check for those 6 months. **The catch is that your monthly checks going forward will be a little smaller because it's like you started your benefits 6 months earlier.** This option can give you quick cash if you need it, but it's worth thinking about how the smaller monthly payments might affect you in the long run.

You can only get a lump sum back to your FRA. So, you must be past your FRA to use this option.

POINTS TO REMEMBER

- If you retire early but then get a new job, you can withdraw or suspend your benefits.

- You can withdraw your benefits once in your lifetime if you haven't already been drawing for more than 1 year. You must pay back all your benefits to get a reset.

- Once you reach Full Retirement Age, you can voluntarily suspend your Social Security benefits to allow them to grow by 8% per year until age 70, maximizing your future payments.

- If you choose to suspend your benefits, any spousal benefits being paid based on your record will also stop until you resume your own benefits.

- A quick reminder: Social Security benefits stop growing at age 70, so there's no financial advantage to delaying beyond that age. You should file by then to avoid losing out on payments.

- You are eligible for a one-time retroactive benefit of up to 6 months if you are at least 6 months past your FRA when you begin Social Security.

CHAPTER 29

TAXES, TAXES, TAXES

I get it. Taxes on Social Security benefits don't seem fair, especially when you've already paid into the system!

"Didn't the government already tax this money? Why am I being taxed again?"

I will attempt to explain these rules and maybe I can help you reduce your taxes if you understand these crazy rules. But remember, I can't make it make sense.

If Social Security is your only source of income, you won't pay federal income taxes. Social Security benefits are only taxed if your **combined income** is over a certain limit. Your other sources of income such as a part-time job, pension, or investments, may cause your Social Security benefits to be taxed. The amount you pay is based on your tax bracket. (Keep reading for more on that.)

Taxes aren't determined by age, so you will never age out of paying taxes. But if your *only* income is Social Security payments, you won't owe taxes and you may not need to file a tax return.

WHY IS SOCIAL SECURITY TAXED?

When you were working and paying FICA taxes (the taxes that fund

Social Security and Medicare), you didn't pay taxes on the full amount of your contributions. If you had an employer, they paid **half of your FICA taxes** (7.65%), while you paid the other half (7.65%) out of your wages. *In the government's view, only the portion of your income that you paid into Social Security was taxed during your working years.*

Yeah, I don't like this either.

💡 *Recent retirees want to know who to blame for taxing benefits and that is President Ronald Reagan back in 1984. In 1993 they increased taxes on high earners under President Bill Clinton. I throw this fun political history in to make it clear BOTH parties are to blame.*

THE BIGGEST MISCONCEPTIONS

- Once you start drawing a Social Security benefit, it is *not* included in your taxable income for federal (and some state) calculations. You've already been taxed on that money once, right?
- At age 70, no one needs to file income taxes.
- Once you lock in your Social Security benefits, if you continue to work, you will not have to pay FICA payroll taxes — that's only for people who haven't started Social Security yet.
- If you are going to keep working, the SSA automatically withholds taxes from your Social Security checks.

Wrong, wrong, wrong, and wrong.

How much of your Social Security income is subject to federal income tax *depends on a variety of factors*, including your federal income tax filing status and your Modified Adjusted Gross Income (MAGI).

Here is the math to determine if some, or most, of your Social Security benefits will be subject to federal income taxes.

- Take ½ of your Social Security benefits,

- Add in your Adjusted Gross Income,

- Add in earnings from nontaxable interest,

- Add in your spouse's income, if filing jointly.

If your **combined income** exceeds the limits in the following chart, then you will have to pay federal taxes on either 50% or 85% of your Social Security.

Calculating Your Social Security Federal Income Tax

Married filing jointly	
Your combined annual income	How much of your Social Security benefit is taxable
$32,000 or less	None
Between $32,000 and $44,000	Up to 50%
More than $44,000	Up to 85%

Individual	
Your combined annual income	How much of your Social Security benefit is taxable
$25,000 or less	None
Between $25,000 and $34,000	Up to 50%
More than $34,000	Up to 85%

Take a deep breath and let me break this down. **Let's look at Kay's situation:**

Kay's Social Security benefit is $20,000 a year. She earns another $30,000 from her pension.

To figure out how much of it will be taxable, she needs to take half of that Social Security benefit ($10,000) and add it to her Adjusted Gross Income (AGI) of $30,000. Then she has to add in her non-taxable interest from her municipal bonds, which is another $2,000.

So, Kay adds $10,000 (half of her Social Security) + $30,000 (AGI) + $2,000 (non-taxable interest), for a total **combined income** of $42,000.

Since Kay's combined income exceeds $34,000 (the threshold for single filers), up to **85% of her Social Security benefits** would be subject to federal income tax. This means a portion of her Social Security benefit will be taxed based on her total income.

People panic here and think that she'll pay an 85% tax rate. Luckily, that is not true! There is no 85% tax bracket. How much Kay eventually pays in taxes is based on her own tax bracket. Let's say she is in the 12% tax bracket. Part of her income will be taxed at 12% and the rest of her income above $44,725 will be taxed at 22%.

Yes, this is more than you really want to learn about our tax system but hang in there, I'm almost done.

Kay will pay:

- 12% of $33,725 = $4,047.
- 22% of $2,275 = $500.50.

Her total federal taxes will be $4,547.50

About half of all people drawing Social Security benefits paid federal income taxes last year. Since the income limits do not go up (they built the program that way on purpose), more and more people will end up paying income taxes on their Social Security benefits in the future.

Did you catch that? The government was very sneaky. By not tying the taxable income limits to inflation, as *wages go up each year*, more people will end up paying income taxes on their Social Security benefits.

Now you know why the SSA sends you a 1099 each year!

> Report the taxable portion of your Social Security benefits on line 6b of Form 1040 or Form 1040-SR.

OPTIONAL FEDERAL WITHHOLDING

If you haven't started drawing Social Security yet, you now have a pretty good idea if you'll pay federal income taxes on your Social Security payments. You may want to ask the SSA to withhold money back from your check to ease up the burden at tax time. *Taxes are not withheld automatically.* You have to request it by filing **Form W-4V**.

- File IRS Form W-4V and submit it to your local Social Security office.

- You can choose a withholding rate of 7%, 10%, 12%, or 22%. Your accountant can help you choose an amount or you can just wing it. Something is better than nothing.

- You can change or stop withholding at any time by submitting a new Form W-4V.

REDUCING YOUR FEDERAL TAX BURDEN

Paying any amount of tax on your Social Security benefits can feel like a big slap in the face. There are a few ways you might be able to lessen the taxable burden.

1. **Lower your income** – If you can adjust the total amount of money that you bring in each year to stay below the threshold, you could pay less in Social Security tax, *or even avoid it altogether.*

2. **Delay taking Social Security payments** – If you have access to other income in retirement from accounts that aren't subject to taxation at withdrawal, such as a Roth 401(k) or Roth IRA, you could take money from those accounts first to live on and *delay claiming your* Social Security.

3. **Pay taxes over time** – Having taxes withheld throughout the year, instead of getting hit with a large bill at tax time, can help lessen the pain.

Does Your State Tax Social Security Benefits?

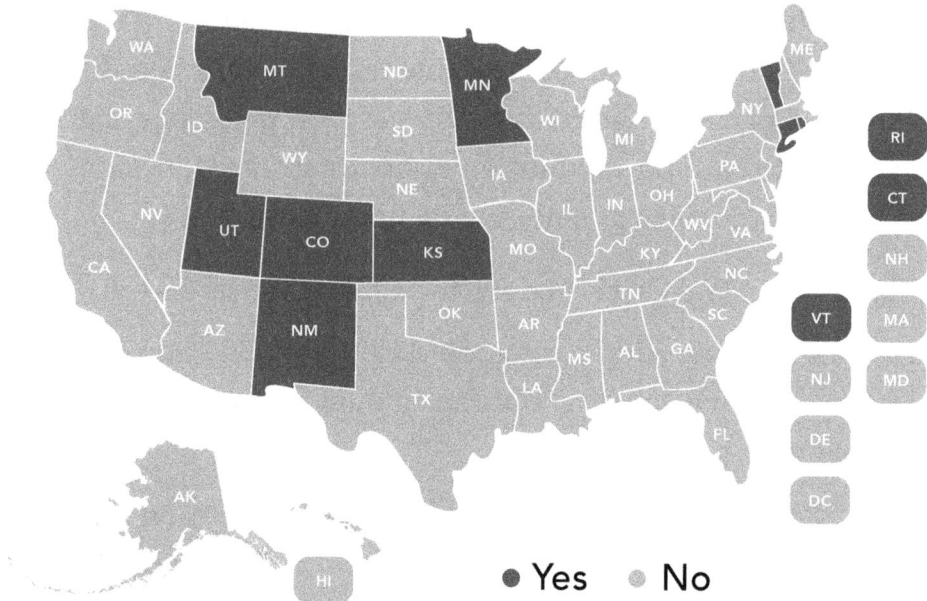

● Yes ○ No

STATE TAXES

In addition to the IRS, seven states also tax some portion of your Social Security benefits. These states include Colorado, Connecticut, Kansas, Missouri, Montana, New Mexico, and Utah. The rules vary in each state, with some offering exemptions or thresholds based on income. This is another topic that is in flux as states need more for their budget shortfalls. More states could tax Social Security in the future.

The good news is that if you live in **Missouri or Nebraska**, your state stopped taxing Social Security in 2024. Consult a tax advisor to get the updated information on your state.

💡 *Most, but not all of these states, only tax those making much more than average retirees. None of these states tax all Social Security recipients. To determine if your state will tax your Social Security, estimate your Adjusted Gross Income (AGI).*

Connecticut

Connecticut taxes Social Security benefits if your AGI is over $75,000; or $100,000 if married filing jointly. People with AGIs above those thresholds may get an exemption of up to 25% of their total benefits.

Kansas

Kansas taxes Social Security for taxpayers with AGIs over $75,000.

Minnesota

Minnesota taxes Social Security benefits for people with AGIs over $82,190; $105,380 if married filing jointly; or $52,690 if married filing separately.

Montana

Montana taxes Social Security benefits for AGIs above $25,000. The income tax threshold is $32,000 if married filing jointly; $25,000 if married filing separately while living apart for the full tax year. For married filing separately while living together *at any time during the tax year*, the threshold is $0. Montana is the harshest state for retirees, but Montana is also 1 of only 5 states without a general sales tax.

New Mexico

New Mexico taxes Social Security benefits for taxpayers with more than $100,000 in income; $75,000 if married filing separately; or $150,000 if a surviving spouse, head of household, or married filing jointly.

Rhode Island

Rhode Island taxes Social Security benefits only if you begin receiving retirement benefits *before* you reach Social Security's Full Retirement Age (usually age 66 to 67) or if your AGI is over $101,000 if you file as single or head of household; $126,250 for married filing jointly; or $101,025 for married filing separately. People under those thresholds can exempt up to $20,000 of their retirement income.

Utah

Utah taxes Social Security benefits for taxpayers who make over $45,000; $75,000 if head of household or married filing jointly; $37,500 if married filing separately. People under those thresholds may qualify for a nonrefundable tax credit.

Vermont

Vermont taxes Social Security for taxpayers with AGIs above $60,000; $75,000 if married and filing jointly. People with AGIs between $50,000 and $59,999 — $65,001 and $74,999 if married filing jointly — get a partial exemption.

TAXES ON RETIREMENT ACCOUNTS

IRAs, 401(k) plans, and other retirement savings vehicles have different tax treatments. Some are pre-taxed and some are taxed *when you take a withdrawal*. This isn't a book about financial planning, but many retirees make expensive mistakes by taking tax-deferred money out and causing a Medicare IRMAA surcharge.

Roth IRAs and Roth 401(k)s are funded by money that was already taxed. If you take $1,000 from a paycheck and put it in a Roth IRA it won't be taxed when you withdraw that money in retirement at age 59.5 or later.

On the other hand, traditional 401(k) and IRA plans are usually funded with pre-tax money, so you'll usually owe income tax on withdrawals in the year you take them. This additional taxable income can drive up your cost of Medicare.

> Consolidation vs. Conversion =
> Taxable Event vs. Non Taxable Event

You may have heard it can be beneficial to convert a traditional IRA into a Roth IRA. That conversion will cause you to pay income taxes. This is not to be confused with consolidating accounts with separate employers. If you have a 401(k) and change jobs, you can bring your money over to the new employer retirement plan. This is not going to create taxes or penalties if done correctly.

But if you convert a traditional IRA or 401(k) to a Roth IRA or Roth 401(k), you have to pay the taxes during the conversion!

💡 *If you are drawing a Social Security benefit earlier than your Full Retirement Age, these withdrawals are considered PASSIVE INCOME and will not cause you a problem staying under the annual earned income limits.*

So, is it better to have a regular pre-tax retirement account or a Roth account?

Both types of plans are great to have. Work with a financial advisor to create a strategy. You will need professional advice when you want to draw out money to minimize your taxes.

PRIVATE PENSIONS AND INCOME TAXES

Like 401(k) plans, pension plans are usually funded by pre-tax money. You'll owe federal income taxes on withdrawals in the year you take them. If you take a lump-sum payment rather than annual or periodic payments, you will owe the total tax bill in the year you receive that payment!

This is likely to trigger a Medicare IRMAA surcharge if you are within 2 years of enrolling into Medicare.

If you take a lump sum at age 62, it won't impact Medicare since IRMAA looks back two years. At age 65, only the taxable income you had at age 63 will matter.

Generally, your financial advisor will caution against a lump sum withdrawal due to taxes!

Regardless of whether you are under 59.5 or over 59.5, there is a mandatory 20% withholding on distributions. And if you take a withdrawal before the age of 59.5, you *may also pay a 10% early withdrawal penalty* at tax time.

A 401(k) withdrawal does not affect your Social Security benefits.

Taking a distribution from your 401(k) does not impact your eligibility for or the amount of your Social Security benefits. But, a 401(k) withdrawal can affect your adjusted gross income (AGI) and how much of your Social Security is subject to federal income taxes!

Don't be like Eldon.

Eldon retired. He didn't want to leave his 401(k) money with his former employer, so he withdrew it all and deposited it into his savings account. He figured he'd get around to making a plan for the money later.

1. This caused him to pay a lot in federal income taxes.

2. It bumped up his tax bracket.

3. It also caused him to have to include more of his Social Security into his combined income subject to taxes.

4. It also caused him to pay about $6,000 more in Medicare IRMAA for one year for both he and his wife.

What should Eldon have done?

He should not have winged these decisions.

He should have worked with a financial advisor to craft a strategy for the money to minimize negative consequences. Sure, Eldon will eventually have to pay income taxes on all his 401(k) money, *but by structuring out the withdrawals over several years*, he could have minimized the issues.

TAX-DEDUCTIBLE MEDICARE EXPENSES

Medicare premiums can be deducted from your taxes *in theory*. But in practice, very few retirees will be able to claim these deductions.

If you have had enough total medical expenses to file an itemized deduction for medical expenses on your Form 1040, your total qualifying medical expenses (including your Medicare Supplement premiums) must exceed 10% of your adjusted gross income.

You may not be able to deduct these expenses most years, but if you have a year with a lot of medical bills, be sure to save all receipts for tax time.

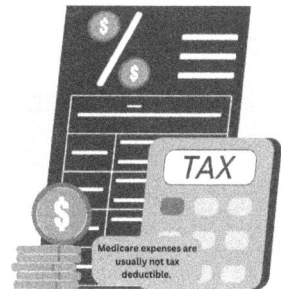

Medicare expenses are usually not tax deductible.

REQUIRED MINIMUM DISTRIBUTIONS

You may not want to take money out of an investment account because you want to avoid taxes. The federal government will *force you to take some money out*. This is your Required Minimum Distribution (RMD). The IRS requires that you take a minimum amount out, so they can tax it. You don't have to spend it. You can turn around and re-invest it.

If you have an IRA, including an SEP IRA and SIMPLE IRA, you are responsible for taking the correct amount of RMDs *on time, every year* from your accounts. If you don't do this, you'll face stiff tax penalties.

The RMD age is currently 73. The age is gradually increasing to 75 in 2033.

RMDs apply to the following retirement plans:

- Traditional IRAs
- SEP IRAs
- SIMPLE IRAs
- Rollover IRAs
- Most 401(k) and 403(b) plans
- Most small business accounts

RMDs don't apply to Roth IRAs and Roth 401(k)s because contributions to these accounts are with *after-tax dollars*.

I will not attempt to show you the math for determining RMDs. I just want you to be aware they may be looming in your future.

Consult a financial advisor, who can also help you avoid steep IRS penalties for taking RMDs that are too small.

INHERITING AN IRA

If you inherit an IRA, you should know that the government has been trying to institute harsh penalties on the inheritors. But everyone is confused so the government has delayed the penalties several times.

If your parents owned an IRA and died after 2020, the government has been trying to force you to take the money out faster so they can tax it. If your parents were already taking RMDs, then you must continue to take RMDs — even if you are not yet the age required to take RMDs. Once you inherit the IRA, you have 10 years to get the money out and into the tax coffers. These new rules stop you from stretching distributions out over your lifetime.

The new rules apply to *non-spouses* who inherit IRAs.

THE TEN-YEAR RULE

Since this new rule took effect, it has created chaos. People think they have to take all of the money out by the 10th year. What the tax man really wants is some of your money each year so it's ALL been taxed by the 10th year.

Good news! If you inherited an IRA since 2020 and are not taking the correct amount of money out, in the correct time frame, your RMD penalties have been waived.

It used to be that the RMD penalties were 50% of the amount that you should have withdrawn. However, due to SECURE ACT 2.0, the penalty for missing RMDs — or failing to take the appropriate amount — is 25% and may even be lower. *In other words, if you inherit an IRA, you need professional advice!*

SIMPLE ESTATE PLANNING

Setting up a **Transfer on Death (TOD)** or **Payable on Death (POD)** is one of the easiest ways to make sure your bank account goes straight to your loved ones when you pass away — no probate, no hassle! All you have to do is tell your bank who should get the money by filling out a simple form. When the time comes, the bank automatically transfers the account to your chosen person, and they won't have to deal with the slow and stressful probate process. It's a quick and easy way to make sure your money gets to where it needs to go.

The best part? It doesn't cost you anything extra, and you can change who gets the money whenever you want. While you're alive, you stay in full control of your account. It's really one of the simplest ways to take care of your loved ones and make sure they don't have to jump through hoops later.

A Trust Is More Flexible

While **TOD** and **POD** accounts are very easy, they do have a few downsides. They only apply to specific accounts, so if you have lots of different assets, or if you want more control over when and how your loved ones get those assets, a trust might be a better choice.

With a trust, you can leave instructions, like making sure your kids only get the money after they turn a certain age or if they meet certain conditions. Trusts also give you more privacy and can protect your assets from legal issues. If you want more flexibility or have a more complicated financial situation, a trust offers a lot more options than **TOD** or **POD** accounts.

There are many estate planning options, depending on your state. You will need to spend some money to ease the transition after your death. While a simple will is cheap to make, it is often *more expensive for your heirs after you die.*

You pay more upfront for trusts, but your family saves money and time later by avoiding the costs of probate.

Many people refuse to consider working with an attorney, but I think it's worth it to get a consultation with an elder law attorney near you.

💡 *A consultation with an attorney is only a few hundred dollars, but if you decide to hire an attorney to prepare legal documents for you, it will cost thousands of dollars.*

If you can't afford to hire an attorney to set up your estate plan, talk to your kids. If they will be inheriting from your estate, they may be able to *pay to help preserve it.* It's a difficult discussion, but everything about estate planning involves difficult discussions.

INHERITANCE

Many people are worried that receiving an inheritance could harm them in the long run. Sometimes that is true. So let me offer some quick advice on how receiving an inheritance can affect different government programs.

In the last chapter, I explained how an inherited IRA could cause you to trigger Medicare IRMAA.

Inheriting your parents' house will be tax-free *until you sell it*. Then you'll usually have a capital gains tax to pay.

How to pass along your house to your kids and minimize their taxes is a conversation you should have with an attorney prior to selling or giving your house away. Not just because of taxes, but also because of the Medicaid Estate Recovery program.

Cash inheritances are easy to understand. Let's look at the impact on different government programs:

Medicare – Usually no impact. A cash inheritance won't cause an IRMAA surcharge. Cash inheritances are tax-free. However, if you inherit an IRA or 401(k), you'll be taxed when you withdraw that money. Those withdrawals can tip you into paying more for Medicare through IRMAA.

Social Security Retirement or **Disability** – No impact. An inheritance is passive income, which can be unlimited.

Medicaid / SSI – Loss of benefits! You'll need to pay back Medicaid for benefits received in the month after you received the inheritance, so be sure to report it as soon as possible to avoid overpayments. Generally, you can't have more than $2,000 in the bank and keep Medicaid. Ideally the person leaving you the inheritance will set up a trust with someone else as trustee to pay you no more than $2,000 so you can remain on Medicaid. Remember, this can vary by state.

LIS / Extra Help paying for your Part D drugs – You can lose benefits when your assets or income increase.

POINTS TO REMEMBER

- Taxes don't stop at any particular age.

- Taxes are based on income.

- Most people will have some of their Social Security benefits included in their federal income taxes.

- A few states also tax Social Security benefits.

- Based on your combined income, either 85% or 50% of your Social Security will be subject to taxes at your tax rate.

- Tax laws change frequently.

- Taxes are not withheld from your monthly Social Security check. If you want the government to withhold taxes, you must request it.

- You can file *Form W-4V* at any time to start, stop, or change your tax withholding.

- The government forces money out of your tax-deferred accounts at a certain age.

- If you don't take your Required Minimum Distributions correctly, you face penalties.

- The age when RMDs begin is currently 73 and moving up to 75.

- A cash inheritance won't drive up the cost of Medicare or cause you to exceed the Social Security earnings limit.

- A cash inheritance can cause you to lose any type of benefits that you qualified for based on your income and assets.

CHAPTER 30

CONCLUSION

Now that you have made it to the end of this book, I want to take a moment to remind you that you're not alone.

Navigating Medicare, Social Security, and retirement benefits can feel overwhelming. With countless decisions to make and an alphabet soup of confusing terms, it's no surprise that many people feel lost or unsure about where to start. If that sounds familiar, take heart — you're in good company.

Confusion is normal. These programs weren't designed for simplicity:

- **Medicare** has multiple parts, each with different costs and coverage.
- **Social Security** comes with tough decisions about when to claim benefits, which can affect your financial future.
- Then, there are **supplemental insurance options, prescription drug plans, and other retirement considerations.**

No wonder this process can feel like solving a puzzle without all the pieces!

The good news? **Help is available.** You don't have to go through this alone or spend hours trying to make sense of it all. Sometimes, all it takes is **a little guidance** from someone who understands the system.

We are Medicare insurance **experts ready to help you — at no cost, no matter what state you live in.**

At **THEMEDICAREFAMILY.COM**, we specialize in helping retirees like you navigate their Medicare decisions. **We work for you, not the insurance companies.** Our goal is simple: **to give you the tools, resources, and expert advice you need to make informed choices about your retirement.**

Your healthcare needs are unique, and you deserve **personalized guidance.** Whether you have **specific questions or just need reassurance**, we're here to help. Take your time, ask for help when you need it, and move forward with confidence.

You've worked hard to get here — **now let's make sure you get the benefits you've earned.**

Reach out to us today at 1-800-970-1964 and take the next step in your retirement journey.

GLOSSARY

You won't find a definition for every term I used in this book. That was a merciful attempt to save 20 more pages. I know you can easily Google any terms I didn't list here. Here are the important terms:

Active Income – Gross active income if from wages, commissions, bonuses, and net-income if self-employed.

Annual Election Period – The Annual Election Period runs from October 15th to December 7th each year. This is where you can change your Medicare Advantage and Part D plans.

Annual Notice of Change – A letter your Medicare Advantage and Part D plan must send you each September to tell you how your plan is changing for the next year.

Assignment – When your doctor agrees to accept the amount that Medicare will pay for your service. This can be an issue with Medicare Supplement Plan N if your doctor does not accept Medicare assignment and you could pay up to 15% extra.

Assisted Living – Room and board, housekeeping, and meals as needed. This type of care is not covered by Medicare nor Medicaid, but your healthcare will still be covered as well as some therapies. You must pay for this type of care.

Benefit Period – Medicare Part A starts your benefit period on the first day you are admitted to a hospital and ends on the 60th day after discharge from a hospital or nursing home. You'll pay a new Part A deductible each benefit period.

COBRA – When you leave your employer group health plan and take a continuation of that same coverage, but you pay the full price for a set time period. COBRA is not creditable coverage for Medicare Part B.

Combined Income – How the SSA determines if some or most of your Social Security benefits will be subject to federal income taxes.

Copay – This is a fixed dollar amount you will pay for certain treatments. Medicare Part D typically has copays for most drugs *and coinsurance for the really expensive medications.* Medicare Advantage has copays to see a doctor and usually a higher copay to see a specialist. Medicare Supplement Plan N has a copay up to $20 to see a doctor and up to $50 to go to the emergency room. Medicare Supplement Plan G doesn't have copays.

Coinsurance – This is the percentage of treatment costs that you must pay. For Medicare Part B, you are responsible for 20%. Medicare Supplement Plan G pays that 20%. Many Medicare Advantage plans charge a coinsurance in lieu of a fixed copay. You typically see this on more expensive procedures like outpatient surgeries, chemotherapy, and radiation treatments.

Common Law Marriage – A few states will allow you to receive Spousal Social Security and Survivor benefits if you can prove you lived as husband and wife per that state's laws. If your state recognizes your union, so will the SSA. Be careful when moving to a new state.

Creditable Coverage – When you have drug insurance coverage that is as good or better than what Medicare Part D offers. Most people use this term to indicate their employer has 20 or more employees, which allows them to avoid late Part B penalties.

Deemed Filing – Social Security's deemed filing rule requires people to file for both their own retirement benefit and any spousal benefits they're eligible for. When you apply for one benefit, you are "deemed" to have applied for the other as well. You cannot switch later unless it is to survivor benefit.

Deductible – This is the amount you must spend out-of-pocket within a certain period *before* the insurance company pays anything. Most plans have an annual deductible, but Medicare Part A has a per-occurrence deductible. This means you might have to pay it several times per year.

Delayed Retirement Credits – The guaranteed 8% return you'll earn on your Social Security for every year you wait to draw benefits past your Full Retirement Age — up to age 70.

Dual Eligible – When you qualify for both Medicare and Medicaid. There are certain plans that are only available if you are dual eligible including some D-SNP and C-SNP plans.

Excess Charges – Something to avoid! When you have a Medicare Supplement Plan N and see a provider who doesn't accept Medicare assignment, he can charge you up to 15% more. This extra is called an Excess Charge.

Extra Benefits – Also known as Supplemental Benefits, are appealing extras that Medicare Advantage plans offer such as Dental, Food Cards, Money Back for Part B, and Transportation. These benefits are optional and vary by plan and year to year.

Extra Help – A Medicare Part D program to reduce the cost of your drugs based on your income. This is also known as a Low-Income Subsidy.

Formulary – The list of drugs that your Medicare Part D or Medicare Advantage plan will cover.

Full Retirement Age – The age when you can get 100% of your Primary Insurance Amount for Social Security. It's based on the year you were born and will be between age 66 and 67 going up in 2-month increments.

Draw earlier than your FRA and get a lower benefit, draw later, and lock in a higher benefit.

General Election Period – The first quarter of each year. When you can enroll into Medicare Parts A and B if you are late.

Government Medicare – Also known as Original Medicare or Traditional Medicare, composed of Parts A and B. You enroll through the government for these parts.

Guaranteed-Issue – When Medicare Supplement plans must take you regardless of your health. I also call this your Golden Ticket.

HMO – Health Maintenance Organization. This is a type of Medicare Advantage plan with lower costs and a smaller network of providers than PPO plans.

Hospice – Medicare Part A covers the cost of end-of-life care when your doctor certifies you have 6 months or less left to live. Hospice is care to keep you comfortable, not to cure your illness.

Initial Enrollment Period – When you are newly eligible for Medicare, you can sign up for Medicare Parts A, B, C, and D within a 7-month window. You only get one IEP in your lifetime.

IRMAA – The surcharge high earners pay for Medicare Parts B and D based on their income from 2 years prior. This is readjusted annually.

Irrevocable Trust – A legal document that allows you to give up control and ownership of your assets to protect them from Medicaid Estate Recovery, probate, and creditors.

Late Enrollment Penalties – Money you'll pay every month for the rest of your life when you enroll into Parts of Medicare later than when you were first eligible, unless you have creditable coverage.

Living Trust – A type of trust you can change at any time while you are alive. It will help you avoid probate but not Medicaid Estate Recovery.

Maximum Out-of-Pocket – Your protection in a Medicare Advantage plan and why these types of plans are very popular. This is the maximum amount you can be charged in a year, not including your monthly premiums or drug costs. Your drug benefit has a separate cap.

Medicaid – A joint program with your state and the federal government. It varies by state. You may get help paying for Medicare if you qualify for Medicaid.

Medicaid Estate Recovery Program – A program required in all states to recover against your estate if you die owing the state Medicaid program a debt due to a stay in a nursing home. This program varies dramatically from state to state!

Medicare Advantage – Private Medicare administered by an insurance company. You won't show your Medicare card as your insurance company will be responsible for all your costs.

Medicare Prescription Payment Plan – Medicare Prescription Payment Plan allows you to spread out the costs of your prescriptions over the year. It doesn't cost you to participate in this program and doesn't save you money, but is convenient for you.

Medicare Savings Program – Every state has a program to help low-income retirees pay for the out-of-pocket costs in Medicare. Apply online at any time.

Medicare Supplement – Also called a Medigap plan. A plan from a private insurance company to fill some or most of the holes in government Medicare A and B. This type of plan is never free and goes up in price annually. Popular plans allow you to see any doctor and hospital in the nation without the red tape of Medicare Advantage.

Medicare Supplement Open Enrollment – This period begins when you enroll into Medicare Part B and allows you to enroll in any Medicare Supplement regardless of your health and with no waiting period for coverage.

Medicare Summary Notice – The government sends you a list of all the care you've received each quarter when you have government Medicare. The corollary for private Medicare is called an **Explanation of Benefits**.

Networks – A list of doctors and hospitals your plan contracted with. If you see an in-network doctor on Medicare Advantage, you'll pay a lower copay than if you see an out-of-network doctor. Some Medicare Advantage plans do not offer coverage out-of-network. Government Medicare doesn't have a network. You can see any doctor that accepts Medicare, and almost all do.

Out-of-Pocket Costs – An out-of-pocket cost is the amount a person must pay for medical care when Medicare does not pay the total cost or offer coverage. These costs can include deductibles, coinsurance, copayments, and premiums. Government Medicare A and B have no maximum cost you can pay in a year. Medicare Advantage and Part D have an annual cap.

Opt-Out Doctors – A few doctors don't like how little Medicare pays, so they opt out. Your doctor may still be willing to see Medicare patients but will expect to be paid her full fee. Medicare doesn't pay for *any portion of the bills* you receive from this type of doctor. The number of doctors who have opted out of Medicare's payment structure *is less than 2% in most states.*

Patient Assistance Program – A program offered by pharmaceutical companies to provide free or discounted medications to individuals who cannot afford them. These programs are typically available to people with low or middle incomes, and some allow Medicare recipients to apply for help with high-cost brand name drugs.

Part A – Coverage inside a hospital, nursing home, hospice, or some home healthcare. Premium-free for most people at age 65.

Part B – Coverage outside of Part A for doctor visits, outpatient surgery, labs, x-rays, etc. Most people pay monthly for Part B directly through their Social Security.

Part B Drugs – Drugs infused or injected while in a doctor's office, typically for cancer, RA, MS, or osteoporosis. These drugs do not fall under the $2,000 spending cap for Part D drugs.

Part C – Another name for private Medicare Advantage plans that are an alternative to government Medicare.

Part D – The Medicare prescription drug benefit. You must enroll with a private insurance company and pay for this coverage.

PPO – This is a type of Medicare Advantage plan with out-of-network coverage. PPO plans cost more than HMO plans but give more flexibility.

Passive Income – Income that won't cause your Social Security to be reduced when you draw prior to your Full Retirement Age. Passive income is unlimited and includes things such as 401(k) and IRA withdrawals, interest, dividends, capital gains, and rents.

Premium – The monthly cost you pay for your coverage. Some Medicare Advantage plans have a $0 monthly premium. Parts A, B, C, and D premiums can be deducted from your Social Security. Medicare Supplement premiums cannot.

Preventative Care – Free screenings and tests that both government and private Medicare allow to keep you healthy.

Primary Care Physician – Your family doctor. You'll need to ensure that your doctor accepts your Medicare Advantage plan. If you have an HMO, your PCP must give you a referral if you need to see a specialist.

Primary Insurance Amount – The amount of insurance the government calculates you are eligible for at your Full Retirement Age. Other people who can draw benefits off you are also based on your PIA even if you draw your own benefit earlier or later than your FRA (except Widow or Survivor Benefits).

Primary Payor – When you have more than one insurance plan, the primary payor pays first, and the leftover charges may be paid by the secondary payor.

Prior Authorization – A nightmare part of Medicare Advantage where your doctor has to ask the insurance company to approve your care. This causes delays and frustrations and is not a problem with government Medicare.

Required Minimum Distributions – The minimum amount the IRS forces you to take out of your tax-deferred retirement accounts so they can tax it. The age you must start this depends on if you inherited the account or own it.

Revocable or Living Trust – A legal document that allows you to avoid Probate while maintaining your control over your assets during your lifetime. This will not avoid Medicaid Estate Recovery.

Service Area – The zip code where you live. You can only purchase Medicare Advantage and Part D plans available in your area. If you move out of the service area, you must change plans.

Skilled-Nursing Care – What we call a Nursing Home, not Assisted Living, but a facility where you get inpatient care usually after a hospital stay.

Special Election Period – When you can enroll into a Medicare Advantage or Part D plan outside of normal enrollment periods. There are over 20 exceptions that create a SEP.

Special Needs Plans – Types of Medicare Advantage plans for groups of people with both Medicare and Medicaid, or those with chronic conditions.

Spousal Social Security – You may qualify for spousal benefits if you don't have enough work credits for your own Social Security retirement benefit, or if your own retirement benefit is less than 50% of your spousal benefit. You may be able to draw off a former spouse if the marriage lasted 10 years and you are currently single.

Step Therapy – A limitation on your Medicare Part D and Medicare Advantage drugs requiring you to try a cheaper alternative first before the insurance will pay for the more expensive drug.

Survivor Benefits – Also known as **widow or widower benefits**. Social Security benefits available to a surviving spouse or former spouse, typically starting at age 60 at a reduced amount. Disabled survivors may be eligible at age 50. Younger survivors may be eligible if they have a child in care.

Suspension of Social Security – You can suspend your retirement benefits and earn delayed retirement credits for each month your benefits are suspended, up to age 70.

Trial Rights – Your once-in-a-lifetime ability to try a Medicare Advantage plan and if you don't like it, you can go back to government Medicare and/or your Medicare Supplement plan without regard to your health.

TRICARE for Life – Military retirees and their spouses may qualify for this type of health insurance coverage that acts like a supplement to government Medicare. You must enroll into Medicare Parts A and B to maintain your TFL.

Veterans Administration – You are not required to have Medicare if you are eligible to get your healthcare from the VA. If you live far from a facility or want more flexibility to go outside the VA, you can choose to enroll into Medicare.

Withdrawal of Social Security Benefits – Once in your life you can "unretire" by withdrawing your benefits if you've received them for a year or less and are able to pay back all that you have received.

Windfall Elimination Provision – This law was repealed in 2025 but no details were available at time of publication. WEP was much hated because it reduced Social Security benefits for certain government employees.

ABOUT THE AUTHOR

Sylvia A. Gordon, better known as Medicare Mama®, loves helping people figure out Medicare, Social Security, and retirement without all the stress. She's got over 1 million followers online who tune in for her easy-to-understand advice and real talk. Through her family business, **THEMEDICAREFAMILY.COM**, Sylvia's been helping folks make smart choices about their healthcare and retirement, one question at a time. She makes educational videos from her hobby farm in Indiana where her animals love to take center stage.

Ready TO TAKE THE NEXT STEP WITH MEDICARE?

LET'S MAKE IT SIMPLE!

Medicare is confusing, but you don't have to figure it out alone. We've spent years helping people just like you make the best choices for their health and budget.

- Personalized Medicare Guidance – We help you find the right plan for your unique needs.

- No-Cost Help – Our services are free to you. The insurance companies pay us, not you.

- Trusted & Experienced – We've helped thousands of people make confident Medicare decisions.

Don't wait until it's too late to make the right Medicare choice! Give us a call today or visit our website to schedule a free, no-pressure consultation.

1-800-970-1964
www.TheMedicareFamily.com
hello@themedicarefamily.com

Your Medicare journey starts here — let's do this together!

The
Medicare
— FAMILY —

www.ingramcontent.com/pod-product-compliance
Lightning Source LLC
Chambersburg PA
CBHW051750200326
41597CB00025B/4500